A PATH
UNEXPECTED

A PATH UNEXPECTED

JANE EVANS

Jonathan Ball Publishers
Johannesburg · Cape Town · London

Originally published in South Africa in 2021 by
JONATHAN BALL PUBLISHERS
PO Box 33977
Jeppestown 2043

ISBN: 978-1-77619-118-5
ebook: 978-1-77619-119-2

Quotes, including from speeches, that aren't directly sourced or
referenced, refer to personal communication with the writer, ad-libbing
in speeches at which the writer was present and taking notes, and/or
communications during Q&A sessions following official speeches.

Every effort has been made to trace the copyright holders and to obtain
their permission for the use of copyright material. The publishers
apologise for any errors or omissions and would be grateful to be
notified of any corrections that should be incorporated in future editions
of this book.

www.jonathanball.co.za
www.twitter.com/JonathanBallPub
www.facebook.com/JonathanBallPublishers
Cover images by Depositphotos and Shutterstock
Cover design by Sean Robertson
Page design by Catherine Coetzer
Set in Dante MT
Printed by CTP Printers, Cape Town

To Anthony

CONTENTS

	Foreword	xi
	Prologue	xvii
1	The farm	1
2	The town	15
3	Sausages and butter: Preserving tradition	19
4	The great divide	26
5	The *pondok*	35
6	The stad	39
7	The toilet-lid covers	45
8	16 June	48
9	The nursery school	59
10	Rebecca	68
11	Milk and oranges	73
12	Josephine	77
13	The washing of hands	83
14	The pothole	86
15	Sickness	90
16	Bonny	97
17	A modest proposal	103
18	Ntataise	111
19	*Papadi*	124
20	Suspicion	131
21	New wings	135

22	Too many questions	140
23	Unexpected progress	143
24	The do-gooder	148
25	Sowing the seeds	154
26	A warning	165
27	Drumbeats	170
28	Far and away	176
29	Patience	182
30	The ambassador	188
31	Woman of the Year	193
32	Flying the coop	198
33	Letsitele	203
34	Sharp sharp	207
35	The shoplifter	213
36	Election day	217
37	Letting go	221
38	Scientifically proven	226
39	Toy trolleys	231
40	Maria and Ishmael	237
41	New York	242
42	An empty space	249
43	A new millennium	255
44	Selena Moloke	258
45	The Queen Mother	263
46	Positive	268
47	The vigil	276
48	Toyi-toyi	280
49	Tomorrow	282
	Epilogue	285
	Addendum	289
	Acknowledgements	291

FOREWORD

How to give outside of a pandemic

I FIRST MET JANE Evans one dark night on a Free State farm. It was my first job after returning from studies in the United States, one that entailed giving what the USAID-funded firm called 'technical assistance' to non-governmental organisations providing education to black South Africans. Nelson Mandela had been released from prison but the first democratic elections still lay ahead. Things were tense in the country and Viljoenskroon, in the northern Orange Free State, was precisely the kind of place in which an armed right-wing group called the Afrikaner Weerstandsbeweging would patrol the town against black locals and the coming 'terrorist takeover' about which these men had been brainwashed.

So, to be honest, on the drive from Johannesburg to the Evans farm I was a little on edge. A black man staying overnight on a white family farm in a rural province known for its racial backwardness was not exactly something to look forward to. The doors of the main house on Huntersvlei Farm swung open and there were Jane and Anthony Evans. That was the other shock. I had thought of these rural farms as being owned by heavy-duty Afrikaner men, the ones who offloaded in central South Africa while the rest of the Voortrekkers pushed on northwards towards Pretoria. I certainly did not expect a Rhodes Fellow with a degree from Oxford and a journalist who once did the women's pages for an English newspaper in Johannesburg to be comfortably ensconced in a small town named for an Afrikaner farmer called Viljoen with a horse named Crown (the 'kroon' part of the town's name).

Little did I know that Jane and Anthony were to become close friends over the next few decades and that we would work together closely in bringing education to young children and training to women who would become leaders in early childhood development in the province and throughout South Africa. Among them would be remarkable black women – at one moment the wives of farm labourers and the next travelling overseas to present their development work at international conferences. That, in sum, is everything you need to know about Jane Evans and the incredible work of transformation that she has accomplished in South African education. This is a book that tells Jane's powerful story in the form of a moving and transforming memoir that at various moments had me in tears and at the end inspired me with renewed hope for our country.

This memoir is, however, different from the many others for which I have written forewords. To begin with, the writing is beautiful, even exquisite, drawing one into the story because of how it is told. No doubt Jane's skills as a writer explain the quality of the story, but it is also because of her sincerity as a person. She does not flinch from telling her story in the context of Old World patriarchy and the chauvinism of influential men as she encounters them in the course of her life. Nor does she hold back from throwing light on the ordinary racism of the rural hinterlands as it impacts the black South Africans who work with the Evans family on their Huntersvlei Farm.

She writes about racism and sexism with the kind of the restraint but also self-awareness that makes the telling so much more powerful than that which comes with the rage and indignation of ordinary writing. I would not judge those who write about hurt and humiliation with the pen of rage but often that kind of writing stirs common passions at the expense of deeper insights into the invisible infrastructures of oppression that sustain the status quo.

Jane's story is therefore not the usual memoir variety of 'then-this-happened-then-that-happened', but an eye-opening account of living and learning in the changing contexts of South Africa before and since the end of apartheid. A simple visit to grieve a passing soul in the township of Rammulotsi, where the black residents of Viljoenskroon live, is described so vividly as to reveal the contrast between privilege and poverty without the need to preach about the blight of inequality.

Which brings us to the central question in Jane's compelling story: How do you give in ordinary times? The COVID-19 pandemic is extraordinary, the first of its scale in a century. At the time of writing more than 46 million people had been infected with the novel coronavirus and more than 1 million had died. Faced with this existential threat to communities and whole countries, South Africa's rich have given spectacular amounts of money to the Solidarity Fund and countless development agencies.

What Jane's memoir reveals is how to give in ordinary times; here, in the Evanses' contribution to education and development in South Africa, I find five useful lessons. First, give where you are. They give on the farm to those who labour and manage in their sphere of influence. So often audiences ask me, 'What can we do to help in education?' Simple: give where you stand, where you work and where you live.

Second, give for the long term. The Evanses' model of giving is to invest in the education of the youngest children knowing full well that, if the foundations are laid for further learning, then the chances of academic success over time are much more likely.

Third, give to build communities. What Jane and Anthony did was to locate early childhood development centres within communities so that everybody gains and develops in the process – the children, the trainers, the parents, the caregivers and those who supply food and equipment.

Fourth, give through involvement. The Evanses could have done what so many other wealthy people do: drop off resources at the point of need and hope for the best. Jane throws herself into the work of early childhood education. She lives and learns with her colleagues. Her contribution, more than financial resources, is herself.

Fifth, give to replace yourself. This is a crucial insight from Jane's contribution to the people on and around the farm. She consciously trains young black women for leadership at the level of governance, management and administration of the project. When Jane stepped back after many years, I know it was difficult for her given her emotional investment. But I also know it was inevitable, for this approach to development is who Jane is as a development activist – somebody who develops others in order to hand over to others.

You will not find a moralising tone in this exceptional memoir. Jane writes about her life with humility and gratitude. In the process, she tells of her place in a broken country and her mission, with Anthony, to rebuild South Africa following the devastation of apartheid.

I cannot recommend this hopeful book more highly in these uncertain and anxious times because, as Jane reveals, we have been here before.

Jonathan D Jansen
Stellenbosch University
May 2020

My dear young people: I see the light in your eyes, the energy of your bodies and the hope that is in your spirit. I know that it is you, not I, who will make the future. It is you, not I, who will fix our wrongs and carry forward all that is right with the world.
– Nelson Mandela

PROLOGUE

IT STARTED SLOWLY. A tremble, almost imperceptible at first. Then the earth began to shiver, as if shrugging off a burden that lay hidden deep within. And then came the shaking. I reached out my arms to steady myself, and watched, transfixed, as the tall glasses of Coke and Fanta, condensation running down their sides, rattled and slid to the edge of the tray on the table in front of us. I stood up. I wanted to run outside. Someone pulled me back into my soft leather chair.

'Jesus, sweet Jesus!' a woman cried out, as she put her hands together in prayer. We were sitting in the home of Rebecca Sothoane, in the township of Rammulotsi in the Free State. She had died at the age of 73, and I had come to pay my respects to her family. Gold-coloured curtains, with delicate white netting behind them, were pulled to the side of each window. The television held pride of place in the centre of the room. And now, with the rumbling, the jittering, the clinking of crockery all around us, it felt as if the walls themselves were going to come tumbling down and destroy all of that in an instant. But just as quickly as it had started, the shaking stopped. The sudden silence was broken by Rebecca's daughter, Josefina, who smiled shakily at me and said, 'It's my mother. She's come to say she's so pleased you're here.'

In fact, on that day in 2014, it had been an earthquake – the strongest to hit South Africa in 45 years, a 5.5 on the Richter scale, jolting the ground all the way from its epicentre in the gold-mining town of Orkney – that had disrupted my visit to Rebecca's home.

And yet, I could feel her spirit, even all those years later, in the way she had moved and shaken my world and helped me find a purpose and mission in life.

It seemed almost impossible that 38 years had passed since Rebecca, a farmworker, hoeing the fields from dawn to dusk, had sat with me, a 28-year-old, brand-new farmer's wife, in my study on the farm. Freshly transplanted from my career as a journalist and women's pages editor for the *Rand Daily Mail* in Johannesburg, I was out of place with the rhythms of life on the land. My world had been one of early morning traffic, exhaust fumes, headlines and deadlines, fast-paced and filled with the cut and thrust of politics and society; Rebecca's world was governed by patterns of weather, the planting of seeds and the harvesting of crops, rising before the sun to make a fire to heat water, cook breakfast and get everyone on their way to school and work in the early-morning mist before her own day could begin. As we sat and talked on the farm, we found common ground in our concern for the generation that would come after us: the children on the farm. Our grand idea, our big dream, was to establish a nursery school for these children, to stimulate them with play, teach them basic concepts, and get them ready for the greater challenges of the school system and life. It didn't occur to us that it might have seemed overly ambitious, maybe even far-fetched, at the time. When I suggested that the children's mothers could perhaps fill the role of teachers, Rebecca widened her eyes and looked at me, aghast. 'Most of them can't read or write!' she said.

Back then, in the mid-1970s, at the height of apartheid, education provided by the government for black children in South Africa was dismal at best, and non-existent at worst. Black children, according to the Bantu Education Act of 1953 – one of the most scandalous of the apartheid laws – were to be exposed to minimal education, the barest necessities to prepare them for a life of menial labour.

'There is no place for [the Bantu] in the European community above the level of certain forms of labour ... What is the use of teaching the Bantu child mathematics when it cannot use it in practice?' said Hendrik Verwoerd, Minister of Native Affairs. 'Africans,' he said, were meant to be 'hewers of wood and drawers of water.' He would become the South African prime minister who turned the racial prejudice that already existed in this country into the atrocity called apartheid.

Apartheid was designed to keep black people uneducated. That most of the children's mothers on the farm couldn't read or write made me more determined. Rebecca and I would do what apartheid would not do. Neither of us could have guessed just how much work it would take, how many challenges and obstacles we would encounter, and just how much of a revolution in thought and deed in the conservative community we lived in lay ahead. We didn't have a name for our idea back then, but within four years of our first meeting our big dream would take shape as 'Ntataise' – Sesotho for 'to lead a young child by the hand'.

Ntataise today is an independent, not-for-profit organisation that has empowered thousands of women, who in turn have touched the lives of over half a million children in some of the most impoverished areas in South Africa. It has set the benchmark for early childhood development (ECD) in the rural areas and has sown the seeds for the nurturing of a wide range of skills, capabilities and opportunities. This is the story of how it came to be, of how my life too was touched and changed, at a time when the ground in South Africa was quaking with the first tremors of political and social transformation. And it all began one day in 1976, when fate led me by the hand, and took me on a journey to a place where, finally, through the strength and resolve of others, I would find myself, under the honey locust tree, leading children by the hand.

1

THE FARM

It was one thing saying, 'I do,' but quite another putting it into practice.

ON A SUMMER EVENING in 1976, as the sun set over Johannesburg, the city of my hopes and dreams, I slid onto the passenger seat of a white Mercedes-Benz parked outside the familiar house I was about to leave behind for good. The car smelled of well-worn leather. All 28 years of my life were crammed into the boot, packed in two worn, blue Revelation suitcases bulging to the limit with my clothes and in brown cardboard boxes stuffed with documents, photo albums and books. There wasn't room for my wedding dress, which I had left in the bedroom cupboard, draped over a hanger, like a ballerina's gown.

I had been married for ten days, and we had just returned from our honeymoon on the Indian Ocean island of Mauritius. As I waved goodbye to my mother, with a catch in my throat and tears welling in my eyes, I was waving goodbye, too, to my life as Jane Klein, women's pages editor of the *Rand Daily Mail*, the bastion of liberal thought at the height of the apartheid era in South Africa. I was about to begin life anew, as Mrs Anthony Evans, the wife of a farmer in the Orange Free State, the rural heartland of maize fields, big skies and small towns, just over two hours away by car. I tried to hide my tears from Anthony, as he folded his tweed jacket and placed it on the back seat before taking the wheel and reversing down the driveway. At the time I didn't think he noticed, but in retrospect I think he did; he didn't know what to do about those tears. He was engrossed in conversation with Abram Mokalodise, his occasional driver, who was wearing a dark suit and tie and leaning forward on the back seat. It sounded like small talk to me but, as I would soon learn, for a farmer it was the biggest talk of all.

'Have we had any rain?' Anthony asked.

'Ja, Baas Anthony,' answered Abram. 'It rained. The mielies are looking good.'

They spoke about children, family, life on the farm. I shifted in my seat, turned my head and watched Johannesburg disappearing in the fire of twilight in the wing mirror.

I had met Anthony only ten months before, at a Saturday night thrash at mutual friends in the city. The Beatles were belting out 'A Hard Day's Night' from a gramophone on a table at the far end of the room. The sour wine flowed from cardboard boxes. Anthony Holiday, the *Rand Daily Mail*'s political reporter, his hair awry, his arms flailing, was trying to make his voice heard above the racket. He was talking, of course, about politics: the rumblings about Afrikaans becoming a compulsory language of instruction in black schools and the treason trial of the SASO Nine, the student leaders of the organisation founded by Bantu Stephen Biko, the Black Consciousness leader who would die only two years later after being beaten by South African security police. As Tony stopped to draw breath, Wessel de Kock, the *Rand Daily Mail*'s news editor, butted in.

'Jane,' he said, 'I thought you were a journalist?'

'I am a journalist,' I replied. 'What do you mean?'

'I hear you're going to edit the women's pages. That's not journalism – not real journalism.'

e

'Of course it's real journalism,' I said. 'It doesn't only have to be about cakes and fashion.'

I was not going to let him get me flustered. My cheeks blazing, I turned away. I felt someone watching me. Most of the guests at the party were journalists, but the man leaning calmly against the wall was most certainly not. He was suave and neatly dressed, his blond hair meticulously combed. He had a wry smile on his face, and his blue eyes were looking straight at me. I blushed and whispered, 'Who's that man?' with a don't-look-now glance.

Of course, Wessel looked straight at him. 'Who, him? I don't know,' he shrugged.

The man walked over to us. 'Jane?' he said.

As a journalist, you get to meet plenty of people. You get to forget plenty of them too. But there was something about this coolly determined man that seemed familiar. It was all coming back to me. 'Anthony? The Free State farmer?'

'Yes,' he said. Did he look relieved that I'd remembered him? 'The last time we met, you were working for South African Associated Newspapers in Rhodesia.' How on earth had he remembered that?

'I'm back at the *Mail* now,' I said. 'Women's pages editor. I used to be the municipal reporter,' I added, in case he gave me that same patronising look Wessel had just given me.

'That couldn't have been very exciting,' said Anthony.

'It was very exciting,' I shot back. Although leaking pipes and zoning areas for business rights weren't particularly stimulating, the underlying politics was.

'Congratulations on your new pages,' said Anthony. 'I look forward to reading them.'

Much later that night, Anthony saw me home. I was still living with my mother. Purple bougainvillea cascaded down the white walls, dim in the moonlight. Anthony wrapped his arms around me and held me tight. 'You're a very pretty girl,' he said, and then he

f
3

left. I turned my key in the door, my heart pounding. What did he mean by that? Would I ever see him again?

'You're very quiet, my girl,' said Anthony. I was jolted back to the present, my eyes drawn to the early evening headlights sweeping the freeway, and then to Anthony, who was looking at me with a frown. 'What are you thinking about?'

'Nothing in particular, just thinking.' I smiled, but I knew he didn't believe me. He reached across and held my hand. I couldn't shake that homesick feeling of leaving my mother and Hilda Chabunku, the woman my mother had employed in my childhood to look after my brother Adam and me while she worked, as they waved us goodbye. I watched the scenery unfold, from mining headgear and mine dumps to scrap metal yards, old car lots, army bases, and fields of maize, wave after wave after wave, beneath the darkening sky. And then the sign that said: 'Viljoenskroon'. We turned right at the T-junction. In the distance I saw corrugated-iron shacks and small mud-and-brick houses. This was Rammulotsi. Its purpose, like hundreds of other such townships in South Africa, was to keep black people away from whites: the reality of legislated segregation. I didn't realise, then, in the gloom of that first evening in Viljoenskroon, that Rammulotsi would become a significant place in my life.

Further along, on the other side of the tarred road from a salt pan dotted with pink flamingos, were more small houses, a few hundred metres in from the main road, this time built of brick and painted white. That was the village where the workers on our farm lived. It was called the 'stad', from the Afrikaans for 'city'. The entrance to the farm was a few hundred metres further on, flanked by strutted wooden gates with shiny brass hinges. The brass letters 'AR Evans' were nailed onto one gate and, onto the other, the name of the farm: 'Huntersvlei'. My new home. But already, far from my own world, my own stad, I felt nervous. This time I would not be going back to

Johannesburg at the crack of dawn on a Monday morning after a weekend on the farm.

'Gosh, they're enormous,' I said, looking at the lumbering shapes in the cattle camps that ran along the wide, well-graded driveway lined with plane trees covered in furry balls of seed, the sort that made you sneeze. It wasn't the first time I'd seen them but they looked even larger in the evening light. 'What did you say they were called?' I said, more by way of making conversation than anything else.

'They're Sussex bulls,' said Anthony, 'and they are cherry-red. They're stud cattle. Highly prized.'

Anthony slowed down. Ahead of us one lay on its side, its stomach ballooning outwards. 'It must be so uncomfortable,' I'd just managed to say when there was a sudden blare of the Mercedes's hooter. I nearly jumped out of my skin. The bull, on the other hand, calmly stood up and wandered off.

'That's to stop him from getting bloat,' said Anthony. I didn't know what bloat was, nor as a matter of fact what made a stud bull different from any other bull. But I made a mental note to hoot whenever I saw a bull lying on its side. I was a farmer's wife. I had lots to learn.

The drive curled along a stone wall, covered in mauve wisteria. I wound down the window and took in the thick, sweet smell, interleaved with what I already knew was the sharper odour of cow dung. At the end of the drive was a large Dutch-gabled farmhouse, rising above an immaculately manicured lawn. We drove under an archway, and I scrambled in my handbag for my tube of bright-red lipstick. Anthony parked the car under a syringa tree and walked around to open the car door for me.

My reception committee was waiting. 'This is Charley Chase,' he said, 'and this is Whip.' The basset hound and the pointer leaped round him, barking, delirious with excitement. Anthony ruffled their backs. I gave them a tentative 'good dogs' and hoped to goodness they wouldn't lick me.

Sybil came out of the house to greet us. Her grey hair was immaculately curled, her slacks and cashmere twinset equally neat. Anthony put his arm around his mother and kissed her. I kissed the soft cheek she turned to me. I had no idea of what my arrival at the farm must have meant to her. I hadn't thought about it. It was only many years later when I was in the same position that I would come to understand the loneliness and emptiness she must have felt. Anthony introduced me to Batla Ndaba, who had worked for the Evans family for years, and Majolefa Sothoane, who had a wide smile and deep brown eyes. 'Hello, Miss Jane,' he said. His voice was warm and welcoming as he took a case from my hand. I suggested he call me Jane but the 'Miss' stuck.

'Calling you Miss is a sign of respect,' Anthony said later. He told me that he and Majolefa had played together as boys and had smoked cigarettes, filched from Anthony's father's pack of Consulates, behind the cowshed. Majolefa's father, Simon Sothoane, was the head cattleman.

'I became "Baas Anthony" when my father died. I didn't want to be called Baas. I just was.' Anthony's father, whom I had never met – he died about a year before our marriage – had been one of the most prosperous and successful farmers in the Orange Free State. He had made his fortune partly from a breakthrough in the production of maize, using new zinc fertilisers.

His name was Rhys Evans and, apart from his farming successes, he had a reputation as a progressive thinker and doer: he had built the first school for the children of farmworkers in the district, and built the brick houses I'd seen to replace the homemade mud houses which all the workers built for themselves and their families. Anthony had big boots to fill and the more I got to know him the more I realised how incredibly well he filled them, with determination and conviction. I too would wind up wandering in Rhys's footsteps; as the years passed Anthony and I would fill them together. For now, I watched Majolefa and Anthony as they carried my suitcases and boxes past the swimming pool. Its water, like the gables, shimmered in the evening light. We walked along a grass-lined path to the Dutch-gabled guest cottage, which was known by all as 'the Cottage'. It was a separate building about a hundred metres from the main house and was built, Majolefa told me, after Anthony's father had been named farmer of the year in 1961. 'There were so many visitors to see the farm, Miss Jane. They came on buses. They used to walk through the main house and some of them took pieces of silver and the silver teaspoons after they'd drunk tea.' After the Cottage had been built, only people who had been invited were welcome inside the main house, he added. This was where we were to stay until our own house was built. Inside, the ruby velvet curtains were drawn and the air smelled musty.

Our procession wound its way up the carpeted stairs. On the right was Anthony's old room. Sybil showed us to the room on the left, which she called the pretty room. It had glazed chintz curtains and matching pink-and-white floral bedspreads. I opened a curtain and let in the evening breeze. It was scented with the tangy smell of lemons, the fat yellow fruit knocking against the window. Sybil had put some pink roses from the garden in a vase on the dressing table, to welcome me to this strange new world.

'My father built the Cottage after the Holden Motor Company in Australia named him South African farmer of the year. We needed somewhere with a space large enough to entertain the huge number of visitors who came to see the farm and his progressive ways of farming, things like adding zinc to the soil.' Anthony was not quite as indiscreet.

'You can settle in tomorrow,' said Anthony as I knelt down to open my cases. 'Let's go and have dinner.'

'Should I change?'

'I don't think so. Not tonight.'

It was a Sunday. Dinner was served in the dining room at a stinkwood ball-and-claw table with a dozen chairs placed around it – five on either side, one at the head and one at the foot. The walls were panelled in a golden-brown wood. 'The wood is kiaat,' Anthony said. I felt like a newspaper reporter, bombarding him with questions, partly because I wanted to know and partly for something to say. We all felt awkward. Blue porcelain willow-pattern dinner plates stood precariously on the china rail that rested on top of the panels. Wooden beams stretched the length of the ceiling. The room smelled of furniture polish, roses and roasting meat from the kitchen. Anthony, who was seated on his mother's right, with me on her left, got up to carve the meat. 'This is beef sirloin, off the farm,' he said. Majolefa, with a red sash draped over his starched white uniform, passed me a plate of pink sirloin, followed by bowls of roast potatoes, beans and mashed pumpkin with white sauce, and a rich brown gravy. All the vegetables, apart from the potatoes, had come straight from Sybil's vegetable garden. I was so overwhelmed, I could hardly eat. I managed the beans, but stirred the pumpkin around and around on my plate, hoping it would go away. The delicate crystal drops from the chandelier seemed to wink at me in the silence punctuated only by our knives and forks and a whirring sound that seemed to come from the kitchen.

Anthony read, once again, the question on my face. 'That's the cold room engine,' he explained. The cold room was a vast walk-in refrigerator with sturdy steel hooks on one side to hang carcasses of cows and sheep, and shelves for vegetables, farm eggs, cream and milk on the other. Anthony and Sybil were at ease in their routine and their comfort zone. My vision of marriage had certainly not included me living with my husband and mother-in-law, even if only for a short time. I don't think Anthony envisaged it either but he'd been caught between us. Cutlery clinked on plates. We sat in silence for a while, and then we all started to talk at once.

'What were you going to say?' asked Anthony.

'No, what were you going to say?' We laughed, and that broke the ice. Anthony and Sybil talked about cricket. I decided not to show my ignorance and kept quiet, nodding and smiling now and again as if I knew what they were talking about. I should have paid more attention to the sports editor back at the *Rand Daily Mail*. I felt myself drifting away, curious to know what was happening in the world of politics just a couple of hours away in Johannesburg. I thought of the conversations we would have in the newsroom, the buzz and banter of politics and sport and plain gossip, the raw and hearty camaraderie of journalists who lived life on the edge of deadlines. I thought about the rat-a-tat clatter of typewriters and the fog of cigarette smoke that filled the air. Anthony turned to me. 'I heard on the radio that students are protesting in Soweto schools, over the use of Afrikaans,' he said. 'I'm not surprised. No one in government is listening to them.'

'Well, they're not going to take that government decree lying down,' I said. The *Rand Daily Mail* was the one paper that let its readers know about the mood, the anger and the growing unrest in Soweto and other black townships.

I had hardly finished speaking before Majolefa appeared, as if by magic. 'How did he know to come?' Anthony pointed to a bell hidden under the carpet near to Sybil's feet, which she pressed to summon Majolefa or Batla when we were ready for the table to be cleared. 'Where does that ring?'

'There's a box in the kitchen with pendulums that swing when someone presses the bell. It shows which room the summons is coming from.' This archaic tradition was not one I was about to embrace, I thought to myself. Our meal ended with stewed peaches, grown in Sybil's garden, and homemade custard. Anthony took a look at his watch. It was nine o'clock, time to go to sleep. In the newsroom, we would still be hours away from putting the next day's edition to bed, but the only thing I was putting to bed that night was me.

Later, I looked at my bedside clock. It was only nine thirty. Anthony was fast asleep. According to the strict traditions of the farm, he would be up and about before dawn, just when the *Rand Daily Mail* would be hitting the streets.

I tiptoed across the carpet and let myself out of the room. The door squeaked slightly. I held my breath, but Anthony didn't wake. I switched on the light in his old bedroom next door; time to explore. Thick linen curtains, matching the green bedspreads, were tightly drawn across the windows. Heavy wooden beams stretched from one side of the ceiling to the other. I stood on a small three-legged wooden stool to get a better look at the framed photographs that covered the wall. There was Anthony as head boy of his high school, Michaelhouse, in the Natal Midlands; there he was leaving South Africa on a Union Castle ship, to take up his Rhodes Scholarship at Oxford; and there he was again, standing with his arms tightly crossed in Harvard Business School's first rugby team. I thought of my BA degree and my ballet certificates, safely stashed in one of my bulging brown cardboard boxes on the bedroom floor.

There were black-and-white photos of the stone house with a corrugated iron roof and wraparound stoep that Anthony had grown up in until the 'big house' had been built when he was sixteen years old. I had grown up in a three-roomed flat in the Johannesburg suburb of Killarney. There was an enclosed verandah for my mother to sleep in, my younger brother Adam and I shared a room and there was a sitting room. Light poured into it, brightening one of the walls, which Peggy, my beautiful mother, had covered in bright, flowering pot plants. In summer, the jacaranda trees that lined the streets outside were a purply blue colour. We used to stamp on the slippery flowers on our way home from school. My mother, Adam and I had moved into that flat not long after my parents had divorced. That in itself had been traumatic. Other people's parents didn't seem to get divorced – not in the early 1950s. I was four years old. We were a close family. My mother made the flat comfortable and charming to look at. Judging by the photographs on the wall and the many aunts, uncles and cousins I had met before our wedding, I knew that Anthony too had come from a close family.

In many ways our families were the same; in others, they were worlds apart. Anthony had been brought up in an Anglican home, with church every Sunday. My family was Jewish, and although we seldom went to synagogue the Jewish traditions and holidays were entrenched in our lives. My father, who had returned from the Second World War as a lieutenant colonel, physically and emotionally scarred but sufficiently glamorous to sweep my mother off her feet, had left our family when I was four years old. Anthony had been born during the Second World War, his father away fighting with the Natal Mounted Rifles in Italy. He lived with his mother and his sister Wendy on the farm and was a none too pleased two-year-old when a strange man called his father arrived home and banished him to his own bedroom at night. He was only eight years old when he went to Cordwalles, a boarding school in Pietermaritzburg. For his whole school and university career he had been away from home. In fact, he had only been back on the farm for a couple of years when I'd met him. I, on the other hand, had spent my whole life in my mother's home. Apart from a year in Hollywood, not nearly as glamorous as it sounds, as an American Field Service (AFS) scholar, I only moved when I married.

As I wandered around the seemingly vast farmhouse, I thought of our conversation at dinner that evening. We had talked about cricket and our honeymoon. Sybil and Anthony had talked about the upcoming Huntersvlei cattle sale. There'd been little talk of politics or what was happening in the wider world. Mealtime talk around my mother's dining room table, far less formal, had seen many a heated discussion about politics, theatre and books. Anthony was, for me, an anomaly. After my father had first met him, he'd phoned to say, 'Don't get too excited. Men like Anthony don't marry Jews.'

'What do you mean?' I'd said, my heart lurching.

'He's too much part of the white Anglo-Saxon establishment.' He didn't elaborate. And yet, Anthony and I could hardly keep away from each other. We shared many beliefs, or were at least prepared to listen to each other. Anthony was far more cerebral than I have ever been. I hardly had to glance at the neat pile of intellectually weighty looking books on his side of our bed to know that he wouldn't be too impressed with the detective stories strewn across the carpet next to mine. I had to up my game to keep up with him. He had a highly analytical mind and saw through to the heart of things much faster than I did. Over the years, we would grow together. His strength of mind and ability to make decisions often calmed my rash reactions to people and situations. Many times I would dash off a furious letter and read it to Anthony, only to have him say, 'Sleep on it.' I was always amazed at how much less aggressive I felt the next day.

I turned around, catching my breath. Anthony was standing in the doorway, tousle-haired, in his shorty pyjamas. I followed him back to bed, admiring, while I was about it, his strong calf muscles. It was so quiet on the farm. I lay with my hands behind my head, staring out of the open windows at the star-filled sky, and listened to the silence. I could hear, in the distance, the newly weaned calves crying for their mothers, and the lonely and forlorn sound of lorries changing gear on the tarred road. Early the next morning, Anthony's side of the bed was empty. He'd gone to work. I remembered his goodbye kiss, as if in a dream. I knelt down next to my cases and began to unpack. I held up one skirt after another, little blouses, high-heeled shoes. Would I ever wear these clothes again? I unearthed a pair of jeans and a T-shirt, wiggled myself into them and wandered barefoot down the stairs. I opened the curtains. Wooden logs filled a brass container next to a vast fireplace. The walls were covered in wooden panelling. A snooker table stood in the centre of the room. I picked up a cue and bent over, taking aim. Click. The balls scattered randomly across the green baize. There was a knock on the glass door. It was Majolefa, telling me that the 'ou Missus' – Sybil – was asking if I was going in for breakfast.

I hardly knew Sybil. She had greeted the news of our engagement with, 'It will be a year's engagement, won't it?' It had been nothing of the sort. Six months later, I'd become the sixth Mrs Evans in the district. It is only now that I can see and appreciate Sybil's capabilities. She wanted to help me settle in, but since Rhys had died Anthony had been the man in her life. And I at that stage wasn't that keen on sharing him. Sybil ran a meticulous home. She knew how to bandage sore arms and dress bloody fingers and knees, presented by a steady stream of people who came from the stad for first aid. I found her aloof, and she no doubt found me young and naïve, certainly in the ways of country life. One day, a little boy from the stad had been invited to play with Sybil's visiting grandchildren. When the lunch bell had rung and he'd been whisked away by his mother, I'd asked why he wasn't staying to eat with the other children. Both Sybil and the little boy's mother looked at me in puzzlement.

I had completely missed the breakfast bell. Meals were a serious matter on the farm. The wooden breakfast table was in a room we called the sunporch, looking out on to the garden. Sybil waved at me to sit down. Majolefa served us hot porridge made from ground grain sorghum. No more chocolate bars and a snatched cup of coffee for my breakfast. This was the real thing, followed by eggs and bacon if I wanted them. Anthony joined us. He was not the lingering type. There was work to be done on the farm. Breakfast was a habit, not an indulgence. Grootman Steenbok, one of Sybil's gardeners, rang the old bell at the top of the drive. Breakfast was over. Anthony kissed me and his mother goodbye and left for his office. 'Pop in for a cup of tea if you feel like it,' was his parting shot. Sybil excused herself from the table, and I left for the cottage to finish unpacking and start writing thank-you letters for our wedding presents.

There were only so many letters I could write. What did farmers' wives do with their time, I wondered. I took Anthony up on that cup of tea. His secretary was clacking away on her typewriter. His accountant was hidden behind a pile of ledgers. 'Is there anything for me to do in the office?' I asked Anthony as I sank into his grandfather's brown leather chair.

'What could you do in the office?'

'I don't know,' I said. 'Type, I suppose, but not very well.'

'Well, many farmers' wives in the district do the typing and keep the farm books. Some of them farm and help inoculate the sheep and cattle.'

'I don't think I'd like to do that.' I pulled a face.

'I didn't think you would.' Anthony grinned. There were perfectly competent men striding around the cattle shed in dungarees and wellington boots, sloshing buckets of water around and pressing cattle and sheep through something called a crush to inoculate them against dreadful-sounding diseases.

'A lot of women bake, cook and sew, and look after their children. And of course there's the sale,' Anthony added. I finished my tea. 'We'll talk about it later, my girl.' He turned back to his work. He didn't mean to be dismissive but he was busy and we'd finished talking. What I was going to do, I'd have to figure out for myself. But in the meantime, on that bright, hot morning, while I wandered around the cattle sheds and the farm workshop with gutted tractor engines lying on the oil-splattered ground, my every sense was itching to know what was happening in the world I had left behind, the city I had last seen in the glow of twilight, veiled in red and orange, as if it were on fire.

2

THE TOWN

*I was out of my depth, out of place in a
town at the heart of apartheid.*

'HEY YOU, YOU CAN'T come in that door. Get out.' The shop
assistant, hands on hips, stood blocking my path. I leapt back, my
hands in the air.

'Sorry,' I said. But she wasn't shouting at me. She was shouting at
the man who had followed me in. He stood his ground as she
pointed to a door at the far side of the shop.

'Can't you read? '*Nie-blankes*'. Non-whites. That's where you must
go.' It was payday Saturday, my first Saturday in Viljoenskroon. The
tall, good-looking man, dressed in black trousers and a white open-
necked shirt, had earlier stood aside for me to go into the chemist
before him.

He replied: 'I will come in whichever door I like.' He didn't raise
his voice. The shop assistant's eyes bulged with fury. Her cheeks
were bright red. Reaching for the telephone, she threatened to call
the police. 'Call whoever you like.' Unhurriedly, he walked across
the shop to the 'non-whites' counter. This man had guts. I caught his
eye and looked at him, deeply ashamed that he had to line up in a

different place and that he should be spoken to so rudely by a white woman younger than himself.

I saw Majolefa in the 'non-whites' queue, and walked across to him. 'Who is that man?' I asked.

'Ishmael Mabitle,' he said. 'He's a schoolteacher.' I would meet Ishmael again and he would become a friend of ours, but I didn't know that then.

Clutching a brown paper bag, my chemist chores done, I stepped outside. The summer heat hit me like a furnace. I stepped gingerly over squashed, empty Oros bottles and dry, curled orange peels that lay discarded in the road. I narrowly missed a sheep, its legs tied with frayed twine, lying bleating on the rough ground. Chickens squawked around me and their feathers flew as they were handed from the old owner to the new. I watched money change hands. I threaded my way through a throng of farmers dressed in khaki shorts. Some had guns tucked into their tight waistbands, held firm by their heavy stomachs. There were farmworkers, the older men wearing jackets and ties and hats, the others in overalls, and women, wearing print dresses, with babies tied to their backs. We'd all come to town to shop. The pavements, with tufts of grass and weeds growing through the cracks, were crowded with people.

Dun-coloured bakkies and tractor-drawn wagons were parked higgledy-piggledy along the tarred main street. They had brought farmworkers and their families to town to do their monthly shop. An old woman sitting on the ground on a flattened cardboard box in the shade of the Huntersvlei wagon, her legs stretched out in front of her, waved at me. I waved back. At least someone in that hectic place was friendly. My search for a bottle of homemade jam with a frilly cover and a packet of sweet fudge in a cellophane bag was unsuccessful. Viljoenskroon was not a town of quaint village stores. Instead I found shop windows filled with tractor spares and fungicides. The buildings were small and functional. I wandered curiously into a trading store wedged between the bottle store and chemist. It was dark and dank. Shelves reached from floor to ceiling, packed with bundles of different-coloured wool, knitting needles sticking out of baskets, and piles of thick grey blankets. Paraffin stoves, enamel mugs and basins stood on the cold concrete floor. Bicycles hung from the ceiling. The shoppers' clothes smelt of wood smoke. With its bright colours, spicy smells and people shouting at each other in Sesotho, a language I couldn't understand, I felt as though I was in a foreign country. It was a far cry from the Sandton City shopping mall with its marble floors, shops with the latest fashions, and buzzing coffee shops and steakhouses. It felt foreign and exotic. Not so my next stop.

'Missus, you're in the wrong place.' I looked up at a man with the bank's logo printed on his shirt. I was by now in one of the two banks on the main street and, as it turned out, in the *Nie-Blankes* queue. I peered through the row of potted ferns he pointed to and saw another, paler, queue on the other side. The bank smelled of sweat and cigarettes. Twice in one day. I couldn't believe it. I thought of Ishmael Mabitle and the calm way he'd replied to the woman in the chemist. I told the man I was fine where I was. Feet shuffled and people in the queue with me sniggered.

The bank manager strode out of his office, tightening his tie. He clearly smelled trouble. All I could smell was his aftershave. 'Is there a problem?' He looked from me to the agitated bank assistant. In small towns like Viljoenskroon, the bank manager was one of the most important people in town, along with the *predikant* (the priest) and the school principal. He shook his head, frowning at me. 'You can't stand here Mrs Evans, you're breaking the law.' I knew it was the law, but what would happen if I stayed there? The walls didn't look as though they were about to cave in. The bank manager, on the other hand, did. He paused, growing flustered. 'Please, Mrs Evans …'

I felt the warm breath of the woman behind me on my neck. 'Go where he tells you, Missus,' she whispered. I turned and looked down the queue at the weary men and women waiting patiently behind me. I was no more than a further delay in an already crowded day.

Embarrassed now as well as angry, I ignored the bank manager's hand, which was eagerly trying to guide me through the pot plants. I was more than capable of climbing through this barrier myself. My last stop that payday morning was the grocery store on the outskirts of the town. There, too, wagons were parked along the roadside. But here there was no issue with separate queues. The storekeeper just didn't allow black people into the shop until, he told me, 'my white customers have finished shopping'. What was it with this town? I drove the six kilometres home past the salt pan, hardly aware of the pink flamingos, diving their long necks in and out of the murky waters. I'd been walking through doors and joining queues for 'whites only' my whole life. But here people relished the apartheid laws and took pleasure in upholding them in the most crass way.

Payday Saturday in Viljoenskroon had thrown me into a community I knew little about. I wanted to know about Ishmael Mabitle, and more about the people who crowded the dark trading store and stood in the long lines in the bank, the men and women huddled on the back of farm wagons, the children clutching adult hands.

3

SAUSAGES AND BUTTER: PRESERVING TRADITION

As the drums beat in the distance, to the pulse of another world, I tried to settle in.

'*DERMS*?' I SQUEAKED, MY lips curled into a wince. It was sausage-making day and I didn't want to be late. I felt curiously excited as I pulled on my by now customary jeans and T-shirt, the everyday outfit of the farm.

Sausage-making was something new to do, and there were new people to do it with. The previous afternoon, I'd watched Majolefa move the cars from the garage to the tractor sheds at the back of the house. The gardeners had got down on their knees and scrubbed the oil-stained garage floor until it almost shone. The long, green garden hose wriggled like a snake as they swished water over the concrete. A heavy machine was hauled off the back of a bakkie and carefully placed on the floor. 'That is the mincer,' said Majolefa.

I tramped across the grass, the hem of my jeans damp with morning dew. Sam, the farm mechanic, was already threading strips of pale pork and red beef, and chunks of thick white fat, into the steel funnel on top of the mincer. A pinkish mixture oozed like braids through the holes of a small steel plate. Sam shaved the mixture into an oval zinc bath. He placed a handful of the knobbly-looking mince onto a plate and marched it off to the kitchen, with Majolefa and me trotting behind him and Anthony striding ahead.

Sybil, elegant in a pink wool twinset and a tweed skirt, was effortlessly directing operations in the kitchen. It smelled of fresh parsley, thyme and pepper. Bowls of finely chopped herbs stood on the long kitchen counter, black patches peeking out of the worn white enamel, waiting to be added to the mixture. 'My grandmother's recipe,' Anthony told me.

'That's a lovely tradition,' I said.

Majolefa and Batla, dressed in their whites, were hovering around Sybil as she tipped one bowl of seasoning into the sausage meat. Majolefa kneaded it like a lump of dough. He looked up, and suggested I take a chance. I squelched the mixture through my fingers. It felt like sticky, wet mud.

Batla looked almost regal. He stood at the stove and clasped the handle of a hot frying pan in one hand, while he dropped little patties of the seasoned mince into the sizzling oil with the other. We watched until they turned golden-brown and crisp. Batla lifted the patties, shook off the oil and almost reverently put them on a plate. There was silence as Anthony bit into one of them. 'Tastes good,' he pronounced, sucking in air to cool his burning tongue. I had to agree it tasted good. Approval given, the gardeners rolled up their sleeves and pummelled the mince, which now more or less filled the zinc bath. Majolefa and Sybil tipped in bowls of herbs. Sam removed the plate and replaced it with a nozzle and a long, white sausage skin, which filled up like a balloon as the slithery mixture snaked its way to the knotted end.

'What is the skin made of?'

'*Derms*, Miss Jane.'

'*Derms*?'

'Intestines,' said Anthony. I watched, queasy, as Sam twisted the writhing *derms* into sausages of identical sizes. Majolefa packed the metres of sausage into plastic bags for freezing.

In all innocence I asked, 'Why don't we just buy them?'

There was a frosty hush, and even Majolefa stared at me.

'Huntersvlei has always made farm sausage,' said Sybil. For her, I came to realise, making sausages, salting hams and corning sides of silverside in barrels of brine was not only about filling freezers and retaining relevance, as she made piles of neatly packed farm meat to go to her daughter Wendy, who now lived in Durban with her husband and three children, and to Anthony and me, but also about maintaining traditions. Traditions were important to her, those she inherited and those she and her husband Rhys had created over the years on the farm. It was a way of keeping control of what was essentially her domain. I'm sure no one wanted me to feel alienated or pushed aside, but that's how I felt. My tummy contracted; I wasn't sure if there was place, here, for me.

Anthony recalled an image from his boyhood. 'When I was a little boy, the sausages were put in a barrel and covered in fat until we needed them. They really were rancid. There were no fridges in those days, and no nearby shops.'

I could almost hear the noise of a pork sausage being prised out of a barrel full of solid fat. A horrifying thought crossed my mind. Would I be expected to make sausages one day?

It wasn't so many years later that I was faced with the dreaded mincer and *derms*. But once I actually had to do it myself, with Majolefa close at hand, I found that there was something comforting about this ritual. It was predictable and, in its way, reassuring. Mixing fresh herbs and bottled spices, a little bit more of this, a little bit less of that, the smile of happiness on Anthony's face when he tasted a new batch of what I still thought were rancid sausages. It was a tradition, part of his childhood.

And then there was butter-making day. The milk separator, an ancient-looking steel bowl with a handle and two spouts, was housed in a small room behind the fig trees and in front of the farm workshop. It was as spotlessly clean as the garage on sausage-making day. Its milky smell reminded me of the bottles of milk with cardboard lids that we drank at primary school each day, with a teacher glowering at us to make sure we drank it all. The milkman poured warm, frothy cream from the Friesland cows into the separator, which he spun round and round with the handle until skimmed milk flowed out of one spout and cream out of the other. Some of the milk went to the big house's cold room, and the rest went home with the milkman and other people who worked in the house and garden. It was unpasteurised skimmed milk, which many of the farm children grew up on – as would our own children in time. The jugs of thick, white cream stayed in the cold room until they were full to overflowing. Then, one day, it was time to make butter out of it.

I can't say I was summoned by Majolefa, but he told me he was going to make butter and said maybe I'd like to learn. It wasn't a thought that had particularly crossed my mind, but if Majolefa was making butter, so would I. The cream, he told me, had to be cold and thick or it wouldn't turn. Some people, he said, made butter by putting a small amount of the cream in a glass bottle, screwing the lid on tight and shaking it endlessly until the hard lump of butter formed. But we were using an electric beater. We poured the cream into a brown mixing bowl, covered the top with a dishcloth to keep the spatter to the minimum and began to beat it. I watched, fascinated, as Majolefa's steady beating turned the cream into a lump of butter, swimming in a pool of weak-looking buttermilk. He strained it, kept the buttermilk aside and washed the butter with cold water. My turn. Within minutes my pretty new apron with embroidered roses, a wedding present, was drenched with buttermilk and lumps of forming butter. It ran over the kitchen counter onto the floor and onto my shoes, and trickled all the way to the door.

'You're meant to cover the bowl with the dishcloth!' Like me, the dishcloth was drenched in buttermilk. Majolefa was too polite to roar with laughter, but Anthony wasn't when he came in to see what was going on. I learnt to make butter in the end but I found it just as rancid as the sausages.

Then there was the cattle sale, the one Anthony and Sybil had talked about on my first night on the farm. I felt the same frisson of excitement I'd felt on sausage-making day. Something different was happening; there was something to do.

Buying and selling cattle was men's work. Serving food was women's. Determined to be useful, I joined my mother-in-law behind the tea tables, flanked on either side by farm managers' wives offering buyers 'tee of koffie'. Everything was impeccably organised, down to the last teabag. Cream-coloured enamel teapots and milk jugs stood beside a steel urn that sporadically belched out clouds of steam. Trays of freshly cut egg-and-ham sandwiches, made with homemade brown bread, and farm-baked scones, cut in half and laden with butter, jam and a good blob of cream, waited on the tables to be eaten. A matching length of floral tablecloth hung over the side of every trestle table.

The well-oiled sale-ring gate swung open. The head cattleman prodded one ton of perfect Sussex bull into the ring. The sale had begun. Anthony, dressed in his tweed jacket, shirt and tie, stood next to the auctioneer on a raised platform at the front of the tent. I was proud of him. He looked smart and sounded confident, totally in control of things, apart from the prices and the number of buyers who'd arrive. The annual Huntersvlei cattle sale was an important part of the farm's business. However confident he may have looked, as the days to the sale had drawn closer Anthony's temper had grown decidedly short. He'd been nervous; what if buyers didn't come? I'd watched curiously a few days earlier as a green metal sale ring was erected behind the feedlot not too far from the house, along with stands for buyers to sit on. A team of cattlemen in red overalls and black galoshes raked the ground and poured buckets of sawdust onto the scraped dirt.

'Ten thousand rand? Who will offer me ten thousand rand? Fifteen thousand? Fifteen thousand for this prime Sussex bull is a giveaway. Who will give me twenty …? Fifty thousand it is to the buyer over here. *Geluk*, Jan.' The auctioneer smacked his gavel on the metal stand.

In the 1970s, that was a good price. As one prize bull snorted its way out of the ring, another took its place. The auctioneer's chant rose and dropped. I sat on the creaking metal stands and watched my first cattle auction, mesmerised, until someone prodded me. It was lunchtime. I scuttled down to join Sybil and her helpers, scooping dollops of sweet-smelling curry and fluffy white rice into plastic containers for the hundred or so buyers and onlookers. There was soon nothing left. The men melted into the nearest pub to celebrate a good sale. Sybil, competent and organised, bustled around, tidying up, then disappeared, pleased with a good morning's work, to her house. I wandered back to the Cottage. The sale was over. In Johannesburg I'd felt like a grown up, busy with work that meant something; on the farm, I felt like that lump of butter I'd tried to make.

The *Rand Daily Mail*'s incessantly ringing phones were part of a different life. In the newsroom, no two days were alike. I didn't know where I'd be going or what I'd be writing about – the excitement, the deadlines, the drama and often the sadness of it all. But it wasn't my world any more and I had to put it behind me. Anthony and I sat on the cottage stoep that evening as night fell. The soft wind smelled of manure from the feedlot and the lemons that lay on the ground outside the Cottage. Anthony idly scratched Charley Chase's neck. The dog whimpered. If he could have smiled he would have. For a man who was so strong in his business world, with such a quick mind and an ability to make tough decisions so fast, I was always amazed at how gentle he was with animals and little children and, when needed, me.

'I'm worried about you, my girl,' he said. 'I was worried before I asked you to marry me. I didn't know what you'd do on the farm and I still don't. You don't smile any more and you're too thin.'

We listened to the farm noises and the drumming and singing that echoed from the stad. It was a haunting sound which, at first, had unnerved me. But I was getting used to its cadence and strange beauty. With each drumbeat I realised that the farm wasn't just about us, but about the hundreds of people who lived half a kilometre from where we sat, listening.

'I'll make sausages, I'll cook for sales.' I broke our silence. 'But it can't be my life's work. It's your mother's work. Because you have a wife it doesn't mean she needs to stop doing it. But I feel on the edge of everything that goes on. As though I'm imposing on someone else's life and that it is expected that I'll just step into the life Sybil has created.'

'It'll get easier when we move into our own house. It's nearly ready for us.' He paused. 'What is going to be your life's work?' We sat quietly for a while, then Anthony said, 'Living on a farm doesn't mean you only have to do things on the farm. Think about what you did in Johannesburg,' he said.

It was as though Anthony had turned on a light bulb. I didn't know what my life's work would be but I'd been so busy trying to find something farmy to do that, in as much as I'd felt part of the real world in Johannesburg, I hadn't seen that there was a real world right on our doorstep. It was Viljoenskroon, ironically, that would introduce me to the real world.

4

THE GREAT DIVIDE

I crossed the line that divided us, but the great divide remained.

'MUST WE GO?' I reluctantly zipped up my smart new jade-coloured dress.

Anthony, dressed in a jacket and tie, was not sympathetic. 'It's a Rotary fellowship evening. Of course we must go.'

I didn't like the sound of 'fellowship'. Sybil sat in the front seat on the drive to town. I sat in the back. I wouldn't have minded if I'd suggested that Sybil sit in her usual place next to him, but the fact that Anthony had just assumed it irked me. I nearly blurted out my irritation but some wise inner counsel stopped me. It makes me think, now, of Anthony talking about the old bull and the young bull locking horns when he returned from Harvard to work with his father. This, in retrospect, was a mother and daughter-in-law both needing and wanting the same man's attention, a son and a husband. Anthony must have felt torn between the two of us.

The dinner was held in a brown face-brick house in Viljoenskroon. Our Rotary Ann hostess greeted us warmly and showed Sybil and me into a room full of women. One of them looked at me and patted the hand-embroidered seat beside her. I felt completely overdressed in my smart cocktail dress. Sybil was greeted like the gracious person she was.

'Good evening, Mevrou Evans.' The younger women stood up for her. She was the grand dame of the district.

I was exchanging ideas with my new acquaintance about where to buy clothes when our hostess interrupted us. 'Ladies, please serve your husbands their dinner.' Serve our husbands food? Couldn't they serve themselves? While women piled lamb stew, rice, peas and sweet pumpkin onto plates for their husbands – who were in a separate room, which smelled of smoke and beer, talking about rugby – I found mine. He assured me he would help himself. Before I helped myself, I made my way to the toilet. I groped in the dark for the light switch. What a sight greeted me. The toilet lid was buried beneath a confection of frills and ribbons, as were the toilet roll and tissue holder.

On the drive home, Anthony and I were silent – Anthony no doubt thinking about work to be done, and me thinking about the toilet-lid covers. As we turned into Huntersvlei, I saw three enormous shapes in the headlights lumbering down the drive towards us.

'Dammit! The bulls are out.' Anthony pulled the car to the side of the drive, switched off the engine and got out. 'Stand here,' he said, pointing me to a spot in front of the car. 'I'm going to chase the bulls back into the camp. Don't let them get past you.'

'How am I going to stop them?' I spluttered. 'Put your arms out, like a scarecrow.' Anthony sprinted up the drive. 'Okay,' he yelled from behind the bulls, 'they're coming.'

I felt my high heels sink into the dirt. I was trapped. I couldn't budge. My heart hammered, but I held my arms out at right angles, terrified. They seemed a million times my size, and snorting. I closed my eyes and waited to be trampled. There was a sudden silence.

Warily, I peered out through one eye. The bulls were trotting back into the camp.

'Well done,' said Anthony.

I'd discovered, after our evening of fellowship, that all Rotarian wives automatically became Rotary Anns. 'I'd rather be a Rotarian,' I told Anthony.

'You can't be, it's men only.' He laughed, and didn't need to add that in South Africa it was white men only.

'We do help any people in need,' Rhys Rolfe, Anthony's general manager, who became a mover and shaker in South African Rotary, told me when I somewhat acidly made my feelings known about the situation the next time I found myself at a Rotary function. That made it almost worse – doing something for somebody was ephemeral; it didn't bring lasting change. Meetings were held once a month at the Rotary Anns president's home in Viljoenskroon, and I was expected to go. Despite the fuss I was making, Rotary wasn't entirely strange to me.

I could still feel the excitement and nervousness racing through me. It was the mid-1960s and I was eighteen years old, an AFS exchange student spending a year at Hollywood High School in Los Angeles. Part of an AFS student's 'duties' included giving talks, no political discussion allowed, to men's service organisations like Rotary, Kiwanis and the Lions Club where, in a vast hotel dining room with chandeliers dripping from the ceiling, what seemed like a hundred men 'roared' a welcome to me. In the 1960s, at about the time when I was there, the women's liberation movement was growing in the United States. By the mid-1970s women were speaking out, demanding rights and equality in all spheres of society. Some may have seen my job editing the women's pages at the *Rand Daily Mail* as a cop-out, but for me it was going to be the vehicle through which I could investigate women's issues, including an article on birth control that had Anthony in such a panic.

'What will everyone in Viljoenskroon think?' he asked me on the day it was published – somewhat icily, I thought. I didn't particularly care what anyone in Viljoenskroon thought about the article; I couldn't think why it irritated Anthony. Then the penny dropped: an injection for women that provided longer-term birth control no doubt meant, among other things, sex before marriage. And I, the editor of the page that had run this apparently outrageous thought, was the woman Anthony would be bringing to live in Viljoenskroon.

'I was trying to make it easier for you to settle in here,' Anthony said years later. 'It is a very conservative community. I didn't mind the idea of injections for birth control – that seemed like a breakthrough – but I thought other people might object.'

When I asked the Rotary Anns president, 'What do Rotary Anns do?', I wasn't the only person asking it. The first proposal to allow women to become members of Rotary was made in the 1950s in the US, where this men's service club had been established way back in the 1930s. It took over fifty years until, in 1987, the US Supreme court ruled that women could no longer be excluded from Rotary because of their gender. In 2019, the time of writing, the Viljoens-kroon Rotary Club has black and white members, men and women. But in 1976, when I asked what the Rotary Anns did, the president answered, 'We cook for the men, and we visit the old people in town. Things like that.' She added, 'Today I've got a new suggestion. Come, sit down.'

Why was it that so much of women's time in this part of the world seemed to be taken up cooking for men, I wondered. I couldn't cook, and I wasn't at all sure that any old person would want to meet me. At one end of the room, a cabinet was filled with china dogs. Someone's knitting lay on a small round table with a crochet doily on it. An open copy of *Landbouweekblad* lay beside it. Panels of embroidery hung on the walls. Before I sat down and she rang the bell (another bell to boggle my mind) to call the meeting to order, the Rotary Anns president announced, 'You are going to write the monthly Rotary Ann newsletter, Jane. You're a journalist.'

'No one has asked me to.'

'I'm asking you now.'

Later, when she'd told the meeting her new suggestion, the president, a determined-looking woman, banged her hand on a table to quell the uproar it had caused. The suggestion was that the Anns serve soup and biscuits to pensioners in the newly completed *lokasie* community hall, deep in Rammulotsi, on old-age pension day. There was no general agreement on the matter of serving soup to pensioners in Rammulotsi, but sufficient agreement for us to go ahead.

First we had to get permission from the township manager to be in the township. He didn't particularly want us. 'You'll disturb the payout,' he told the Rotary Anns president. 'In any case, what does a bunch of white women want with the payout for black pensioners in the *lokasie*?'

What *did* a bunch of white women want with the *lokasie*, I wondered. There was no political point to make, apart from the women whose husbands wouldn't 'allow' them to go into a 'black' area. It was one of the many ironies of the time that, while most of the Viljoenskroon Rotary Anns didn't question apartheid, there was among them genuine concern for the hundreds of cold and hungry people who would be queuing up for hours on end to get their pensions.

Not long after my first Rotary Anns meeting, wanted or not, our small group of Rotary Anns was on its way to Rammulotsi. It started out cold that pension day and I had a nervous feeling in my stomach. I felt as though I was part of a tour group. We stared out of the bakkie's window at residents of Rammulotsi and their homes, and they stared right back at us. 'Watch out!' A dog had run in front of our bakkie. The Rotary Ann driving it swerved to miss him. She drove past the small, oblong, brick houses, mud huts and patchwork homes made of worn corrugated iron and brown cardboard that I had seen from the main road some months before. Our heavily laden bakkie juddered over rocks and splashed through puddles of rainwater.

The township manager had eventually given his permission for us to be there. Women with metal buckets balanced on their heads, and children pushing drums in rusted wheelbarrows, queued at scarce water pumps and taps and stared at us. This was the Viljoenskroon township, the *lokasie*, the place where black men, women and children who did not work and live on the farms lived. The words 'township' and '*lokasie*' contained all the worst connotations of racial segregation. The road from Viljoenskroon to Kroonstad separated black people from white people. There were few coloured people in the Orange Free State and Indian people were not allowed to overnight in the province. The road separated houses with the bucket system for toilets, no electricity, no water apart from communal taps, a township with no tarred roads, from homes surrounded by green grass, beds of flowers, water, flush toilets and electricity.

This 'satellite' town was one of hundreds throughout South Africa. Often less than a kilometre divided the township – an under-developed conglomeration of houses and shacks with no or inadequate municipal services housing people struggling to maintain their dignity and feed and educate their children – from the nearby rural town. The townships' role, in the main, was to serve the neat towns and people living in comparative luxury just a thousand-odd metres away. Although the areas are no longer racially segregated, the inequality remains. The roads today are such that in both Viljoenskroon and Rammulotsi it is often safer to drive at the very edge of the roads to miss the potholes. Farmers and local businessmen fill them in and after the rains wash them out, they fill them in again. (In May 2019, the day before the national elections, residents of Rammulotsi, desperate to be listened to, to be given a plot of land for a house, electricity and water, would burn down part of the hall we were then driving to, and the old township clinic next door. We weren't to know that then.)

An official directed our vehicles through the crowd of men and women who arrived on foot and on the back of farm wagons to collect their pensions. On that day in 1976, our small group was waved to an empty space at the back of the new, cavernous community hall, well out of the way of the important-looking men at the front who were organising themselves for the monthly payout.

Early-morning cold crept in from the high corrugated-iron roof and worked its way up through the concrete floor. We set about our work with determination. Many willing hands helped us unload the bakkies. We'd brought everything from tables, pots and gas cookers to barrels of water, sacks of soup powder, boxes of biscuits and boxes laden with polystyrene mugs. 'Kom, kom, we haven't got all day,' a voice yelled to the hundreds of people waiting in the chill as the hall doors opened. A procession of men and women, blankets wrapped around their shoulders, obediently moved through the open doors past the indifferent officials, who ticked their names off lists and handed out brown envelopes. Pensioners from surrounding farms and Rammulotsi, some bent with age and arthritis, leaned heavily on sticks or their children or grandchildren's arms. They tucked their envelopes into blouses, or thrust them deep into the pockets of threadbare trousers, hoping they wouldn't be stolen on the way home.

The line of people waiting for soup grew like an unravelling ball of string. There seemed to be no end. We cooked and ladled soup and handed out thick oatmeal biscuits until the cold air turned hot and muggy with body heat and the midday sun beating down on the roof. Even the officials made their way to our tables. I tasted the soup. It didn't taste much like the beef and vegetables described on the label, but it was hot and warming. '*Dankie* Mme, *dankie* missus.' One pensioner after another nodded their thanks. I was shaken by the poverty and pain etched on so many of their faces. I don't know what I'd expected.

I'd felt that same feeling once before. I was a five-year-old girl. Hilda had stood clenching a wet handkerchief in her hands, tears pouring down her face. Only hours before she'd watched her son Jackie, an eighteen-year-old man, being manhandled into the back of a police van because 'he didn't have his pass'. All black people from the age of sixteen were legally obliged to carry a pass – a '*dompas*', or 'dumb pass', as it was called – if they were in a 'white' area. South African jails, I learnt as I grew up, were full of people arrested for not having their passes, one of the most hated corner-stones of apartheid. Hilda, Adam and I had stood around my mother as she dialled police station after police station, the numbers sliding around our old black Bakelite phone, until she found Jackie. I didn't know what was going on but I knew something bad was happening because Hilda was so frightened and my mother looked worried. 'What is a pass?' I'd asked my mother. 'Do I have one?' She'd explained as best she could.

A woman holding tightly on to a younger woman's arm hobbled painfully to the table. Her toes peeped through worn slippers and a *tjalie* was tied around her green dress. She said something to me in Sesotho as she grasped the mug and biscuit in her wrinkled hands.

'What is she saying?' I turned to ask one of the women behind her in the queue.

A deep male voice said, 'She says thank you. She hasn't eaten all day and she is very hungry.' It was Ishmael Mabitle, the man I'd met at the chemist. He wasn't a pensioner, but he said he had seen us and had come to say hello. I was pleased to see him. His warm smile broke the feeling of hopelessness that filled the hall. 'Hello,' he said, 'I remember you.'

I can't remember how much he said the pension for the men and women in the hall was, but I do remember him saying, 'It's a pittance and often the whole family, sometimes eight, nine, ten people, rely on it for food for the month.' I looked at the woman and her daughter drinking the last drops of soup from their mugs.

'How did it go?' Anthony asked me when I got home.

'It went well. I suppose.'

'You only suppose?'

'We gave everyone soup and biscuits. Even the officials came for a mug. I don't know how the pensioners felt about it, but that man I told you I'd met in the chemist, Ishmael Mabitle, came to say hello. He said people were hungry and pleased to have something to eat and drink.'

Forty years later, pensioners in Rammulotsi still queue from early morning to get their money. Today, whatever colour people's skins might be, they queue together. Many people have their pensions paid straight into a bank account.

'I didn't know what a bank account was when I first came to work in your house,' Maria Moloke, whom I would soon come to know, told me years later when she was old and arthritic herself. 'Now we queue at the ATM with everyone else, waiting to draw our money.'

If anything, the queues are even longer. Life in Rammulotsi has not got easier. South Africa's rural towns still seem to be forgotten. I see children and elderly people scavenging for food in the vast, overflowing rubbish dump on the edge of Rammulotsi. Men without work sit on the side of the road into the town , hoping someone will pick them up in a bakkie for a day's work on a farm. Others stand outside the grocery store, begging for food.

5

THE *PONDOK*

After the heat of a merciless summer,
we settled into our new home and waited
for the dust storms.

AT LAST, A HOME of our own – that is, if I didn't include a cook, a housekeeper, a woman who washed and ironed, and two gardeners. Alina Marumele, Maria Moloke, Bertha Serapelo, Moses Nthethe, Andrew Moloke and I stood in the non-existent garden of our newly built house and stared at one another. Any traces of cement and bricks had been swept away. The house smelled of fresh paint. It was early autumn. The leaves were turning brown and crisp and falling to the ground. The last of the dry maize plants, heavy with cobs, waited to be harvested. Their leaves sounded like a baby's rattle as they blew in the wind. The days became shorter and colder. I wore a jersey over my T-shirt. I had no idea how important a role at least four of those people would play in my life as we solemnly shook each other's hands. But on that chilly autumn day, I wondered what on earth everyone was going to do. It was another oddly-shaped piece in the strange jigsaw puzzle of this new and often disconcerting life I had to slot into.

'Why,' I asked Anthony, 'do we need so many people to work for us?'

'We don't,' he answered, 'but this is the way we do things on the farm. Everyone here wants to work.'

My problem was that Bertha, who was to cook, couldn't cook – and Maria, who could, told me she was the nanny.

'I haven't got any children,' I told her.

'You will have,' she replied. I blushed. Nothing could be further from my mind.

'I'm expecting a baby,' she told me later, as we stashed groceries into a cupboard.

I stared at her. 'Your first?'

'No, my fifth child.'

Five children. I looked at her in awe. 'Who looks after them when you're at work?'

'Andrew's mother.'

Maria rose each day before sunrise to make a fire to boil water for her family to wash with. She cooked a breakfast of pap and milk, then filled her husband Andrew's 'skoff tin' with pap and beans for his lunch. She filled a bottle with hot, milky tea and wrapped it in newspaper to keep it warm for him. Only once he and her children were ready for school did she get ready for work. She told me she repeated the whole process again in the evening.

I waited anxiously for the women to arrive each morning. The house was quiet and empty. Anthony had long gone to work in his office across the road. Hardly had Maria and Bertha put down their pink-and-blue checked plastic bags with their jerseys in them than I was in the kitchen with my cup of coffee waiting for them to make themselves a cup of tea and be ready to talk. I'd find out how their children were doing, and news from the stad. Maria took me and Bertha under her wing and taught us to cook. We started with crusty brown bread. I never really got the hang of it.

Alina, a kind woman with a gentle smile and voice to go with it, established a routine in the laundry outside. She also unpacked her pride and joy, a gold-and-black Singer sewing machine, much like my mother's. It looked so familiar and made the same whirring noise when she turned the handle. It made me quite homesick.

Our house was christened the 'two-pitch *pondok*' by Philip Watermeyer, an architect friend of ours. This meant he thought it was somewhat unimaginative. A long rectangle, it had a sitting room stretching across one end and our bedroom balancing it on the other. In between was a narrow passage with a study and two bedrooms to one side and a kitchen and bathroom to the other. Straight up and down, no fuss and strictly practical.

'Who designed it?' asked Phillip.

'I did,' said Anthony. He was inordinately pleased with himself and had appointed himself 'project manager'. I'd walked in, one morning while building operations were in full swing, on an obviously fraught scene.

'*Ag*, Anthony, it's almost straight.' Oom Koos, the elderly (in my 28-year-old eyes) builder, was measuring the top line of the avocado-coloured kitchen tiles with a spirit level. 'It's just a little out.' He scratched his head.

'My father would have asked you to re-lay them, but leave it,' said an agitated Anthony. The next morning Oom Koos, who had been building houses on the farm for many years, had removed the offending tiles and laid them again so that the spirit level was straight. 'If it wouldn't have been good enough for Mr Rhys Evans, it's not good enough for me,' he told Anthony.

What nearly unhinged me was the garden. Anthony had great expectations of my ability to 'project manage' its creation. 'I don't know the first thing about gardening,' I said in panic.

'Find out,' he replied.

The Free State dustbowl surrounding our new house didn't look like a promising place to start. With great difficulty in a conversation conducted over the party line, I consulted Sima Eliovson, a dear friend of my mother's and one of South Africa's leading horticulturalists. I announced smugly to Anthony that evening, 'We're going to have a ha-ha.'

'What on earth's a ha-ha?'

'A moat at the end of the garden. We'll take away the fence and have a fabulous view of the cattle.'

'We can see them perfectly well as they are.' Anthony's expression was about as promising as the garden. I'm sure he had visions of his prize cattle, legs up in the ditch.

In the event, we planted a thick carpet of wheat around the house, which Anthony said would keep the dust down in the August winds. And when the winds howled over the lands, gathering up the dry soil and turning the sky thick and brown, dust getting into our nostrils, ears and eyes, the wheat did hold the soil around our house in place until the winds died down and the summer rains came.

6

THE STAD

I moved my hand along the rough wall to feel for the light switch. There wasn't one.

'SOMEONE WANTS YOU. COME quickly.' Maria Moloke grabbed my hand.

The farm stirred each day to the pace of an age-old routine. I heard tractor engines splutter to life, men and women chatting on their way to work, and cattle bellowing in the feedlot. The smell of fresh air and manure blew through the window and mingled with the steam curling from my mug of coffee. I held it in my hands and looked outside my study window at the late-autumn landscape. But that morning was different. I hurried to the back door with Maria. I don't know why we ever built a front door. We never used it. It was Selena Nthethe, Moses's wife, her eyes darting frantically from Maria to me. She held out a bundle wrapped in a *tjalie*. The bundle moved and gave a faint whimper. I cautiously turned back the rug. Inside was a baby, its lips caked with dried vomit, lying limp in its mother's arms.

'What's wrong with her?' Maria peered over my shoulder. She said something to Selena in Sesotho. 'This baby is very sick.' She pointed to the silent woman, 'She wants you to take them to the doctor.' The two women, one carrying the whimpering bundle, hurried with me to my car. My heart thudded as I drove. I'd never dealt with a sick baby before. She was so little.

The wait was interminable. I paged through the out-of-date magazines on the wooden table in the 'white' waiting room. Eventually, the doctor called me. The baby, he explained, had diarrhoea and was dehydrated. He handed me a brown paper bag, filled with medicines that the baby needed to drink – or, he said, she would die. She was starving from drinking diluted baby formula. I wondered why he wasn't explaining all this to the baby's mother, rather than to me. I felt totally inexperienced and, quite frankly, terrified.

'Why isn't her mother feeding her breast milk?' I asked.

'Listen to the adverts for baby formula on the radio. Everyone thinks formula is smarter and better than breast milk. Baby formula is expensive, so mothers often dilute it with unboiled water. Nearly every day, someone brings a dying baby in to see me.'

This baby was not going to die. I clutched the paper bag and we all clambered back into my car. On the way home, we stopped at the grocery store, where they let us all in with no apparent problem, and bought bottles, steriliser and tins of formula. It was too late for this baby to drink breast milk.

Maria was the star of the day. She coaxed drops of the rehydration mixture into the baby's tiny mouth. We mixed the formula and watched her suck weakly at the bottle, but at least she was sucking. Once the baby had settled, I drove her and her mother to the stad. Maria was not to be left behind. She got into the car beside me. She directed me down rows of small, whitewashed brick houses with fenced gardens, past a long building, which she said was the farm school, to the Nthethes' house.

Men and women walked in the dirt roads, calling to each other. Children, lots of children, kicked balls and pushed wire cars, raising small clouds of dirt. The smoke from cooking pots hung in the air, mingled with the dust. A windmill clanked as its blades turned in the wind. I followed the two women across a well-swept dirt yard. The house was dark and smelled of food and smoke. Four rooms led one into the other. A table with a grey Formica top and four chairs filled the kitchen. An old woman with a scarf on her head sat heavily on one of the chairs, her slippered feet resting on worn linoleum. A little girl clutched the folds of her dress and stared at me with large brown eyes. She shyly touched my hand. At the back of the house was a yard where the family's cattle lived.

I put the packet of medicines in their brown paper bag on the table and looked around me. The walls were plastered with a mixture of what Maria told me was mud and cow dung. Selena had etched patterns into its surface to decorate the walls. I moved my hand along the rough wall to feel for a light switch. There wasn't one. There was no electricity in the stad. Through the open back door, under a black three-legged pot in the backyard, I saw the ashy remains of the morning's fire. Flies from the family's cattle hovered over the blackened pot. At the back of the fenced-in property was a black plastic structure that looked like an enclosed sentry box. It housed the long-drop toilet. Eight people slept in this house with its one double bed and no electricity or running water. I said to Selena I would fetch her the next day to help mix the baby's formula.

'It wasn't that long ago that every man we employed was given a few days to build his own mud house for himself and his children,' Anthony told me that evening when I told him about my visit to Selena and Moses's house. 'That meant if he left the farm he could take the zinc roof and doors with him to build another house for himself and his family. Each family built their own long-drop and my father sent water tankers to the stad for everyone to collect water.'

'How could people live like that?' I asked.

'That's the way they did things.'

'And these houses like the ones Selena and Maria live in today?'

'My father built them while I was away overseas. They were a great improvement, but not enough.'

'How many people live in the stad?' I asked.

'Five hundred.'

'And on your other farms?'

'About a thousand.'

'That's a lot of people. What happens when someone gets sick?'

'They go to the doctor or the clinic in Rammulotsi. We send farm transport.' He thought for a moment. 'There's a lot of sickness. The flies are terrible and the houses aren't big enough for everyone who lives in them.'

'What are you going to do about it? You can't leave it.' I thought of the flies in Selena's kitchen.

'I'm not going to leave it. The flies come from people's cattle. There are too many cattle in the stad, they roam all over the place. I know they are people's security and help pay for their children to go away to high school, but it can't stay as it is.'

'You can't take them away.'

'We may have to.'

'And the sickness?' I asked.

'I'm appointing a nursing sister to work on the farms.'

'Isn't that quite revolutionary?'

'Not so much revolutionary as essential. It wasn't only my idea. There's a liaison committee on the farm that I set up so that the workers and I could talk honestly to each other.'

'I suppose it's all men?' I said.

'Of course they are all men. Let's take it step by step. They asked me if we couldn't get children immunised on the farm instead of going to the clinic in the township because it was so crowded and I suggested we look for a full-time, qualified nurse to look after all the health problems in the stad.'

'And?'

'I'm trying to find a nurse.'

Anthony, in 1976, was 34 years old, not long out of Harvard Business School and doing his best to put 'B-School' principles to work on a South African farm. He had in effect been away from home – excluding school and university holidays – since he was eight years old. His life had been a mixture of boarding school and life on a farm where workers depended on the farmer for their houses, grazing for their cattle, a school for their children, wood for boiling water and cooking, maize meal, and lifts – to town, to the clinic, on Saturdays to the shops and over weekends to play soccer on neighbouring farms. Thrown into the mixture were four years at two of the world's leading universities. However matter-of-fact he may have sounded, appointing a nurse and establishing the liaison committee were, in the context of the time, revolutionary. As I got to know more about life on farms, I came to understand that Anthony's relationship with the workers on his farms was, in those dark apartheid days, not the norm.

I had married Anthony as he was becoming immersed in bringing modern business life to the farm. I was so busy thinking of myself that I hadn't given much thought to how strange he, too, must have found it coming back to the farm. But over the years we worked together on improving life on the farm for the people who worked and lived there, which included education.

And so, in the late 1970s, Sister Florida Tseki came into all our lives. She was a large, formidable woman, more at home speaking isiZulu than Sesotho, but Anthony's men's liaison committee approved of her and she quickly became a fixture in the Rhys Evans Group. She was the first person to move into a new stad house, complete with electricity and running water. For the rest of the stad, there was – when I arrived in 1976 – one tap for every four houses; it boggled my mind. By 1978 there were water and flush toilets inside the houses. At much the same time, the stad houses were extended to give everyone more space. But the difference between Sybil's and our homes and the houses in the stad remained vast.

7

THE TOILET-LID COVERS

With no call for froth and frilliness in the big city, a social enterprise stops before it starts.

ALINA MARUMELE TOOK HOLD of the frilly toilet-lid cover I held out to her. She rubbed it between her fingers, turned it inside out and pulled the elastic.

'Ai, Mrs Evans, what is it?' she asked. She might well have. The laundry smelled of the clean, freshly ironed sheets that she had neatly folded on the table.

'Come,' I said. She followed me into the house, which still had that new carpet smell, and into the bathroom. I fitted the cover over the toilet lid. I stood back to admire it. In every house I'd visited since my first reluctant trip to the Rotary Fellowship evening, the toilets had been decorated from cistern and lid to tissue box and toilet-roll holder in similar frothy, frilly covers.

If Free State toilets were decorated in such a way, why shouldn't they be in Johannesburg? It seemed to me to be too good a business venture to miss. And who better, I thought, to make these intriguing covers than women in the Huntersvlei stad? It would give them a chance to work beyond the lands and make more money for their families. It didn't occur to me to ask anyone if they wanted to join my fledgling sewing enterprise; I just went ahead. I could hardly thread a needle, but Alina, who did our washing and ironing – dear, kind Alina with her Singer sewing machine – could. She looked at me and the toilet-lid cover dubiously. There was a world of difference between our white ceramic toilets and the long-drops in the stad and buckets in the township. Maybe she didn't want to dampen my excitement, or maybe she was just trying to humour me, but she agreed to make them. She told me I would have to supply suitable fabric and thread.

I dangled, some weeks later, one of Alina's completed toilet-lid covers in front of Anthony and told him my plan.

'Who's going to buy them?' he asked.

'I don't know, everyone, I'll sell hundreds. In Johannesburg, in Durban, in Cape Town.' I imagined lines of Huntersvlei women turning out toilet-lid covers and earning money to buy extra clothes and food for their children. 'There must be shops in Sandton City that will want them,' I said.

'Maybe you should contact their buyers first.' I didn't find his lack of enthusiasm at all daunting. Who would be able to resist our toilet-lid covers?

The two-hour drive to Johannesburg went quickly and I headed straight for the shiny new and vast shopping complex of Sandton City in the north of Johannesburg. I hadn't, as Anthony had suggested, contacted any buyers beforehand. Adrenaline pumping, I almost floated into the first store, pulling my suitcase of goods behind me. I announced to a saleswoman that I'd come to see the manager. She looked at me suspiciously and disappeared. After what seemed an age, an older woman appeared, radiating reluctance. She took one look at the toilet-lid covers and said with an incredulous gaze that she didn't think they would sell in her store.

My reception at the second store was much the same. I stood on the shopping centre's gleaming marble floor, people pushing past me, my case at my feet, not quite sure what to do next. A sign saying 'Bathroom Boutique' glared at me from across the passage. Not quite so confident this time, I went inside. Against the smell of scented soaps and lavender, I hauled out my toilet-lid covers, which were by now distinctly rumpled. For the third time I heard someone say, 'What are they?' After much discussion about the merits of toilet-lid covers, and why it was imperative for people to have them, the manager of the boutique asked me to make her 12 sets in any colours I liked.

My car and I seemed to fly from Johannesburg to Huntersvlei. I had an order, without any appointments. I couldn't wait to tell Anthony and Alina. In time, of course, we would need to buy more sewing machines and we'd need a space for the women to sew. I pushed open the back door. 'I've got an order,' I yelled.

'I'm afraid you haven't.' Anthony, still in his farm khakis, hugged me. He handed me a slip of paper. 'Cancel order,' the message read.

'They'll just have to go on our toilets,' I said, ruefully. And there they stayed for the next seven years, until we moved to the big house and they were worn with washing and age.

As for me, I'd just have to come up with another plan. Maybe this time, I'd ask the women in the stad if they'd like to go into 'business' with me first.

8

16 JUNE

In the drift of smoke from distant fires, a light shines on an opportunity to make a difference.

IT WAS WEDNESDAY 16 June 1976. The lush green maize lands had given way to vast brown emptiness. The tractors and combine harvesters would soon stand silently in the sheds, giving everyone the time to rest and recoup their energy. We'd been married for four months. The day was cold and grey clouds blotted out the sun. I was standing at the study window nursing my usual cup of coffee and thinking how dramatic the change in seasons was when Anthony strode into the room. He didn't usually come home before lunch. My heart leapt; it always did when I saw Anthony, for the 40 years we were married. He walked past me and turned on the radio, our link to the wider world. There was no television on the farm. It had only been introduced to South Africa in January that year, and we hadn't yet installed it.

Anthony twiddled the dial until we heard a disembodied voice on the BBC World Service. 'The student protests in South Africa's vast black township, Soweto, have turned violent. Police have opened fire ...' We listened in growing horror. The presenter's voice was all but drowned by the sounds of gunshots, sirens, feet pounding the roads, as thousands of unarmed black students marched in an orderly protest at being forced to learn in Afrikaans, for them a foreign language and yet another ploy by the South African government to impede their education. The bullets mowed the students down with deadly violence, like the harvesters mowed down the maize plants on the farms with deadly accuracy.

'What do the police think they are doing?' I looked at Anthony. 'The students are unarmed, it was a peaceful march. How can they fire on them?'

'They do what they like.' Anthony was grim. 'They are frightened of losing control.'

'I wish I was back at the *Mail*,' I said, pacing to the door and back to the window.

'Why?' he asked. I couldn't explain to him the adrenaline rush, the sense of purpose that came with reporting on shattering events like this, of being part of a newspaper that told society and the world the truths of apartheid. On that day I wanted to be one of those journalists, bringing the screams of children being beaten by out-of-control policemen raining blows from their batons on heads, arms and legs, injuring and killing them, to the attention of the world. I wanted to report, even if in a one-dimensional way, what was happening. As shocked and sickened as I felt, I couldn't feel what those young boys and girls, men and women felt – I'd never been in their shoes.

'I feel so useless here.'

'Don't feel useless. Come with me – I'm going to the stad. I'm worried about the farm children who go to school in Rammulotsi.'

There were no telephones in the stad, and no cellphones, no social media – only party lines in the farm offices. There was no way anyone could contact family and friends in Soweto or even in Rammulotsi without actually going there. The children at the

Huntersvlei primary school had been to school that day. They were playing as usual in the streets, pushing wire cars, kicking soccer balls and shouting to each other. Men and women were huddled together. Some were warming their hands on fires and listening to radios balanced on upturned drums and fence posts. Anthony saw Abram Mokalodise and stopped the car. We both got out. The people Abram stood with shuffled around the fire to make room for us. They were talking to a boy dressed in his Rammulotsi high school uniform. The words tumbled out of him. Abram translated what he was saying.

'The teachers told us to go home. They told us we must stay inside our homes, they said there were terrorists coming, Umkhonto we Sizwe, and that we must hide. But it was lies, all lies, those were police informers making trouble.'

'We didn't know what was going on. The only news we got was from the people in the stad who owned radios. We were worried sick about our families in Soweto.' Bonny Ntsoeleng was one of the youngsters milling around in the stad that afternoon. It was many years later, when we'd become friends, that she would tell me how uncannily normal things had seemed in the stad that day. 'My cousin was in the Soweto protest. We only knew he'd been shot when he arrived at Huntersvlei with the bullet still in his shoulder. He was so frightened. He'd got to us by train and hitching lifts. He told us what had happened, how they'd been shot at. He died not long ago and we buried him with the bullet still in his shoulder.'

In Viljoenskroon, where we drove to next, the streets were quiet. A few white men dressed in their customary khaki clothes patrolled the pavements, clasping the handles of their guns. Across the road in the Rammulotsi township the police were out in full force. They waved us back. The party line rang incessantly that evening. White farmers and their wives phoned one another, terrified that the protests would spill over onto their farms. But there were no protests in our district, not on that day. I remember fear, confusion, uncertainty and shock in all sectors of our splintered community at the news filtering through – an unnatural quiet, the calm before the inevitable storm.

The *Rand Daily Mail* was meant to be delivered to Viljoenskroon by van from Johannesburg each day. Sometimes it arrived, sometimes it didn't. The next day it did. I snatched a copy off the shelf and sat in my car outside the grocery store, paging through it, horrified. A photograph of Hector Pieterson, a thin, thirteen-year-old boy shot by South African police, dying in his friend's arms, his distraught sister running next to them, dominated the front page. As black children lay dying in Johannesburg's Baragwanath Hospital, the anger spilled from one black township to the next. The struggle for liberation was no longer taking place outside our borders. It had become an internal fight. Police retaliated with devastating violence.

I sat in my car, the newspaper spread over my knees, thinking how far removed from the chaos and violence in Soweto my school days had been. Kingsmead – where I'd sat each day, my dark-green tunic pulled hastily each morning over a smocked light-green blouse, in well-appointed classrooms with twelve to twenty other girls – was a private girls' school in Rosebank, a comparatively well-off Johannesburg suburb. When the bell rang we'd move with decorum, our school bags in the left or right hand – one hand in the morning and the other hand in the afternoon – from classroom to classroom or to the library with its shelves of books. There'd be a mad dash to the tennis courts, swimming pool, or hockey or netball fields. We took it all for granted. It was part of the bubble we lived in.

I thought about Anthony and the things he'd told me about his school days. I tried hard to picture him as a five-year-old with his sister Wendy being driven to school in Viljoenskroon, then a tiny collection of houses, bumping along the dirt roads on the back seat of an old farm cart, a blanket pulled over their knees, 'Old John' sitting on the rickety front bench flicking the reins to get Diamond the horse to get a move on.

Anthony was barely eight when his parents had sent him to Cordwalles. It was an 80-kilometre drive from the farm, with not a tarred road in sight, through countless farm gates that needed to be opened and closed, to the Kroonstad station where Anthony and Wendy boarded the train. A little boy, skinny legs sticking out of his short pants, shivering in the cold early morning, he'd stand on the station platform in Pietermaritzburg waiting to be met, a whole term ahead of him until he made the return journey to the farm for his holidays. Anthony took the train to school in Natal until he was 18.

The picture of Hector Pieterson lay staring up at me from the passenger seat. It jerked my mind back to the present as I started the car. Things had to change and I wanted to be part of that change.

I'd barely got home when Anthony pulled up at the house. 'I'm going to our primary school. Would you like to come with me?'

'Why do you call it our school?' I said, getting into his car. I'd seen the school before, but this was my first official visit and the first time I'd really become aware of the system of farm schools.

'It *is* our school. The government doesn't provide primary schools for farmworkers' children. They say it's the farmers' responsibility. They pay some of the teachers' salaries and half the cost of the school buildings.'

'Who pays the rest?'

'We do.'

'Who appoints the principal and teachers?' I asked, aghast.

'I do – the principal at any rate, and he consults me on the teachers he wants.'

'Shouldn't an education department be responsible for the appointment of school principals and teachers?'

'Government doesn't particularly care about farmworkers'

children's education. I'm the school manager. My father, Rhys, built the original school in the Huntersvlei stad. It was a small brick building and, in 1963, the only school for farmworkers' children in the district.'

'Is that the same school I saw in the photo in the big house? It seems much bigger.'

'It *is* much bigger. I added more classrooms so that there is one per standard. I also built houses for the teachers to live in during the week. Most of them go to their own homes in other towns over weekends and school holidays.' Anthony drew up outside the primary school.

The situation on many farm schools was, I learnt as the months went on, worse than awful. Not only did some children have to walk kilometres a day to school and back, but when they arrived it was to roughly converted farm sheds with one teacher for two or three standards. The existence and quality of farm primary schools did rest with the farmer. Over the years I would visit farms in all areas of the country and see farm schools that ranged from classrooms with broken windows, not enough chairs and desks and no toilet, to a school like that at Crocodile Valley Citrus Estates, with large, airy schoolrooms, plenty of desks and chairs, food and a teacher per standard – everything one would expect from a school.

June 16 was one day behind us. Like us, Mr Sello, the school principal, meticulously dressed in a jacket and tie, was shaken to the core by the unrest and the police's violent retaliation. He came out to greet us. He grasped my hand in both of his. 'I'm pleased to meet you, Mrs Evans, and pleased you've come to visit our school. Come in.'

I followed him along the concrete walkway and looked through an open classroom door. Feet shuffled and chairs scraped as girls in black gym dresses and boys in shorts or long pants seated at wooden desks stood up for me. Embarrassed, I said, 'Please, sit down.' Some of those children looked far too old to be in primary school, teenagers sitting side by side with ten-year-olds.

Mr Sello's office had just enough space for his desk and our chairs. He said that about three hundred children attended this school, two hundred from Huntersvlei and a hundred from neighbouring farms. 'Some of them walk five kilometres or more to school and the same distance back in the afternoon. Many of them haven't eaten and don't have shoes. They arrive tired and hungry before the day has even begun. Some of the children come to school mainly for the food. The farm feeds all the children thick, hot soup and bread. Hungry children can't learn. Some of the children, those who are lucky, bring their food from home.'

But they too were hungry and joined the long lines of boys and girls who held out enamel mugs, or mugs made from empty jam tins with wire twisted around them for handles, to the women who cooked and ladled soup from big three-legged pots. There was so much I wanted to know.

Mr Sello scratched his head when I asked about the differing ages of the children I'd seen in the classroom. 'Every year children fail and every year they return to us.' Language, he said, was as fraught an issue here as it was in Soweto. Until their fourth year of primary school, the children were taught in their home language. After that, there were abrupt changes to learn in Afrikaans. 'It's an impossible situation. Children already struggling to learn in a foreign language are being taught by teachers who are often unable to speak the language themselves. We are doing our best.' Teachers were required by the Department of Education and Training, which was responsible for schools for black children, to have a minimum of Standard 8 (today Grade 10) and some training in teaching, Mr Sello told me.

I left the men to discuss the events of 16 June and crossed the dirt road to the clinic and Sister Tseki. Outside the clinic I watched two little boys who sat on the ground drawing in the sand. One boy – Majolefa was his name, his legs streaked with dried mud, one bent under the other, his feet bare – stared at me with deep brown eyes. He wore a faded T-shirt and shorts. He clutched a rough stick in his small fingers and continued to draw pictures in the sand. That solemn little boy worked with such concentration. He seemed so unconcerned, so trusting and so innocent. I wanted to freeze that moment and preserve the innocence and childhood trust, and hope that life would be good to him. The other little boy stood up and ran screaming to his mother when he saw me. He buried his head in her skirt, hoping, no doubt, that I would disappear. I wanted to hug him, to tell him it was only me, I wouldn't hurt him. I couldn't bear to see his smile disappear, the light in his eyes turn to fear.

'The only white person these children see is the doctor,' Sister Tseki said brusquely, opening the clinic door. 'He thinks you're going to give him an injection.'

A queue of women sat on benches stretched along the red, polished-concrete clinic stoep. There were old women, young women, women with babies on their backs, toddlers tugging at their hands. Three- and four-year-olds pushed homemade wire cars in the street and flicked water at one another from zinc baths balanced on chairs in gardens where women swished their washing back and forth. When I saw those children, something inside me, a memory, clicked: these children were the same age as the children I had seen in the African Self Help Association nursery schools in Soweto when I'd been a 16-year-old schoolgirl just 12 years earlier.

It wasn't a compulsory school outing and there'd been few takers. It was my first visit to Soweto. 'Non-Bantu entering this area must have a permit': a large sign in English and Afrikaans was the first thing I remembered seeing as we'd driven into the sprawling conglomerate of South Western Townships. The sign was meant to intimidate white people visiting Soweto. But that was nothing compared with the passes that every black person over the age of 16 had to carry to show that they were allowed to be in a white area, the *dompas* that had had Hilda in tears so many years earlier when her son Jackie had been thrown into a police van. What I remember most about that day was the bleakness, the brown colours, the dirt roads, offset by the warm greeting of the nursery school supervisor when she took my hand in hers in welcome. It was the first time I had met black people who were not domestic workers, and my first visit to a 'black township'.

I had felt a shiver of curiosity, and strangely humbled, as I walked into the first nursery school I had been to since I'd left my own nursery school many years before. How different the circumstances. Our drive that morning had taken us from the tree-lined, tarred suburban streets of white Johannesburg where I had grown up, with well-built schools, houses with gardens, and shop windows laden with the latest fashion and plenty of food. It was overwhelming privilege compared to this place of cheaply built 'matchbox' houses, hostels over crowded with men far away from their homes and families, washing blowing in the wind, children running in the streets. The drive had taken us all of half an hour. Soweto was only some twenty kilometres away, but a foreign place to the vast majority of white people. 'I didn't know about apartheid when I was growing up. We didn't talk about those things in my family,' a friend confessed to me not so long ago. How could she not have known about apartheid?

The African Self Help Association was an extraordinary enterprise where black women from Soweto, and white women from the northern suburbs of Johannesburg, worked together to provide 'day nurseries' for over two thousand young children while their mothers worked. It was a two-pronged initiative. On one hand, care and education were provided for the children by women from Soweto, and on the other, women with access to the business world cajoled business leaders into providing funds to build the nursery schools, and to buy food for the children and finance training in early childhood care and development for the women who ran the schools. That Soweto visit was to become a defining moment in my life, although I didn't know it at the time.

The Association was not a charity: it was a group of women from vastly different backgrounds – some privileged, others struggling against the tremendous odds of poverty, hunger, illness, insufficient housing and humiliation – working together as equals to meet the women's needs and to look after and bring early learning into the lives of an increasing number of black children growing up in an iniquitous system of racial segregation. I knew at the end of that visit that I wanted to do something like the work of the African Self Help Association.

Dawn Haggie, the Association's chairperson, was a remarkable woman and one of the first people I'd interviewed for the *Rand Daily Mail* women's pages. The idea of my becoming involved in preschool education had been as unlikely at that time as the idea of my herding lumbering bulls back to their camp.

'Why aren't those children in nursery school?' I asked Mr Sello when I finally walked back into his office. 'There must be something more for them to do than draw in the sand ?'

'Which children?' he asked.

'Those little children playing outside.'

'Nursery school? There isn't a nursery school for them,' he said. 'There are no nursery schools for farmworkers' children. Now that you ask me, I don't know of nursery schools anywhere in the rural areas, not for black children.'

'Is this because the government doesn't provide for them or because nobody has thought of it?' I asked.

He shrugged. 'I really don't know, Mrs Evans.'

Combine harvesters still chugged on the lands on either side of the road as we drove home. The air was filled with fine dust from the thousands of maize kernels rushing like floodwaters down the harvesters' chutes into a lorry waiting to take them to the imposing grain silos across the main road from Huntersvlei.

'It is difficult enough getting government support for primary schools for farm children. We haven't even thought of nursery schools for children on farms,' said Anthony. But thinking about nursery schools was exactly what I was doing. 'You're very quiet. What are you thinking about?' Anthony turned his car into the driveway at the back of our house.

I looked at him. 'There is such a difference in the way we live compared to the families in the stad. Those families are so poor. If the government doesn't provide nursery schools for farmworkers' children, we'll just have to do it ourselves, just as you do for the primary school,' I said.

'What do you know about nursery schools?' Anthony asked.

'Not very much,' I replied.

'Find out what it entails, then let's talk about it. If the provision of education for the majority of children in this country doesn't change, there will be ongoing June the 16ths.'

A week later, triggered by the Soweto violence and a fierce determination for there to be a nursery school on Huntersvlei – not because the children playing in the dirt looked particularly unhappy but because children were children, and all deserved the same chance in life – I was on my way to Johannesburg to meet Dawn Haggie, Chairperson of the African Self Help Association.

9

THE NURSERY SCHOOL

With the help of formidable activists in the field of early learning, a vague vision stirs into the possibility of practice. It seemed like a worthy idea, but who would teach the women who had to teach the children?

DAWN HAGGIE WAS AHEAD of her time. As a young woman in the early 1940s, well aware of the inequalities and vast disparities of South African society, she had become an assistant to Margaret Ballinger, that feisty, powerful Scottish woman who fought for the rights of black people and had been elected to Parliament as a representative of the black community in the Eastern Cape in the late 1930s. No black men or women were allowed to represent their own communities; the government stipulated that a white person had to do it for them. She was a gutsy and outspoken member of Parliament, a real irritation to the government of the day.

When Alan Paton, author of *Cry, the Beloved Country*, established the Liberal Party in 1953, Margaret Ballinger became its first president. The multiracial party stood for 'one man, one vote', anathema to the government. After years of government harassment, it disbanded in 1968 when legislation made it illegal for political parties to be multiracial. The liberal party and women like Margaret Ballinger are not thought of enough these days, but they laid the ground for women of my generation – along with Helen Suzman, who was one of the bravest and most intrepid women I ever met. Dawn Haggie, still chairperson of the African Self Help Association whose nursery schools I'd visited in Soweto so many years before, was a true philanthropist. Rich or poor, black or white, she welcomed you with equal warmth to her home, Glenshiel, one of the grand old Johannesburg Randlords' homes and today home to the Order of St John. We sat in the garden of the gracious stone mansion, drinking tea from elegant porcelain cups. I told her what I wanted to do. I asked her for advice. 'Let me pour you another cup of tea,' she said, before we settled down.

A few days later, I stood on a bare patch of ground outside the clinic. This was my first engagement with women on the farm. I don't know what made me think they would give up their time to meet with me. 'Mrs Evans, you're the boss's wife, they'll come. They want to know what you look like,' said Rebecca Sothoane.

The minutes passed and still no one came. Rebecca was Maria Moloke's sister-in-law and was standing in for her while Maria was on maternity leave. I liked Rebecca, with her sing-song voice and constantly surprised look. At last, above the faraway hum of tractors, I heard voices. Women came in twos and threes, chatting and laughing among themselves. Their *tjalies* wrapped around their waists, they stood together until their clothes melted into a patchwork: young women, old women, mothers, grandmothers and curious onlookers, not to forget the babies on backs, or children playing at their mothers' feet. Rebecca waved at everyone to stop chattering. I stood beside her, intimidated by this gathering of curious women, who were openly staring at me. Rebecca translated my bumbling mixture of English and Afrikaans into Sesotho, and the women's Sesotho responses into Afrikaans. I wished I could speak Sesotho; I wouldn't have felt like such an outsider.

An old woman (I thought she was old then; she was probably no more than sixty), leaning heavily on a stick, fixed her eyes on mine and asked, 'Is a nursery school a crèche? I've heard about crèches on the radio,' she said.

'A crèche looks after babies and little children. It feeds them and keeps them clean and safe. It doesn't help them learn. No, a nursery school is not a crèche,' I answered. I had everything Dawn Haggie and Denise Parkinson had told me about early learning at my fingertips, ready to share with the women sitting in front of me.

'Then what is it, why are you concerned with our children? Why do you want them to go to a nursery school?' There was a murmur of agreement from the other women. We stood in the hot sun, sweat trickling down our faces.

My mouth was dry and there was an edge of desperation to my voice as I tried to explain: 'A child's learning is like building a brick house. The first bricks are the foundation, the beginning of the house, the strong, solid base on which the next bricks will be built. If the foundation is weak, the building will be weak.' I was warming to my subject. 'A nursery school is like that foundation. It is, along with what children learn at home, the first brick of learning, a child's future learning will be built on that foundation. If it is weak, the child's later education will be weak.' I paused to take a breath.

A woman asked, 'Why do you want a school like this for our children?' Most people there nodded their heads. 'Why?' The farm, for me, was a lonely place, but it wasn't loneliness that drove me – it was those little boys drawing in the sand. If a nursery school had been good for me when I was little, if nursery schools were good for children in cities, then they must be good for children on farms. At that time I didn't really understand how vitally important early

61

learning was for young children, especially children from disadvantaged backgrounds, but that didn't deter me. 'A nursery school will give your children a better start to their education. All children deserve that,' I said. Then, 'We can do it ourselves, together – that is, if you are willing to work with me?' It would be nice to say my eyes blazed with determination, but my voice wobbled, I was nervous and I was shading my eyes from the sun. I felt as I had done as a 14-year-old waiting in the wings at a ballet eisteddfod for the bar of music which would propel me onto the stage. The winter sun blazed down. The women were sitting on the clinic benches and fanning themselves with their hands and pieces of cardboard. The voices rose around me as the women talked among themselves. Rebecca clapped her hands. From her obvious command of the situation and her wide smile, she seemed to be enjoying herself, which is more than I was doing. Silence fell, punctuated by phlegmy coughs and a hand swiping at a noisy child.

Someone asked if the children would get something to eat at the nursery school.

'Yes, of course they will,' I answered.

'Will we have to pay?'

I really didn't know, but I promised that, if there was any cost, it wouldn't be very much.

Someone asked, 'Who will teach the children?'

It was the heart of the matter, the crux of the challenge. The question would lead to the dawn of a new world for many South African women in rural areas, and for me. Dawn and Denise's words rang in my ears: 'The quality of teaching and learning offered to two-, three- and four-year-olds is what turns a nursery school from a place of care to a place of early learning. The children are not the challenge, finding teachers and getting parents to understand about early learning will be your greatest challenge.'

There weren't any qualified Sesotho-speaking nursery school

teachers – certainly not in Viljoenskroon, nor, I imagined, in the rest of the Free State. I thought of Denise and the African Self Help Association's training programmes, developed for women with little access to formal education. 'Some of you will be the teachers,' I said.

At that, everyone had something to say. It was an uproar.

'They say they don't know anything about teaching and there can't be a nursery school because there won't be proper teachers,' said Rebecca.

'We'll teach them to be proper teachers,' I answered.

'Mme Jane,' Rebecca added, 'you go home. Let us talk this through our way.'

I didn't want to go home. Maybe I wasn't explaining it very well. Maybe I should try again. It was suddenly very quiet. Rebecca, her arms folded across her chest, stared at me, as did everyone else. Most reluctantly, I left.

What was taking Rebecca so long? I switched on the kettle, tapped my fingers on the orange kitchen counter. But as I waited, clutching a cup of hot coffee, I thought about the women in the stad. The disparity in our lives was stark. The odds were stacked against those women, young and old; they were poor, obviously hungry, judging from the constant mention of food, and certainly not about to trust me. What would it take for me to gain their trust? Where was Rebecca? The more I looked at my watch, the slower the hands seemed to move.

Finally, the door squeaked on its hinges. Rebecca looked serious. My heart sank. I wanted this nursery school more than anything I'd wanted in a long time. I thought of those exhausted women outside the clinic with toddlers tugging at their sleeves, the children racing their handmade wire cars along the dirt road.

'They want the food for their children. They don't mind the books and crayons, but they want the food. So if there's food, Mrs Evans, we want a nursery school.'

There it was, food again. Rebecca jutted out her chin and continued, 'We will choose the teachers. You must find out what we do in the nursery school and teach us.' I wanted to punch the air. 'But their husbands have to agree first.' My heart sank yet again.

'I'm sure that won't be a problem,' I said airily.

'Why do they have to ask the men?' I asked Anthony.

'Well, that's the way things work,' he said. 'The men make the final decision. I'll ask the men's liaison committee what they think of the idea.' I sat perched on the arm of a brown leather chair in Anthony's office. Anthony was behind the large mahogany desk, twiddling a pen. The desk had been his father's and would, in time, have one of our children sitting behind it. 'The men say there's a perfectly good school on Huntersvlei and they aren't quite sure why we need another one. Let me finish,' he said as I started to talk. 'It's what they believe. They don't think children learn at all until they go to primary school. Until then, their lives are only about growing.'

'But ...' he held up a hand, '... if the children will get extra food, and their wives are able to work instead of looking after the children all day, then they said, why not.'

The women's husbands had agreed. I didn't care why. I just felt incredible relief.

The women in the stad formed a committee to choose the teachers. Rebecca and Anthony said I should let the women get on with it and that I should trust their decision.

Despite my bravado, I didn't have a clue what size a nursery-school building should be. I didn't know how many teachers we'd need and what food we'd serve. Above all, I had no idea of how or what I was going to teach the women, let alone the children.

'Ja, well, you can't just start a school, Mevrou Evans. You need to follow regulations.'

I sat opposite a government official in his bleak Kroonstad office, a good hour's drive from the farm. The office and its yellowing cream paint looked sterile. The window panes, behind their sturdy burglar bars, could have done with a good clean. I told him that I was trying my best to follow regulations, but every time I spoke to anyone in his offices I got passed on to someone else, thus my visit to him.

'There's already a nursery school in Viljoenskroon. Why do you need another one?' he asked me. 'This nursery school isn't going to be in Viljoenskroon. It'll be on the farm, for farmworkers' children.'

'You didn't say it was a black school.' He sounded surprised.

'It's not a black school. It's a nursery school for farm children. Anyway, does it make a difference? They're little children.'

The official shrugged his shoulders and thumbed through a book of regulations.

He told me the amount of floor space that was required per child, which I confess I can no longer remember beyond the fact that it was considerably less than the number of square metres recommended in the South African Association for Early Childhood Education's handbook. Those measurements, he said, were for white children.

I asked if we would get a subsidy. 'Not for the school you're starting,' he replied.

I got back into my car, infuriated at the government's lack of concern for farmworkers' children or interest in helping me. And yet, I was delighted too. It had been obvious from my conversation with the official that we could do more or less as we liked. We would not at this stage be subjected to government bureaucracy. I went in search of Anthony. I couldn't find him and had to make do with Rhys Rolfe, Anthony's general manager, who was helping himself to a rusk from a plate on the secretary's desk in the farm office.

'I hear you're starting a nannying service,' he grinned.

'I'm doing nothing of the sort.' I edged past him. 'It's a nursery school.'

'Same thing,' he said. At least the official in Kroonstad had known what a nursery school was, even if he wasn't going to support it.

'A nursery school teaches children the things they need to know before they go to primary school. It makes them ready for school,' I told Rhys.

'So who's going to teach them?'

'Women from the stad.'

'They can hardly read. How could they be teachers?'

I didn't bother to answer him.

I got home to find Rebecca and Bertha waiting for me. They had news. They sat side by side on the angular blue couch in my comparatively empty new study. They stared alternately at the beige carpet and at me.

'But you work here, Bertha. You didn't say anything about wanting to work in the nursery school.' I was flabbergasted when Rebecca told me who had been chosen to be teachers.

'I really don't like cooking.'

I sympathised. I wasn't too keen on it either.

'Let her, Mme Jane, the others want her.' Rebecca, who was the leader of the nursery school committee, hadn't finished. 'Bertha will be one teacher and Alina's daughter-in-law Maria Thekiso will be the other.' Bertha had married the son of a Huntersvlei stalwart and lived with her parents-in-law in the stad. Maria Thekiso had grown up in the Huntersvlei stad, and had gone to the farm primary school and then high school in QwaQwa, a cold, isolated 'homeland' three or four hours' drive from the farm.

Criteria for choosing teachers had been sketchy. Rebecca and I had agreed that the prospective teachers should be able to read, write and speak Sesotho, that they should live on the farm and like the idea of working with children. They waited for me to say something.

A journalist, a cook and a farmworker. Little did any of us know that, between us, we would take early learning and preschool education to places it had never been before. The ripples from that informal meeting on Huntersvlei would reach deep into some of the poorest rural communities in South Africa.

'Congratulations, Bertha,' I said.

10

REBECCA

*From the mud of the ground up, the dream
of a better tomorrow begins to take shape.*

REBECCA KNELT ON A plastic mat and splashed water from a jam tin onto the sand. It fell like rain. She followed this with a dollop of mud, which she scooped out of a bucket and dumped on the wet ground. Leaning forward, she smeared the mixture over the soil with both hands.

We had decided to hold the nursery school in the empty room next to the clinic. 'If the nursery school lasts, I'll build a special nursery school building. I promise,' Anthony had said.

'What are you doing?' I stood at the door.

'I'm smearing the floor.'

'With what?' I knelt down and gingerly rubbed the mixture through my fingers. It felt to me much like the sausage mixture, thick and sticky.

Rebecca sat back on her heels, wiped her forehead with the back of her mud-covered hand, adding to the streaks of dried mud already there. 'Cow dung, soil and water.' Her overall was tucked high on her legs, protecting it from the mixture. A nursery school with a dung floor? 'It gets nice and hard when it dries.' She stood up and wiped her hands on a damp grey rag.

That was not the point. What about hygiene? What was wrong with nice clean tiles? If something spills on it?

'It dries again.'

'Doesn't it smell?' I wrinkled my nose.

'Mme, it doesn't smell.'

We walked outside into the sun and she said to me, 'When I was a little girl I watched my father make mud bricks to build our house here on the farm, out of a mixture just like that.' She pointed to the bucket of mud and dung. 'He put the bricks in the sun to bake and when they were nice and hard he and my brothers built the hut. He smeared the mud walls with the same mixture. It was an extra coat to protect us from the weather. It filled in all the cracks and it was hard like plaster when it dried. And you know, Mme Jane, it didn't matter if it rained or if the wind blew, the house stood firm with all of us warm inside. My mother smeared the floors inside the house and even the inside walls and she drew patterns on them. We slept on the floor, on mattresses we made by stuffing hessian bags with mielie leaves.'

'Didn't they scratch you?' I asked.

'It scratched a bit but we made blankets out of bits of material which we put on top of them. My grandfather said that's where people slept and he wasn't going to sleep in the air like a chicken.'

'Do chickens sleep in the air?' I asked, feeling stupid.

'Our chickens did. They slept in wire cages which hung from the roof. That meant nothing, no cats, could eat them during the night.'

'Did you go to school on the farm?'

'There was no school on the farm then. I went to school in Vierfontein, near the coal fields. It's about thirty kilometres from here. I stayed there during the week and came home over weekends. Then my mother got sick when I was in Standard 6, and I had to leave school to look after her and run our house.' Rebecca shrugged. 'I was sad to leave school but I had enough to eat, a house to live in and my family so I didn't worry. When I got married I came to live here at Huntersvlei in a brick house. I smeared the walls inside my house with mud and cow dung. I drew patterns in the mixture like wallpaper. Just like my mother did.'

Despite what Rebecca had said, a mud floor was not exactly what I'd had in mind. But it seemed I was in the minority.

'How,' I asked Anthony that evening, 'can we possibly have a nursery school with a mud floor?'

'Why not? All the houses in the stad have a mud floor. My grandparents had a mud floor.'

While Rebecca smeared the floor, Moses and Andrew dug deep into the playground's hard, brown soil. They took away mounds of stones and low-spreading bushes covered with *dubbeltjies*, nasty little thorns that dug into the soles of my shoes and clung so painfully to bare feet. On the levelled ground we planted long lines of kikuyu grass, which would be tough enough for the children to play on. And in the middle of this playground we planted a line of honey locust trees. These trees, I was told by the nurseryman, would grow fast, and soon give us shade from the hot summer sun. The sturdy, thorny trees with their long, brown pods were about as far away from their native North America as I felt from Johannesburg.

We were both planting our roots in foreign soil.

Alina gathered a small group of her friends. They sat inside our laundry, cutting out pinafores for the nursery school children from the mounds of crisp red, green and yellow material I'd deposited on the ironing table. It wasn't toilet-lid covers, but it was women sewing. By the time Christmas came, piles of pinafores lay neatly stacked under the ironing table, waiting for the new year.

Christmas also brought its own traditions. When Anthony and I arrived at the big house on Christmas day, a long line of tables had been set in front of the Cottage, covered with Sybil's rose-patterned tablecloths. The swimming pool reflected the morning light and I felt the day's promised heat on my bare arms. A distant hum from the stad got louder and turned into voices, hundreds of voices.

Moses heaved cardboard boxes off the back of a bakkie, its muddy wheels leaving marks on Sybil's pristine lawn. He threw them one by one, as effortlessly as soccer balls, to Elias, who threw them to Majolefa, who put them on the tables and slit them open with a sharp kitchen knife. Hundreds of packets shaped like Christmas stockings and filled with sweets tumbled onto the table. Someone else opened the bottles of Coke. The bent metal bottle tops fell onto the grass and glistened in the sun. As children and their mothers arrived to greet us, I was on my hands and knees, scrabbling for bottle tops to make musical instruments for the nursery school.

There must have been two hundred children and at least a hundred adults who poured onto the lawn. Every child under the age of 12 – and, it seemed to me, some considerably older – had come for a packet of sweets and a bottle of Coke. The younger children clung to their mothers' or grandmothers' hands. Many of the mothers were high-school age themselves and wanted their own sweets and Coke. There seemed to be far more people than sweets. Anthony and I placed packet after packet into the small hands clasped together in front of us. Some of the children wore shoes, others were barefoot. Worn, darned or new, their clothes were all their best clothes, their church clothes. It was, Majolefa said, a very special occasion. As each little boy or girl bobbed to say thank you, I wondered what on earth we'd do if all the younger children came to the nursery school: it wouldn't be big enough.

Majolefa said I shouldn't worry. 'Lots of these children are from Rammulotsi. They come and stay with their families on the farm over Christmas. They all get sweets.'

I recognised many of the women who were dressed in their

church uniforms: black choir dresses and red shawls. They said they wanted to sing for us, a Christmas greeting from the stad. Mothers and children, hands sticky with chocolate, sat on the grass to listen. A few older women sat on chairs on the lawn. Anthony's family – aunts, uncles and cousins – sat on the Cottage stoep. I felt embarrassed by the pile of torn Christmas wrapping strewn across the floor. 'You shouldn't be embarrassed,' Rebecca told me later. 'Everyone likes coming here. It is a celebration. It's a chance to sing together and to say thank you to each other.'

The strong voices of the Huntersvlei women's choir lifted into one of the most poignantly beautiful songs I know. Shivers ran through me. 'Nkosi Sikelel' iAfrika': this was my Christmas present from the choir. As the women's voices rose, I sensed something of the changes that would be coming. And just as change would sweep the country, so it would come to the farm. I looked at the children. Perhaps the nursery school would improve their chances in life. But the thought nagged at me well after we'd stuffed the torn wrapping paper into black refuse bags: would I be seen as a white do-gooder, and was everyone saying yes to the nursery school to humour the boss's wife?

I didn't want to be seen as a person who did things for other people. I wanted us to work together.

11

MILK AND ORANGES

Amid the clouds of dust and the chaos of children crying, a new school of thought opens its doors.

'GO AWAY. MOVE.'

A motley group of stad cattle eating tufts of grass at the nursery-school gate totally ignored my flapping hands.

'Hai, hai!' It took an authoritative roar from Rebecca to get them clattering off to another part of the stad.

The sky stretched over us like a vast blue dome that morning. I smelled dust and smoke from the cooking fires and the herby smell of gum trees. I unhooked the chain and opened the gate to the nursery-school grounds. The swings, made in the farm workshop out of car tyres and heavy chains, were wet with dew. The jungle gym and slide were newly painted. The sun's early rays warmed the sandpit: a tractor tyre filled with clean river sand mixed with coarse salt to kill any nasty bugs, exactly as I'd read in a book – one of a pile of books on nursery schools and early learning that lay next to my bed, along with the detective stories. Buckets and spades stuck out of the fine grains.

The long wire handles of a fleet of homemade wire cars rested against the fence next to a pile of bouncy rubber balls. I unlocked the playroom door. I had to have one last check before the children arrived – if the children arrived. The mud floor was covered by thick plastic fertiliser bags, scrubbed until every last speck of fertiliser had been removed. Fathers had made child-height wooden tables and benches in the farm workshop. They had painted them bright red, blue and green. Thick wooden blocks of different sizes and shapes had been neatly stacked by Rebecca along a wall. Children's books were displayed on upturned cardboard boxes, and ragdolls lay in cardboard beds, each with its own little blanket and pillow. I picked up a doll and hugged it. It felt soft and smelled, like so much else in the stad, of wood smoke. I was so proud of the playroom, mud floor and all.

By this time Rebecca, Bertha and Maria were bustling about the clinic in the plain-coloured overalls which they had chosen to wear. They lined up cream-and-green enamel mugs and cut oranges into quarters. The clinic was about the only place in which we could keep flies away from the food. Sister clucked around, making sure we didn't make too much of a mess. I was nervous; for all of us, this was something out of the ordinary. I felt responsible for the success of the nursery school. Everyone's anticipation was high; it had to work. What if no one came? What if they'd changed their minds?

Puffs of dust appeared. I unclenched my fingers. The puffs of dust turned into clouds. Out of these clouds mothers and grand-mothers appeared, children tugging at their arms in, it seemed to me, the opposite direction from the nursery school. 'Mpho, Modiehi, Majolefa,' yelled older brothers and sisters to their siblings. They'd ducked out of the primary school across the road. The opening day of the nursery school was too good a spectacle to be missed. The headmaster tore across the road. 'Get back to school, now,' he commanded. Some went back; others hung on to the fence, peering at the growing chaos inside. The first children straggled through the gate, followed by more. And more. And still more.

I had no idea how many children had arrived, but it didn't matter. I was just so relieved they'd come. We'd begun at last. I joined in the desperate attempts to bring some kind of order. Everyone wanted milk and oranges.

'I've told them if their names aren't on the list they'd better go home and get a mug,' said Rebecca, but no one budged. Mugs magically appeared from surrounding houses and were passed to Rebecca through the fence. That was fine, but where was the extra milk to come from?

Anthony's truck squealed to a stop outside the gate. He'd come to see how we were getting on, and he couldn't have been more welcome. 'Serve them less in the meantime. I'll get milk from the cold room.' He got right back into the truck and drove off to the big house. Those ancient-looking steel milk cans in Sybil's cold room, filled with warm, frothy milk from the farm's Friesland cows, had at last, as far as I was concerned, come in useful.

My overriding memory of that first day isn't the homemade toys I'd spent weeks making. It isn't the mothers and grandmothers yelling at their children to be quiet. It is the sound of children crying. Every child seemed to be in tears, holding on to his or her mother, terrified of being left behind.

If I'd thought there was chaos before, it was now bedlam. Hardier children clambered over the jungle gym and swings. Others held on to their departing mothers and howled. Inside the playroom, every girl wanted a doll. Boys clung on to the blocks and were not about to share them. The nursery school I'd imagined had children gathered quietly around their teacher, listening to a story. I can still remember the dress I wore that day – blue and sleeveless, with a white stripe down the front. I can still, all these years later, feel the panic as I frantically threw a ball to any child who'd stop crying for long enough to catch it.

Only while they all drank their milk and ate their oranges was there silence. The primary-school children had grown bored and had long since gone back to their classrooms. In the sandpit, a few little girls started to play.

'How did it go?' Anthony was waiting for me when I got home. I thought of the crying children, the shouting mothers, the battles for toys in the playroom.

'It was fantastic,' I said, and faded into his arms.

12

JOSEPHINE

*Like a vision, a saving grace, she appeared
from the big city, with bountiful lessons to teach.*

'THERE ARE 77 CHILDREN. We can't fit them all in.' Rebecca helped me unload pockets of oranges the next morning. 'We're going to have to send some home.'

We were certainly not going to do that. Not after we'd managed to get them there. I'd been at the grocery store as it opened and had piled sacks of oranges into my car. In the playground, mothers and grandmothers looked from Rebecca to me. Inside the playroom, children clung to whatever toy they could find. There was not a spot to sit on any of the benches. Children sat on the mud floor, crying. I wanted to cry too. Eventually, Rebecca broke the standoff.

'We could divide them into two groups, half in the morning and the other half in the afternoon? That's what high-school children do.'

An afternoon nursery school? I'd never heard of one, but it's what we did. From the next day the younger children came in the morning, the older children came in the afternoon. It worked. It didn't take long for the children to get over their tears and fears. They soon got used to me and flocked round, yelling, 'Mme Janey, Mme Janey,' and holding my hands, pressing their little thumbs against mine.

The children were happy and I was so busy I didn't have time to think. But the teachers were worn out. Every day was as chaotic as the first and there wasn't enough of anything – apart, of course, from children who kept arriving. The reason? Food. Parents wanted their children to get the same thick soup we'd served on pension day in Rammulotsi, and the same nourishing biscuits And then, of course, there was the midday snack of oranges and milk.

Despite my joy at the number of children at the nursery school, I felt that some of them were too old to be there. 'Shouldn't some of these children be at primary school?' I leaned over Rebecca's shoulder, watching her tick the daily register. 'Why aren't their birthdays filled in?' There were lots of gaps under 'date of birth'.

'Most of these children don't have birth certificates.'

'So how do they know how old they are or when to go to school?'

'They don't really, but when they put an arm over their heads and can touch their ear with their fingers then they are big enough to go to primary school. Also, the primary school won't admit children if they are not six about to turn seven.'

Every morning I was at the nursery school as it opened, trying to organise the children's play programme. The more I told the teachers what to do, the more they told children what to do, the less anyone wanted to do it. As an educator I was failing, miserably. I sat at night reading piles of books on early learning. On one hand it was all about pedagogy, the theory and practice of teaching. On the other were practical ways of challenging children to think and develop. It was all new terminology, but of one thing I was convinced. It didn't matter that we were 80 kilometres away from the nearest toyshop – we didn't need to buy toys. There were so many playthings we could improvise or make ourselves.

I rifled through my kitchen cupboards for pots and pans. I collected empty Omo boxes and yoghurt containers. A perplexed farm workshop manager watched me as I rummaged through boxes of nuts and bolts. Anthony eyed egg boxes littering the study floor. I had cut and painted them, turning them into centipedes. 'What if they don't want to play with them?' But they did. Little boys were enchanted and crawled around the playroom yelling, 'Vrrm-vrrm!' My centipedes became much-used cars, but that didn't solve my problem.

Some things I had got right – like, thanks to Anthony and Rebecca, consulting the parents before I went ahead with the nursery school, and consulting Sister about food. ('Don't provide full meals, just nutritious snacks,' she'd said. 'Otherwise parents won't feed their children at home.') We had a building, toilets, a fenced-off play-ground, but we still had a fair amount of chaos each day: children running around wanting whatever their friend was playing with, children who could not or would not listen to the teachers.

I had a sneaking suspicion we were getting it all wrong. This was not a school. Children were not meant to sit in rows with their fingers on their lips. They were not all meant to be told what to play with or what to draw or paint, nor were they all meant to do the same thing at the same time. I called Dawn Haggie at African Self Help. Hearing the near-hysteria in my voice, she said, 'Would you like one of our trainers to spend some time at the farm?'

'That would be fantastic,' I said, feeling incredible relief. When I told Rebecca of Dawn Haggie's suggestion, she looked almost more relieved than I'd felt. Part of my frustration was that I didn't know enough about early childhood development or teaching to give the learner teachers sufficient help myself. It was one thing reading about what to do, but quite another interacting with adults and helping them learn how to interact with children so that the children would, in fact, learn.

It didn't occur me that the nursery school might not succeed, and I don't know how I would have felt if it hadn't. I suppose I would have been incredibly disappointed, not so much for myself but for the women who were entering this initiative with verve coupled with hesitant excitement – and, of course, for the children. I wanted things to happen immediately and very often I wanted them to happen my way. I felt not only frustrated but overwhelmed by the task I'd set myself. It took me time to understand that I couldn't do everything immediately and that I really couldn't do it all my way – or myself. I often learnt the hard way to consult whoever I was working with and to turn to people who knew what they were doing for help: thus the arrival of Josephine Mnyakeni, an experienced African Self Help trainer who entered our lives when we most needed her.

Josephine was sitting with Dawn in Glenshiel's exquisite garden when I arrived to fetch her. She didn't seem to mind leaving her family for a month and coming to the depths of the Free State. It was, she assured me, an adventure. 'I'll come and visit while she's there,' said Dawn.

Rain pelted down at the Huntersvlei nursery school when we arrived a few hours later. Josephine stepped gingerly through the playground puddles, her smart black town shoes turning a soggy brown. Thump. A one-armed teddy bear hit her squarely in the stomach. She picked it up from the floor where it fell. I caught a tennis ball in mid-air. The playroom windows were closed against the rain and the room smelled stale. The children were hyped up with excitement at getting a 'real' teacher. Our teachers were anxious.

'What if she doesn't like what we are doing?' asked Bertha. 'Hai, hai, shoosh.' She clapped her hands. The noise of the rain on the tin roof and the shouts of children flinging toys at one another drowned her words. I looked sheepishly at Josephine, wondering what she made of it all. Our playroom was a far cry from the well-equipped African Self Help preschools she was used to in Soweto. She smiled at me, then lifted up her arms in greeting. Only the noise of the rain remained. The 'real' teacher got to work.

Josephine's time with us passed too soon. She left the nursery school, its teachers and me different people; we finally had the makings of a 'proper' nursery school. She would be a constant visitor to the Huntersvlei nursery school over the next few years. It was over twenty years later, when Rebecca had retired, that she had said to me: 'You know, Jane, Josephine and the nursery school changed my life. When I was younger I didn't want anything but what I had, but after I joined you and after Josephine came to stay with me I saw there was a whole other world outside and I wanted more – not for me, but for my children. I wanted them to have a good education'

It was my first visit to Rebecca since she'd retired and moved to Rammulotsi. We sat in her living room on her leather chairs, a soft breeze blowing through open gold-coloured curtains with white net curtains behind them. She'd poured me a cup of tea and offered me a biscuit. 'Now I own my own house, we have our own bedrooms, beds to sleep on, lots of blankets. No more homemade mattresses on the floor.' She laughed her familiar high-pitched laugh. Her hair was grey but her face was barely lined. 'My daughter's a teacher, my sons have jobs. What else could I want?' She'd paused. 'I didn't realise the difference it was making to me and my family's life at the time we were all growing together, but none of this would have happened for us without Ntataise. I didn't mind working in the lands but I'm pleased my children didn't have to.' She'd made me think of the honey locust trees and all that had happened in the Huntersvlei nursery school playground under their growing branches over the years, of myself and my children growing older and growing up. 'I loved my work with Ntataise. I grew with it,' she said.

'Do you think we've made a difference to the children who came to the nursery schools?' I asked her before I left.

'We've made a big difference, Jane. Think not only of the children who have been to the nursery schools, but the hundreds of women who have developed themselves through our training. They've got careers, money; they are someone special in their communities and they've got certificates from the government. They got a chance to improve their qualifications and they started preschools that were never there before.'

13

THE WASHING OF HANDS

In a simple, everyday ritual, a hands-on lesson in the art of understanding.

'COME, NOW.' I CRUMPLED Rebecca's message into a ball. I was feeling sick. A crisis at the nursery school was the only thing that could have dragged me out of the house. My heart was in my mouth as I drove to the stad. It didn't appear to have descended into its early chaos. I couldn't see or hear any children when I drew up outside. This was hardly surprising: there weren't any. If I hadn't wanted to throw up, I'd have laughed. Except that it was no laughing matter.

'The children aren't coming,' Rebecca told me. Her mouth was a straight line as she stood and pointed at the mothers and grandmothers who sat on the children's benches, which had been carried outside. The wood groaned under their weight. 'They say we've told their children not to eat until they have said a prayer and washed their hands. Now they won't eat at home unless their hands are washed and they've said a prayer. The parents say the children now think they are teachers in the home. And they don't like it.'

'Isn't there enough water?' I asked her.

'Water's not the problem. There's water – it's just that not everyone washes their hands before they eat.'

There were still communal taps in the stad in those days. I often saw children rolling drums full of water home. 'You should, perhaps,' said Anthony later that day, 'have told the parents what you'd be teaching their children. And why you are teaching it.' He disappeared behind his newspaper.

He was right, of course, but that didn't help the immediate situation. Praying had been introduced by Rebecca; it was hand-washing and water that concerned me. Washing hands at the nursery school was a rudimentary affair. All the children lined up – boys in one row, girls in another. Bertha supervised the children at the pit toilets with their specially made child-sized seats. Rebecca stood a short distance away with a large enamel jug. After using the toilet, each child put out his or her hands and Rebecca poured water over them. The child then rubbed them around a cake of soap before stretching hands out for more water. Initially, because Sister Tseki had told us that using one towel for everyone was unhygienic, each child had his or her own towel, which hung on the chicken-wire fence. This had turned into such a shambles that Rebecca had got rid of the towels. Instead, the children ran around the playground waving their hands in the air until they dried. I still wave my hands in the air to dry them. It seems healthier than sodden towels or hot-air-drying machines.

I looked at the glaring women, about to say I was sorry – not that children had to wash their hands, but that we hadn't discussed it with them first. Rebecca stopped me. There was more to come. 'They also say we must cut up the children's oranges and they must eat them at school. When we give them to them whole, they take them home and their brothers and sisters sell them to their friends.' I thought that was quite entrepreneurial but solemnly listened. We resolved the matter by agreeing to supervise children eating their oranges and that Sister Tseki would explain to mothers why hands should be washed before eating. I'd had this drummed into me at Saxonwold school when I was nine years old and polio was a scare.

Thirty years later, when all the workers had moved off the farm into their own houses in Rammulotsi, Anthony and I attended the opening of the new Huntersvlei preschool in the township. Dikeledi Nthethe Mokwanasi, Moses's daughter, whose sister Maria Moloke had coaxed rehydration liquid into so many children years before, was now a municipal ward councillor and mother of two children. She had been among that first 1977 intake of children. She was one of the speakers for the opening.

'I'd arrive at the nursery school each morning,' she said, 'and Rebecca would put her hand on my stomach and rub it. Water, she'd say, water, that's all there is in this stomach. You need food and the nursery school gave me food.'

We had given her food, just as we'd given it to countless other children after her. And she had learnt, she said, to wash her hands before she ate. She looked at Rebecca and me, sitting in the front row. 'Mme Jane, it was apartheid years, but you hugged us and touched us.' Is that what the children had thought? That I wouldn't touch them because they were black? They were children – I didn't care what colour they were. I didn't understand the depth of suspicion with which whites were regarded. It was as Sister Tseki had said: 'The only white person these children know is the doctor.' He gave them injections. He hurt them. Did they associate white people with hurt?

14

THE POTHOLE

I drifted in and out of the cloud, as the doctor told me the terrible news.

'WE'RE GOING TO HAVE a baby,' I blurted to Anthony one chilly July day. As usual, he was in his office sitting behind his father's old desk, pen in hand. I burst into tears. 'I don't want a baby.'

He wiped a tear from my cheek. 'Don't look so sad. It's wonderful news.' He hugged me tight. A baby seemed like such a binding thing – not to Anthony, but to the farm and the isolated countryside – not something I was ready to do. I felt utter panic. I wanted to have a baby, but with my mother nearby. I felt concerned that my link with Johannesburg would be broken, the warmth and comfort I got from the familiarity of my mother's home and my friends. That tiny little baby growing inside me did not give me a sense of purpose or make me feel the wonder of bringing another generation to the farm. I felt so conflicted; it would be some years before I allowed myself to feel that I belonged on Huntersvlei.

Poor Anthony; he tried his best to look sympathetic, but the instant I fell silent for long enough to draw breath, he beamed. 'We ought,' he said when he'd finished hugging me, 'to tell our mothers.'

The baby flurry gained momentum from that moment. Sybil summoned us to the big house later that day. Majolefa had taken the Evans family crib, an old-fashioned wooden crib with a short, white broderie anglaise skirt, out of the cupboard where it was safely stored. It smelled of camphor and mothballs. Anthony, his sister Wendy and all her children had slept in that crib.

'I want our own crib,' I said to Anthony when we were alone that night. The panic I felt intensified. I was being swallowed by Evans traditions.

'But we all slept in that crib. What's wrong with it?'

'I want to choose our own crib.' I wanted something new, that was ours. After some back and forth of what I can only call negotiation between a determined Sybil and an equally determined me, we reached a compromise: we'd surround the old crib with a new skirt of my choosing.

In the event I needn't have worried. The farm that Anthony had bought on the doorstep of Spioenkop, a historic Boer War battlefield in what was then Natal, was neglected and the roads rough. I'd gone with him to visit it. The farm's gently rolling hills, with the towering Drakensberg on the horizon, were quite different from the flat Free State veld. I sat in the back of the manager's Land Rover. He and Anthony sat in front, talking about the changes they were planning. No one saw the pothole until we landed in it with a sickening thud that juddered through my body.

I don't remember much about our frantic drive to Johannesburg a few days later or being admitted to the Park Lane Clinic, where my gynaecologist was waiting for us. I drifted in and out of a white cloud. Anthony hovered at the side of the hospital bed and held my hand. The doctor told me, through the fog of anaesthesia, that he hadn't been able to save my baby. I'd had a miscarriage.

I looked at Anthony. He looked at me with such love and concern that tears rolled down my cheeks, yet again. 'I'm so sorry. It's all my fault,' I said huskily. 'I didn't want a baby, so it went away.'

I would never know if it was the pothole that caused it, and I didn't know which was worse: hearing that I was having a baby, or hearing that I'd lost it. The days and weeks that followed were among the lowest I can remember. I felt buried in a thick fog of total misery.

'You've had a traumatic experience. I'm sure it'll come right,' Anthony said. But that determined, confident women's pages editor had got lost somewhere in the brown veld of the northern Free State. The happiness and sense of purpose the nursery school was giving me was put on hold. I sat at the dinner table, cut my food into tiny pieces and tried to swallow, but it wouldn't go down. I woke up in the middle of each night feeling helpless and sick. I was thin, I was frightened – and I was no longer pregnant.

My mother came to stay with us. She and I walked down the Huntersvlei front drive. The plane trees dropped fluffy balls of seed at our feet. Bulls snorted at the dogs that ran alongside us and she demanded I tell her what was wrong. It wasn't Anthony, I loved him. It sounded so lame, but I was homesick. I was the newest of six Mrs Evanses in the district. The older ones, wives and cousins, had carved out their lives, made their places, absorbed the traditions. I liked the traditions, but this was an Evans stronghold and I wasn't going to give up my independence. I felt it was assumed that I'd just slip into farm life and the way things had always been done. I didn't make it easy for myself. I knew it was the life I had chosen and that Johannesburg wasn't as incredible as I made it out to be, but I just couldn't let it go. I was holding tight to my own identity. The more swamped I felt by Evans traditions, the more I resented Viljoenskroon. It was totally irrational. Anthony understood how I felt but he wasn't sure how to help me.

Alarmed at my lethargy, my mother suggested a few days in Johannesburg. Anthony was as distressed as I was about having lost our baby. Since I had arrived on the farm, the lure of Johannesburg had created a tug-of-war not only in me but between the two of us. In retrospect, it needn't have been like that. Each time I went to Johannesburg, he thought I wouldn't return. Neither of us knew any better; we hadn't yet learnt how to compromise.

I lay on the bed in the consulting room of Mosie Suzman, a Johannesburg physician, and told him I was dying. 'That you are not. I suggest you take these.' I left his rooms an hour later, clutching a bottle of pink beta blockers. When I returned to my car, I found an equally pink parking fine tucked under my windscreen wiper.

'Don't go away again,' said Anthony when I returned. 'I don't like it when you're not here. We'll have a baby, but at the right time.'

The two women closest to me during the awful time of my miscarriage, apart from my mother, were Monica Masukela, the woman who was our new cook, and Maria Moloke, who had long since returned from maternity leave. They were both mothers and knew all about morning sickness. I hadn't had to tell them I was pregnant; they had known. When I lost the baby, they brought me tea and looked after me. When I couldn't eat, they cooked soup using vegetables from the garden and baked homemade brown bread. They kept the house tidy and Anthony fed. I waited for them to come to work each morning. They made our empty house feel alive.

Rebecca, Bertha and Maria Thekiso kept the nursery school going; I didn't have the energy. I wallowed in sadness until one morning, not long after my miscarriage, Monica came to work on her own.

15

SICKNESS

A mix-up over medication brings home the
ravages of a rampant illness.

'MARIA'S BABY IS SICK. She's staying at home to look after her,'
Monica told me.

The little girl had been sick before and I didn't think too much of
it – not until that evening, when there was a loud knock on the door.
Rebecca stood outside, her face lined with worry. 'Ai, Mme Jane.
Maria's baby's died.'

The night watchman drove Rebecca back to the stad. I lay awake
thinking of the pretty baby girl and how proudly Maria had brought
her to the house to show her to me. My miscarriage and the misery
that had submerged me seemed so insignificant.

I knocked hesitantly on Maria's front door the next morning. A
child let me in. Maria sat on an upholstered chair in her small,
darkened sitting room. She rested her head on her hand and stared
at the floor, her body slumped in anguish. She stood up when she
saw me. She didn't say anything, just pushed me gently towards her
bedroom.

I'd never seen a dead person before. I felt curious and afraid. I felt desperate for Maria. The room was dark. A mat covered the mud floor. A low double bed, the mattress sunken in the middle, and a wooden wardrobe filled the room. I heard children playing on their way to school. Somewhere a clock ticked. The perfect baby girl, skin smooth, eyes closed, lay naked on a sheet on the bed. Her arms lay neatly at her sides. I couldn't believe she wouldn't open her eyes and hold out her hands. After I left the baby was gently placed on her sheet on the floor, to keep her body cool.

Upset and angry, I stopped at the clinic on my way home. Babies shouldn't be dying – not in this stad, not anywhere. Outside the whitewashed building, women and children were lining up to see Sister Tseki. I pushed past them into the room where Sister was laying things out on her table. I demanded to know why the baby had died.

'Diarrhoea and dehydration,' she answered without any hesitation.

'Couldn't you have saved her?' I exploded.

We glared at each other. She said that by the time Maria had called her, it was too late. 'They always call me when it's too late.' She shook her head. 'Poor hygiene, unsterilised bottles, dirty teats, flies, uncovered food, mean babies and children die. There are too many cattle in the stad, they bring the flies.'

If Sister Tseki had been proactive and not reactive, maybe the baby would have lived. But I couldn't blame her for the baby's death. I was angry with the system.

'What are you going to do about the flies in the stad?' I asked Anthony that evening in anger.

'It's not that easy. We'll have to get rid of the cattle. It's not only the flies that are the problem. We're running out of grazing for the numbers of stad cattle.' Every family owned cattle that grazed in their yards and common stad land. 'Cattle are a family's wealth and their security. They give the family milk and when school fees are needed an animal gets sold. But it's time to make a change.'

Change came after lengthy negotiations with the liaison committee, which agreed that, if Anthony set up an education fund to pay for the children to go to high school and if he provided them with transport to Rammulotsi and back each day, they would slowly get rid of their cattle – but the pigs and chickens would stay. And so a new vehicle arrived to join the tractors in the sheds: a blue-grey bus with the odd dent, which took high-school children to school, rattling over the stony farm roads for many years, a firm feature on the farm.

Sister waved me down as I drove on my way to the nursery school in the midst of these discussions. She was dragging a struggling young man by the ear. 'He's got worms,' she said, thrusting a bottle under my nose. She let him go and he scampered back to the stad, rubbing his ear.

He was not the reason she wanted to see me. Diarrhoea and dehydration were only two of the health problems in the stad. She got into the car and sat next to me, the bottle with its unappealing contents on her lap. The purpose of her visit was to tell me that one of the tractor drivers had tuberculosis, and that she'd arranged for the adults on the Rhys Evans farms to be tested by the provincial TB services. 'I'm sure,' she said bluntly, 'he's not the only one.'

TB was nothing new in the rural areas. This highly infectious disease was not helped by generally poor health, bad eating and the impoverished circumstances in which people lived. The province's mobile TB testing unit parked outside the Huntersvlei nursery school on the appointed day. The X-ray unit was manned by a nurse and doctor. Queues of men and women from all our farms waited their turn to be X-rayed. This was a voluntary exercise for anyone on the farms, but it seemed that most of the adults were there. Tractor-drawn wagons parked along the verge of the road leading past the primary school; drivers sat in the shade eating pap out of skoff tins. There was almost a holiday atmosphere, but I wondered how everyone really felt.

When the results of the TB testing had finally reached us, I'd been appalled. Far too many people had TB. The bad cases were admitted to the TB hospital in Allanridge, not too far away from us. Sister said she would treat the other affected men and women at home with medication to be provided by the provincial health department. And provided it had been.

'Mevrou Evans, there are boxes for you from Bloemfontein, lots of boxes, and they are clogging up my waiting room.' The stationmaster phoned me in a highly agitated state. It was all very well to demand I fetch them, but what on earth was I going to do with them? Almost as agitated as the stationmaster, Moses and I heaved the brown cardboard boxes of TB medication into the farm bakkie.

'Why,' I asked a doctor in Bloemfontein over the usual crackly party line, 'has the Department of Health sent such a vast amount of medication?' There was no mistake, I was told; those pills were meant for us. I couldn't understand it. Neither could Sister Tseki, but there was nothing to be done. We rapidly turned our attention to finding a place to store the boxes. I arrived home later, flustered from commandeering storage space wherever I could find it, when the phone rang.

'Mrs Evans?' It was the doctor, the one I'd spoken to earlier in the day. 'It seems,' he coughed, 'we've sent you the province's entire supply of TB medication.'

They wanted it back. Sister was reluctant to see it returned. It gave her a feeling of confidence having it so near at hand. I was delighted to see it go. Pills might cure TB, but they weren't going to prevent it.

There were families on the farms with six, seven and even eight children. 'The men won't hear of birth control,' said Sister Tseki. 'They believe the more children they have, the more will live and the more there'll be to look after them when they are old.' The mortality rate was high and there were far too many little graves in the farm's graveyard. If the men wouldn't hear of it, the women would. Many of them wanted to take the pill, but in secret. They were, Sister Tseki said, worn out by childbirth, feeding and caring for families in small homes with little income. The government clinic in Viljoenskroon was to supply Sister Tseki with the birth control pills – not, I was praying, in such enormous quantities as the TB treatment.

The clinic nurse arrived at Huntersvlei in her white government car early one morning. I was in the nursery school playground; Sister Tseki was in her clinic. The nurse drove past the nursery-school and wound down her window: 'Hello, Mevrou Evans. I have come to do birth control,' she yelled in Afrikaans.

Heaving a megaphone off the seat beside her, she thrust it through the open window. Letting out the clutch she lurched into the stad, her voice booming through the megaphone: 'Birth control, it's time for birth control. Come to the clinic for birth control.'

She sounded like an ice cream vendor. I watched women who had been talking in groups in the road run inside their houses, close the doors and draw the curtains. Sister pushed me aside, tore out of the clinic and ran down the road after the white car. Her feet hit the sand road like an enraged bull. Stones scattered under her feet. Eventually, she gave up, bent over and panted.

'What did you think you were doing?' she demanded when her colleague arrived at the clinic. 'No one will come for birth control now. It was private, between the women and me. Do you know how long it's taken for me to get them to trust me? You were meant to give me the pills.'

Nurse Y pursed her lips and her face turned red. She straightened her uniform and stormed out. Clearly, no black woman was going to talk to her like that.

'Now, Mrs Evans, I've got to start all over again. And,' a furious Sister Tseki added, 'apart from birth control, it isn't enough just to treat TB, diarrhoea and dehydration. We've got to prevent them. We need bigger houses, clean water in each house and electricity.'

All of which Anthony was in the process of providing for the 60 stad houses at Huntersvlei and similar numbers on the other three Rhys Evans farms. There were, however, different ways of approaching problems.

'What a day,' Anthony said.

'What happened?' It was already dark outside. I drew the curtains and sat in the chair opposite him.

'The Huntersvlei liaison committee came to see me.'

'That sounds ominous.'

'It was a bit. They told me in no uncertain terms that, while they welcomed the sister to do inoculations and fix colds and cuts, they didn't want anybody treating people in the stads like children. Nobody was to tell them their homes were dirty, and above all nobody was to tell them how to live their lives.'

'Do they mean us?'

'Yes, in a roundabout way. But there was a peace offering of sorts.' Anthony shifted in his chair.

'What was that?'

'They said if we wanted to do something for the adults in the stad they would like a clubhouse, a place to relax, with dartboards and beer. Rhys has done this at Sandfontein, one of the other Rhys Evans farms, and it's worked well.'

While Anthony looked into the provision of a clubhouse, Rebecca, who was back working in the lands, took matters into her own hands. In her spare time, she invited small groups of mothers and grandmothers to the nursery school to talk about health, hygiene and nutrition. She offered everyone something to eat and drink and turned the gatherings into well-attended social events, albeit events with a purpose. Maria, grieving for her little girl, was back at work, slowly regaining her strength. The dark cloud that had all but swallowed me after my miscarriage had lifted. I watched health and hygiene slowly improve. Sister got on with major health matters and Rebecca shared information with mothers and grandmothers. By the end of Sister's first year with us, babies stopped dying; the next time we saw TB on the farms was many years later, linked to HIV.

It was spring. The peach trees in the garden were laden with fresh, pink blossoms. The days were longer, the sky bluer, the birdsong noisier. Every day, there seemed to be more boys and girls standing with their faces pressed against the fence, watching their friends play on the jungle gym and swings. The playroom was just not big enough for them all and the new year was fast approaching. I don't know if Anthony found my rather formal notification that I needed a meeting with him as ominous as the meeting with the liaison committee, but I walked into his office with a determined look on my face.

'Yes, my girl,' he said, clasping his hands behind his head. 'What is it?'

'The nursery school. It's been almost a year and it's going so well.'

'I promised a second building?'

'Yes, you did.'

He kept his promise and we built the second nursery school, roomy and sunny, with a separate kitchen and storeroom on the far side of the playground. I helped the teachers unpack boxes of mugs and plates, which we lined up on the kitchen shelves. Gas cookers and the big stainless steel soup pots were at last out of the children's reach. I couldn't stop smiling.

Rebecca announced to me that we needed more teachers and that she was going to be one of them. I was going to have to choose the other. In the event, the other teacher more or less chose herself.

16

BONNY

*I didn't know how babies were made.
Nobody told me.'*

WE SAT IN THE sparse shade of the spindly honey locust trees. Bonny Ntsoeleng cradled her tiny new baby girl in her arms. The baby's soft cheek peeped out from a cuddly warm shawl. I gently stroked it and felt her breath on my finger. Children's voices filtered through the playroom windows.

'My granny, Stompie, told me I mustn't talk to boys. She said I mustn't go near boys. But I didn't listen. My boyfriend, Jane's father, and I went into the veld together and I didn't think anything of it. You know how I learnt where babies come from?'

I shook my head.

Bonny, a pretty, slender young woman whose dark eyes were framed by long lashes, was nothing if not forthright. 'One day in class, there,' she pointed to the primary school behind us, 'the teacher was telling us how animals made babies. I put up my hand and said, "That happened to me." Everyone stared. The headmaster said I must go and see him in his office. He talked to Stompie. He said I must not go back to school until my baby was born.' Bonny stood up and rocked Jane, whose whimpers had turned into full-throated yells.

'She was the first baby girl born in the stad after your wedding so I called her Jane, after you. The first boy born in the stad was called Anthony,' Bonny continued. She was so much younger than me but already had a baby.

'What did you do before Jane was born?' I asked her.

'I was at school, here on the farm.'

'And now?'

'Mme Jane, and now I don't know. I want to go back to school. I am only seventeen. After Jane was born, I thought I was going to go to school in QwaQwa. My mother told me Stompie would look after Jane. I'd packed my clothes. Our neighbours came to say goodbye, to wish me well. I was dressed to leave, my case was packed, then Stompie came into the room. She said to me, "Where are you going? Who is going to look after this baby?" I said, "My mother said you would. That's how things work. My mother negotiated for me." But do you know what she said?'

I shook my head at Bonny's indignation.

'She said to me, "I am not going to look after any baby." Everyone was passing the house, calling me to come, they were going to the station in the bus. I was going to miss the train. I cried, Mme Jane, I cried and cried.'

I nearly cried just listening to her. Bonny's mother Miriam Lengau, I knew, had been Anthony's nanny when he was a very little boy, before she had married and left the farm. Now she was nanny to Anthony's sister Wendy's children, and lived with them in Durban. 'How long have you lived with Stompie?' I asked.

'Since I was eleven. My mother went away to work when I was four. First she left us with my father's family in Wepener. No one really looked after me. I went with my sisters to school. I sat outside the school gate playing with nearby children until they came out at home time. Sometimes someone gave me something to eat.' She paused. 'Then the school was built at Huntersvlei and my mother's parents lived here so I came to live with them. I worked so hard. I helped cook, clean the house, collect the water, and I looked after my younger brothers. I still do.

'One day,' her voice dropped; I leaned closer to hear, 'I forgot to close the door of the house. The pigs got in. We cooked our soup and porridge in three-legged pots in the middle of the room. They pushed over the pots, dug up the mud floor to get to the food. Hoo, I was in such trouble.' Bonny's laugh was like honey, thick and rich. 'My grandpa usually slaughters a pig in winter. We cook the meat then put it in a container and pour melted pig fat all over it until it is totally covered and no air can get to it to spoil it.'

'It keeps it fresh. Anthony said that is what his grandmother used to do,' I exclaimed. I thought of sausage-making day only a few months before. Bonny and I had that in common.

As Bonny rocked her now-whimpering baby, I thought how incredibly different our upbringing had been. Bonny loved her mother as much as I loved mine. Mine had also worked, but didn't have to go away; she was always there for me. There had been no waiting at school gates. Someone had cooked me meals, hugged me when I was sick or sad. Unlike Bonny, I didn't know my grandparents – immigrants from Eastern Europe – they had all died long before I was born.

'I'm used to hard work. I want to work in the nursery school,' Bonny told me.

It was July and I was pregnant. I looked at Bonny's frank, expectant face; I looked at little Jane. This young woman had plenty of self-confidence and was not about to take no for an answer. Rebecca and the rest of the committee said they wanted Bonny as the new teacher. And so, while I went to Johannesburg to have my first baby early the following year, Bonny and hers became part of the extended Huntersvlei nursery school, with Rebecca firmly at the helm.

The crib shook. Its new occupant, Robyn Winifred Evans, was beside herself, and so was I. I bent over and tucked Robyn's flailing arms into her blanket before I picked her up. I settled into a soft armchair to give her her early morning feed.

For a while I heard nothing but the urgent sucking of a hungry baby. It is one of the most moving noises I've heard. We had prepared impeccably for this baby. A white chest of drawers was filled with Baby-gros, little cotton vests and soft crocheted blankets. A pink plastic bath stood on top of the chest. But nothing could have prepared me for becoming a mother. My whole world had changed the moment this tiny person had arrived in it, screaming. I was consumed by a more intense love than I had ever felt before. That little squirming being was mine and Anthony's to look after, to feed, to keep clean and loved and warm and safe. She was so helpless and so dependent.

Writing this when Robyn is a mother herself, I think of Anthony arriving at the Park Lane Clinic and peering over the nurse's shoulder to watch Robyn being weighed before and after her feed to see how much she'd gained. He literally beamed with pride. 'This little girl has had plenty to drink. I always said small-breasted girls produce more milk. You'd make a good dairy cow.'

I'd thought with distaste of the black-and-white Friesland cows that were milked daily in the sheds behind the big house. There were moments when I could understand them, their udders full to bursting and bellowing in pain. Anthony was so pleased with me that everyone on the farm knew I was breastfeeding my baby.

'Why is this so important?' I asked.

'Companies that sell powdered formula are making great inroads in the rural communities. People think formula is better for their babies and the health services are struggling to convince mothers that breast milk is best.'

'That's what Dr Issy said to me when I went to his rooms with Moses's child. I'd forgotten about that.'

'I'm telling everyone you're breastfeeding Robyn.'

'That's so embarrassing. I wish you wouldn't.'

'Why not? It's natural, something to be pleased about.'

'I'm really not too keen on everyone discussing whether or not I'm breastfeeding.'

Breast milk or not, nothing else I did for Robyn seemed to be right. She would hardly have finished feeding when she would start to cry again. I put her over my shoulder, rubbed her back, then laid her over my knees and gently patted her. Nothing helped. I stood on the carpet in my bare feet, holding her. My hair felt lifeless and clung damply to my cheeks. Robyn screamed and screamed. Her little face screwed up and turned red, her tongue in that little mouth seemed so small and pink. I wanted to scream too. I didn't know what to do.

'Give her to me.' I hadn't heard the door open or Maria come into the room. I put Robyn into her outstretched, capable hands. 'Shh little baby, shh,' she said. Maria sat on the chair I'd just vacated and patted Robyn until she stopped crying. She swung Robyn onto her back, tied a blue-and-brown checked *tjalie* around her and fastened it tightly with a large silver safety pin. Robyn nestled against Maria's warm back, and went to sleep. I tiptoed past the picture of Jemima Puddleduck on the wall and quietly closed the door.

I don't know what I would have done without Maria's help. While my new baby slept in her springy, navy-blue pram or on Maria's back in between feeds, I set about making things for the nursery school children to play with. I was missing my writing and when I had finished I arranged my homemade toys on the lawn, photographed them, wrote detailed descriptions of how to make them and an article on why there should be nursery schools on farms, and mailed it all to *Farmer's Weekly*.

The nursery school had been open for over a year and I'd begun to see the benefits. The general chaos had gone. I'd seen how children had adapted to being away from their parents, how they learnt to share while they played and how much they loved playing with the equipment we'd made or bought. Above all, the teachers seemed to have got the hang of it. If we had a nursery school on Huntersvlei, there was, I thought, no reason why other people shouldn't introduce nursery schools on their farms. I'd help them.

Every week, I would wait for the new edition of the magazine to arrive in the post and page through it hopefully. Week after week there was nothing. Until, at last, Anthony strode in with the post: 'Congratulations. That's an excellent article,' he said, holding it out to me. I was absurdly excited. For me, getting something published has always seemed an amazing achievement. Seeing my byline gave me a thrill. Because of my innate shyness, this was a way of showing I did have a voice.

For days, I'd run to answer the phone every time it rang, convinced that someone would be phoning to ask me how to start a nursery school. It never was.

The first request for help was not from a farm at all.

17

A MODEST PROPOSAL

I rolled the unfamiliar phrase around in my mind. Early childhood development. Was that what we had been doing all along on the farm?

THE VILJOENSKROON 'LOCATION' ADMINISTRATION offices in Rammulotsi were secured behind a high wire fence in the sprawling township. Sturdy metal gates were intended to keep people out, or in – I was never quite sure which. The gate was secured with a padlock that swung to and fro in the wind, clicking like a metronome. The fence separated the offices from the decaying rubbish that lined the township's potholed dirt roads.

The township manager, a white man not much older than me, drummed his fingers on a broad wooden desk. He wore a white shirt and nondescript tie. His jacket hung over the back of his chair. '*Ag* Mevrou Evans, I hear you're doing such good work on the farm, it's time we had a nursery school here in the *lokasie*. We want to build one there, over the street.' He pointed his chin in the direction of the windows, out of which I could see an empty plot of land covered in long grass and weeds.

He asked me if I would help set up the school. I looked closely at this man, who lived his daily life behind the high fence that separated him from the black population whose lives he controlled. His concern about the township children seemed incongruous. Our nursery school might not have qualified teachers or the right sort of toys, and the daily timetables may have left quite a lot to be desired, but it was working. There was something where there had been nothing before. I said with great confidence that I would love to help.

'I had the oddest meeting with the township manager in Rammulotsi today,' I told Anthony that evening. He was sitting on a rug playing with Robyn. 'He wants to build a nursery school opposite the municipal offices. Apparently, along with the plot of land there is a budget. He wants me to help.'

'Why is that odd? I think it's fantastic.'

'It's odd because it seems such an unlikely thing for him to want to do. He did say, however, that there isn't enough money to build the sort of nursery school he wants to build.'

'That's his problem, my girl. I'm sure he'll be able to get it from the province.' Anthony turned his attention to Robyn and her rattle.

'It's not exactly his problem any more. I told him I'd try to help him raise the extra funds.'

Rattle forgotten, Anthony stood up and looked at me. 'How are you going to do that?'

I took a deep breath and walked through the main entrance of the University of the Witwatersrand's Business School in Parktown, Johannesburg. My smart beige skirt, black jacket and high-heeled shoes made a good change from everyday farm jeans and takkies. I was about to meet the Business School director, Dr Simon Biesheuvel.

My introduction to him was one of those magical moments of life-changing serendipity. Apart from heading the Wits Business School, Dr Biesheuvel was the South Africa advisor for an organisation called the Bernard van Leer Foundation, which I learnt in time was one of the major funders of early childhood development in the world and highly respected for its work.

'The Foundation,' Dr Biesheuvel told me once I was settled into a firm, upright wooden chair, 'receives its money from the Van Leer packaging companies worldwide and is a major funder of early childhood development projects in many countries, including South Africa. What makes this Foundation different is that it supports new groundbreaking models of early learning in disadvantaged places, including teacher training. We do this,' he added, 'because we believe that good-quality early learning will make for a child's success in his future education.'

He was a short, distinguished-looking man with a Dutch accent, doing his best to put me at ease. He must have seen my clasped hands and heard my voice wobble. I'd never tried to raise funds before. 'The Rammulotsi nursery school ...'

He cleared his throat when I'd finished telling him why I was there and said, 'It is a worthy venture. But I'm afraid it is not ground-breaking.' Cars hooted in the street outside, curtains billowed in the breeze. I looked at the shelves of books that lined the office walls. My fundraising career was at an end before it had even started. I felt my face tightening with disappointment. 'But,' he added 'from what you've told me you're doing pioneering work in early childhood development. Maybe we could fund the development of a model for early learning for farmworkers' children? They are among the most disadvantaged children in this country.'

'Why would the Foundation support something on private farms?' I asked

'Children's education at any level shouldn't be the farmers' responsibility. Send me a proposal. You're doing something inno-vative, something that hasn't been done, as far as I know, on South African farms before.'

I drove the two hours back to the farm, oblivious to the building rush-hour traffic on the outskirts of Johannesburg. I couldn't wait to tell Anthony. My thoughts were in a whirl. Writing proposals wasn't one of my major skills, but I was not about to let this deter me. In any case, I was sure it was one of Anthony's.

He was going to hate it. I knew he was going to hate it.

No, he wasn't, he was going to love it. Love it, hate it – the words clashed in my mind. I sat in the chair I had occupied a few weeks earlier. The painstakingly typed pages of my proposal sounded crisp as Dr Biesheuvel paged through them. There were no emails in those days. I hadn't sent it on before. He just had to like it.

'It's an interesting model.' He placed the proposal on his desk. Did that mean yes or did it mean no? It meant neither. What it did mean was that Ann Short, head of the Van Leer-funded Early Learning Resource Unit (ELRU), would visit the Huntersvlei nursery school to find out what we were doing and how we were doing it. The ELRU was a Cape Town-based non-governmental organisation (NGO) and a leader in the non-formal South African early childhood development (ECD) field. I knew nothing about NGOs. In fact, I knew very little about ECD in South Africa at that time apart from the fact that there was no state provision for ECD for farmworkers' children and that, unless things had changed drastically over the twelve years since I'd visited the nursery schools in Soweto, there wasn't support in the urban 'black' areas either.

In 1977, at the time when Rebecca and I were dashing around buying oranges and scrounging extra mugs for milk, nursery school education was not a major government consideration in South Africa for any race group. What funding there was went to nursery schools or preschool education for white children, which then was the responsibility of provincial education departments. Eric Atmore, a man who would become a highly recognised authority on ECD in

South Africa and a colleague of mine, told me that the provinces were allowed to establish their own preschools as needed, which led to the growth in the number of government nursery schools for white children and allowed for subsidies for privately run 'white' nursery schools. Government support for black preschool-aged children, he said, came from the Department of Social Development and was for crèches – custodial care.

What nursery schools there were for black children, I discovered, were mainly in the urban townships and were driven by the communities themselves, churches, welfare and NGOs. Research into ECD – or ECED, early childhood education and development – internationally was showing the importance of good-quality ECED, specifically for children from disadvantaged backgrounds. I had a lot to learn.

In her late twenties, slightly older than me, with short, straight, brown hair and an intense, no-nonsense face, Ann Short arrived at Huntersvlei on a crisp, early-winter's day for her first of many visits. It was June 1979. After a while, I became used to both her self-conscious giggle and her incredible intellect. But on that first day, we were all on our best behaviour. Rebecca, Bonny, Bertha and Maria had dressed in African-print dresses. I wore my 'lucky' blue dress, the one with the white stripe. I don't know why I thought it was lucky – it just felt right whenever I put it on. I had worn it for the opening day of the nursery school, which had been a special day.

For most of the morning, Ann did what she'd come to do – observe. She did this by sitting in the playroom on a nursery-sized chair in total silence. I found it quite unnerving. Inside Rebecca's playroom, 25 children sat at the wooden tables behind 25 large pieces of computer paper, drawing with fat wax crayons. This stranger, unlike most visitors, did not coo at the sight, nor did she call the children adorable.

'Why are these children all doing the same thing?' She broke her silence at last. Had I not heard of free-choice activities? I most certainly had not. I didn't know what she was talking about.

As for the buildings, she demanded to know why they weren't facing north and making the most of the sunlight. She told me that the teachers might be very nice women who looked after the children well enough, but they didn't know very much about early learning. She sounded just like Rhys. Whatever we were trying to do, we weren't, according to Ann, doing it very well.

Her report arrived in the post a week later. I paged through it, a sick feeling settling in my stomach. It said that the daily programme was too teacher-directed, the buildings faced the wrong way and our teachers were badly in need of professional training. I was devastated. I thought Ann would understand what we'd achieved. The children were fed and stimulated and we were giving them a great deal more than they'd ever had before. We'd created the nursery school out of nothing. There was no way Dr Biesheuvel would approve a grant, not based on her report.

'Have you read the last page?' Anthony asked shortly after I had I thrust the report in front of him.

'What last page? I read it all.'

'You couldn't have.' He handed it back to me, pointing to the unread page.

I scanned the page. 'She suggests that the Van Leer Foundation should support the proposal – it shows, she says, potential.' I looked at Anthony. 'That's incredible. She is so critical.'

'Why don't you take Ann's report as constructive criticism?' Anthony said as the sunlight faded outside. 'Don't you agree with her observations? I think they're very perceptive. You've said yourself that the nursery school is about so much more than care, toys and food.'

He was right. I needed to swallow hard and take the criticism. Even if I didn't like it, I knew she was right. Now I had to wait to see whether the Van Leer Foundation would accept her recommendation.

Dr Biesheuvel's letter finally arrived. I opened it slowly.

'Dear Jane ...' I read the neatly typed pages. My hands shook as I fumbled through them. I had to read the letter twice to make quite sure. I tore across the road to Anthony's office and waved the letter in front of him; this was becoming a habit of mine. 'They'll do it!'

'Calm down,' he said. 'Who'll do what?'

'The Bernard van Leer Foundation,' I told him, quickly reading the letter a third time to make quite sure I hadn't made a mistake, 'will fund everything that we asked for in our proposal. They like our model.'

The model that I had so painstakingly worked through with Rebecca, a number of farmers in the district and Anthony, called for the establishment of nursery schools on six farms in a 20-kilometre radius from Huntersvlei with support from the farmers and farm communities concerned. Two women from each farm would become nursery-school teachers and the new Trust, which I would establish to administer the Van Leer funds, would employ two Sesotho-speaking, qualified Grade 1 or 2 teachers to be the trainers and teach the teachers – or teacher aides, as the women would ask to be called – about preschool education. The trainers would visit each nursery school once a week, driving a nursery school on wheels: a panel van specially kitted out with learning equipment for each nursery school and boxes to transport food without sacks of milk, soup and oranges rolling around in the van. The trainers would give the teacher aides weekly hands-on support at their own nursery schools, in addition to regular lectures and practical training sessions at Huntersvlei.

'The Van Leer grant will be for three years,' I told Anthony.

'That's fantastic. What will it pay for?'

'Everything we asked for.'

'Like what?'

'It'll cover the salaries of nursery-school teachers on six farms, play equipment, and the salaries of the two trainers or supervisors.' I could hardly contain my excitement. 'And it will also pay for the nursery-school van – our very own mobile nursery school.'

The Foundation would also throw its considerable experience behind the pilot project. It was to be a low-cost, high-impact nursery-school programme. It would rely on the goodwill of farmers, the buy-in from farmworker communities, and the strength and passion of untrained, often poorly educated, women who wanted to learn and to make a difference to themselves and the parents and children in their communities.

This was beyond anything I'd ever dreamt of doing. I felt excited and overwhelmed. A new future for many women, including me, and children had fallen into my lap. We were about to become an NGO and join a vibrant group of women and men, filling a gap left wide open by the national government and making ECD a reality for children in some of South Africa's most impoverished communities.

18

NTATAISE

Maria tells her story, as the nursery-school project finally gets a name.

IT WAS 1979. BLACK high-school pupils throughout South Africa were boycotting classes, continuing to demand a better education. Police were retaliating with bullets.

Our farm nursery-school project was pushing ahead. Rebecca and Bonny were in Soweto, learning from Josephine what a 'proper' nursery school should look like. Anthony and I sat on our front stoep with Ishmael Mabitle and watched the moon rise in the vast Free State sky. Its early light glimmered on the shallow water covering the salt pan across the main road from the farm. The evening air was warm and smelled of summer. There was a faraway rumble of thunder, the promise of rain.

As a boy growing up in Rammulotsi, Ishmael had unpacked goods in a local grocery store, and had later become a teacher. He was an inspector of schools, a well-known figure in Rammulotsi and a regular visitor to the Huntersvlei primary school – and thus Anthony. I got my wish to meet the man I'd seen in the chemist that day, and we became friends.

The Johannesburg-based Bernard van Leer Foundation lawyer had drawn up a deed for the trust that would administer the Van Leer funds. We called it the Rural Preschool Development Trust. Together with Van Leer, we'd agreed that trustees should include people from different sectors of the Viljoenskroon community. Ishmael had agreed to be a trustee, as had Abel Dlamini, principal of a nearby farm primary school. Anthony and I were trustees, as were Sandra and Andries Botha, neighbouring farmers.

This seemed the easy part. Now, I had to find trainers and five other farms to join the proposed project. Ishmael had joined us that evening to discuss what was becoming, to me, an increasing challenge: where to find supervisors cum trainers. Ishmael put his glass of Coke on the white metal stoep table. 'What sort of person are you looking for?' he asked.

'Ideally, qualified Sesotho-speaking nursery-school teachers who will train the farm women and help them establish nursery schools,' I said.

'And not ideally?'

'That is the challenge,' I replied. 'I don't know of any qualified Sesotho-speaking nursery-school teachers. In fact, I don't know of any qualified black nursery-school teachers.'

'I'll think about it. We'll find the right people,' Ishmael replied.

'Look nationally,' said Ann Short when I asked her. She suggested a woman in the Eastern Cape, who would later go on to become the premier of that province.

But when we put her name before the farm women, they were not interested in her. 'We don't want someone from anywhere else. It must be someone from here,' said Rebecca. 'We want someone who can speak Sesotho. She must understand us. We want one of us.'

I swung from being excited to feeling desperate. 'I don't know where to look,' I said to Anthony.

'Stop looking for what there isn't. Look for what there is: a primary-school teacher, a nurse, or a social worker.'

'I don't know why I didn't think of that.'

Confident, I pinned up notices at the farm nursery school, the primary school, the high school in Rammulotsi, the grocery store, the Methodist and Dutch Reformed churches, the clinic, the police station and the municipal offices in the location, in the town, anywhere I could find a noticeboard: 'Rural preschool development organisation requires the services of two suitably qualified women to supervise the establishment of farm nursery schools on farms in this district. Primary-school teachers will be given preference. Driving licence and Sesotho essential. Contact me at ...'

The days became weeks.

'I haven't had even one application,' I said to Anthony.

'Not one?'

'Not one.'

'If no one applies you'll just have to cancel it,' the nurse in the clinic said cheerily when I popped in to Viljoenskroon yet again to ask if anyone had answered my notice. That was not an option; it never occurred to me to cancel the project. The right people were there somewhere – we just hadn't found one another. But we would. We had to.

Not everyone thought that way. 'Haven't you got enough to do with one nursery school? What about Robyn?' asked a disapproving neighbour.

'What *about* Robyn?' I said to Anthony, indignantly. 'How I bring up my child is none of her business. Robyn and Maria come with me to the nursery school every day.' I loved what I was doing and I was filled with determined energy, but I did need to find a supervisor or trainer.

Rebecca delivered the message almost as an afterthought.

'Sharp sharp.' I was pressing one last little thumb at the nursery-school gate goodbye when she said, 'Oh, and Maria Mohlahleli wants to see you.'

'Who is Maria Mohlahleli?' I asked.

'Elisa's granddaughter. You know, Elisa, who does the old missus's washing? She wants to talk about the nursery schools.'

A few days later, I heard the hum of tractors in the distance, the incessant birdsong and my year-old daughter chatting to 'Nanny Maria' in the garden as Maria Mohlahleli and I sat in my study drinking tea from the blue willow-pattern cups that Anthony's mother had bought, wrapped in straw and carefully packed away to wait for Anthony to acquire a wife.

'Rebecca says you are Elisa's granddaughter.' Maria and I sized each other up. She balanced a plate with a chocolate biscuit on it on her knees. Cattle clattered past our house on the dirt road, kicking up clouds of dust. Their sour, musty smell filled the room. We both took another biscuit from the plate on the coffee table.

Maria was poised and reserved, but she broke the awkward tension between us. Pointing at the white gable peeking out from behind the gum trees, she said, 'I used to go and work there in the big house during the holidays, to earn extra money.'

'What did you do there?'

'I went with Elisa, my grandmother, to play with Mrs Evans's grandchildren who were visiting her with their mother, and to clean the windows. They were naughty and didn't listen to me. I said I wasn't going to work there any more. But I was asked to come back and do housework. I saved what I earned for my teacher's course.'

'How did you feel working there?' I tried to imagine what I'd feel like.

'It's funny but I felt privileged. The other girls and boys I knew on the farm were working in the lands. We were not allowed to go through the gate to the big house. All my friends in the stad wanted to know what was inside the house, how it looked. I was so surprised that everyone there was so nice. The bedding was so nicely done, there were embroidered sheets and pillowcases and there was lots of different food. I was shown how to dust carefully. Sometimes I envied them but that's the way it was. White people had those things.'

I told her I had worked in Woolworths in Johannesburg during my holidays, in the men's underwear department. 'Where did you grow up, Maria?' I asked.

'I feel as though I grew up all over the place. My father, who was a farmworker, kept moving my mother, my brothers, sisters and me from one place to another looking for work and as a result I didn't go to school. When I was eight years old Mr Rhys Evans built the primary school at Huntersvlei. My grandfather, Matol Scheepers, worked here. He helped build the school and when it opened my parents sent me to live with my granny and grandpa here on the farm.'

'I know where Elisa's house is, the house not too far from the reservoir?' I said.

'Yes, that's where I grew up. But when I came to live with them they had a mud house, and later she got the brick house she lives in. We had three rooms with mud floors and a zinc roof. The kitchen with mud walls and a grass roof was outside. There were so many of us sleeping there. The three youngest grandchildren slept on the bed with Elisa. The rest of us crammed into two rooms on the floor. Our pillows were old coats and clothing. In winter we needed these to cover ourselves. Then we used our arms to support our heads. We made duvets out of the old clothes and when it was really cold we sewed empty hessian sacks together and filled them with leaves.' She smiled as she reminisced. 'I loved mealtimes, when we were all together. We ate out of one big bowl. Pap, and sometimes there was milk or dried meat and wild spinach.'

'I loved mealtimes too with my mother and my brother Adam when I was growing up. There were only the three of us.' I reminisced too. Mealtimes, especially evening meals, had seemed so safe and secure.

Maria continued. 'Then my mother died. My father married again and lost interest in us. It was tough. Elisa loved me, encouraged me and saved every penny she could to help pay for me to go to high school. I liked studying. Nothing was difficult for me and the teachers treated me well. Elisa worked so hard to help me through school. I wanted to do well for her.' Elisa, she said, had also helped her to attend the teachers' training college in QwaQwa, that bleak, isolated homeland in the shadow of the Drakensberg mountains a few hours away from Huntersvlei. 'The people in the stad used to give me a few shillings here and there. We were all one big family. Everyone in the stad was proud if one of us could be educated.'

I thought of Maria's story and the vast inequalities in our lives, the difference between being a young white woman and a young black woman growing up in South Africa in the late 1970s. Maria was 26; I was 31.

'I got my teaching certificate in QwaQwa and now I'm teaching Grade 3 children at the Ntsoanatsatsi Lower Primary School in Rammulotsi. For the first time in my life I can do something worthwhile for my grandmother. She's done so much for me, Mme Jane. Elisa is old now and doesn't work. I share my salary with her.'

'How did you hear about the Huntersvlei nursery school?'

'I heard about it from Elisa and I sent my daughter Daphne there. Everyone is talking about it. It's something quite new, we don't have anything like that in the township. That's where I live with my husband and Daphne.'

The more we talked, the more I liked Maria. Behind her reserve there was warmth and compassion. Everything Maria had told me made me like and admire her. I just hoped she liked me. We talked for a while about my idea for farm nursery schools and I asked her what she knew about nursery schools.

'I only know what Daphne's shared with me, the little poems she recites. The one I especially like goes like this: "I'm as thin as a rake, as tall as a tree, as round as a ball. I'm bouncing like a ball."'

That became our favourite. I still remember Anthony convulsing with laughter at Bertha, Rebecca and me bouncing like balls at the year-end Huntersvlei nursery-school concert.

'Apart from helping Elisa, why are you interested in this work?'

Putting down her cup, she looked at me, her dark eyes earnest. 'It's time to give something back. This community raised me and now it's my turn to help it, just as it helped me.'

The second supervisor came to me from an unlikely source. Lydia Khoabane ran the showroom at a local pottery. Considerably older than Maria and me, she was a large, comfortable-looking woman and the only black person I had met in this district who had been to nursery school, in the days of mission schools. (Before the formation of the Department of Bantu Education, the root of so many of this country's problems, a number of black schoolchildren had attended schools run by Catholic mission societies. While in part funded by the government, they retained a measure of autonomy and didn't tolerate racial segregation.)

I'd met Lydia at the pottery. She was a forthright, no-nonsense person. We got chatting one day.

'I hear you're looking for someone to work with nursery schools, Mrs Evans?' she said as she tied string around the parcel she was wrapping for me. 'I'd be interested.'

'Do you know anything about nursery schools?'

'Not too much, but I work with women at church. I'm sure I could be a big help with parents and I did go to a nursery school run by missionaries.'

It was a leap of faith for these two women: both gave up secure jobs to join me in this unknown venture. All I could offer with certainty was a salary for three years and the promise that I would do everything I could to work with them to make the project a success. We were reaching for the stars, but the three of us, together with Rebecca and her team, would reach for them together.

'Now you want me to run a nannying service?' Rhys banged his fist on his desk. The small office to the side of his house was cloyingly hot in the morning sun. He stared at me in disbelief. Outside, his pet peacock gave a strangulated cry. I could hear sheep bleating in the kraals.

I had to find five farms to join Huntersvlei in the nursery-school project. Why we decided on six farms I can't for the life of me remember – that was the number in the proposal and that's the number it would be. I had started with Rhys because he was Anthony's general manager and I'd thought that, by now, he would have seen at first-hand what we were doing. Yet, no matter how I explained, he still would not accept the fact that a nursery school was not a nannying service. I paced up and down, highly agitated, knocking into a tray of coffee and rusks on the side table. Even that couldn't move him.

'I'll think about it. A nannying service ...' he muttered again as I left.

I knew a few farmers in the district but took advice from Anthony about which farmers were most likely to be persuaded. This project was only going to work if the farmers agreed and if the parents from their workforces would support a nursery school. As annoying as Rhys had been, my reception there had been mild compared with the greeting I'd received at some farms.

'Don't you tell me what's good for these children,' yelled one khaki-clad farmer. 'I'll tell you what's good for them.'

At another farm, I was stopped in the driveway by a furious farmer shaking a stick. 'If I find any piccaninnies near my house I'll shoot them,' he yelled at me. At that moment, he looked quite ready to shoot me too.

But, of course, it wasn't all like that. The other farmers I approached were more concerned about the costs, what buildings they'd use to house the nursery school and who would run them. No one was entirely convinced about farm women being the teachers, but they were all concerned about their workforce. The nursery schools might bring extra stability and it meant more women to work on the lands. Like Rhys, most of them didn't really believe in the importance of early learning, but they agreed to try.

'What do you think?' asked Anthony.

'There is so much in the books I'm reading which suggests otherwise. It's early days in much of this research but all indications are that good-quality nursery schools and early learning are having a significant impact on children's development, especially children from disadvantaged homes. As for the women, we'll teach them.'

The process I followed in getting the project going might have been topsy turvy, and I hadn't approached farmers until the Van Leer Foundation had agreed to fund this project. But from the moment the Rural Preschool Development Trust deed had been signed and Maria and Lydia appointed, it was a scramble. Maria and Lydia had hardly worked their notice period with their current employers than they were on a train to Cape Town and ELRU to attend a training-of-trainers course.

I'd been so busy convincing farmers, who never were really convinced of the educational advantages of a nursery school, that the five weeks of Maria and Lydia's training in Cape Town had passed in a flash – for me, at any rate. For Maria, it had been an eternity. 'Mme … it was tough. Everything was so strange. I'd never stayed in a hotel before. There was no pap to eat and it was so different. I've never been so far away from my family either and I felt so homesick.' The three of us were having our now-regular Friday-morning meeting. Sometimes this took place in my study, but this morning we sat on the Huntersvlei nursery-school lawn. The long, brown pods from the honey locust trees – which had grown and looked, by now, like sturdy toddlers rather than wobbly babies – made a crunching noise when we stepped on them.

The food and environment were not the only things Maria found different in the Cape. 'When I went to school we did what our teachers told us to do. We didn't question them or give our own ideas. At ELRU we were asked what we thought, we were encouraged to challenge the women training us.'

One of the reasons Maria would do so well was that she did have her own ideas and was given the chance, and encouragement, to use them. The ELRU was teaching her how to express them. 'And early learning isn't about children sitting in neat, quiet lines. It's all about play, play and more play. Children,' Maria told me, 'learn through their play. I never thought of playing as learning, it just seemed a way of keeping children busy. The idea is new to me. It's quite challenging, but I'm beginning to understand it.'

It was something new for me too – and as Maria said, it wasn't only the playing but the way the teachers asked questions, presented play activities and talked to children. In time to come, Maria would tell me that that first nerve-wracking trip and training course at ELRU had given her the confidence she needed to cope with all that lay ahead.

It was time for me to introduce Maria and Lydia to the farmers, for the farmers to introduce them to the men and women on their farms and to find women who wanted to be trained to be nursery-school teachers.

'Shouldn't you give the project a name before you do that?' Anthony asked me. 'You can't keep calling it "the nursery-school project".'

'That's such a good idea. I don't know why I didn't think of it. Have you any suggestions?'

'I don't, but see if Rebecca, Lydia, or Maria do. Don't you think it should be a Sesotho name?'

'Let's make it a competition, and ask the children and their parents to think of a name,' said Rebecca.

This engendered much enthusiasm, but none of us could agree on a suggested name until Lydia blurted out one morning: 'Ntataise! Let's call it Ntataise.'

'What does Ntataise mean?' I asked her.

'It's a Sesotho word. It means "to lead a young child by the hand".'

And Ntataise the nursery-school project became.

Maria and Lydia held the first meeting to introduce Ntataise and the idea of nursery schools to parents on farms other than Hunt-ersvlei in a primary-school classroom at Skietlaagte farm, some twenty-five kilometres away. I watched as about fifty men dressed in heavy dark-blue overalls straggled in from a long day's work on the lands. Women, some with blankets tied around their waists, some with babies on their hips, sat crammed together on narrow benches behind wooden school desks. A chilly breeze blew through the open schoolroom door. Outside in the twilight, children kicked soccer balls, and crickets' piercing rasps punctured the air. I squashed in at the end of a bench, my jersey pulled tightly round my shoulders.

The men and women looked at us warily. They had come because the farmer had told them to. But the nursery school couldn't open without the parents' buy-in. Most of the Sesotho words washed over me. My Sesotho lessons with a nearby school principal were going slowly; I wasn't a great pupil when it came to learning languages. We held my lessons in Anthony's office with a small blackboard and my teacher striding around the room with a piece of chalk in his hand. All went well until he started teaching me words that Maria Moloke told me, in no uncertain terms, were intimate parts of the body and not things that young women should be learning from a man.

I didn't progress much further in my Sesotho studies until I registered for a distance-learning course with Unisa some years later, and even then I wasn't an adept pupil. I was lost in this reverie when I heard the words 'teachers' and 'training'. The quiet of the evening was shattered.

'Eh-eh,' said a man in the front row. He stood, rested one hand on the desk in front of him, and violently shook his head. Wives turned on their husbands, wildly gesticulating. Lydia spoke over the hubbub, asking people to be quiet and give her a chance to explain. The meeting broke up in disarray.

Lydia pushed her way through the throng to reach me. 'They don't believe children can learn before they go to school,' she said. 'They say children are just there to get bigger and when they've grown enough they can go to school.'

It obviously wasn't just a Huntersvlei belief. But what they were suspicious about was the training. What was this training in any case? What were we going to teach them? The men didn't want their wives to go away, even if it was to Huntersvlei. Who would cook for them and look after the house if the women went away – and what if the women came home knowing more than they did?

It wasn't only the men. Many of the women said there hadn't been schools for them to go to. Others said they'd had to stay at home and help their mothers, and had only been to school for a few years. They were ashamed and frightened of training because they couldn't read and write properly. They didn't know what a nursery school was and were scared of Maria because she was a 'proper' teacher. They thought she was 'higher' than them and that she might criticise them.

The reaction was the same on all the farms. Rebecca said I shouldn't worry. 'Don't be in such a hurry,' she told me. 'This is something new. People need to talk about it.'

Maria and Lydia went back to each farm again, and sometimes again, meeting with the women on their own or in groups. They explained the reasons for having a nursery school and talked about what the prospective teachers would learn. The nursery school would give them jobs, salaries and standing in their communities. We invited anyone who seemed even a teeny bit interested to Huntersvlei to see the nursery school in action, to share a cup of tea with us. Only a few women came forward.

In the end, either the farmers or the farm communities chose the rest of the teachers. 'They chose women who'd been to school,' said Maria.

The women who put themselves forward were gutsy, in my opinion – as were Maria and Lydia and the Huntersvlei teachers. In the wider world, far away from this tiny, isolated farming community, the feminist movement had grown. Gloria Steinem had the United States Congress in a quake with an explosion of demands for women's rights. In South Africa, women were beginning to flex their muscles. They wanted to be treated equally: equal pay for equal work, and jobs that were traditionally reserved for men (white men). They wanted childcare so that they could go to work. It wasn't necessarily the US women's movement that influenced the women in Viljoenskroon, but the realisation that women had a role to play in society in addition to looking after children and running households.

Eighteen women joined Ntataise: fourteen as trainee teachers and four as nursery-school cooks.

19

PAPADI

The biggest lesson to learn was that play could be learning too.

NOVEMBER 1980. SCHOOL BOYCOTTS continued. The country's bubbling discontent was a volcano waiting to erupt.

At Huntersvlei, we were preparing to host our first training course. Behind the primary school, Anthony had built the requested 'clubhouse'. Painted white to match the rest of the buildings, it came complete with dartboard, brown armchairs and waist-high wooden counter that served as the pub. Beer was delivered every Friday on a farm *trokkie*, and by Monday the fridge was empty. This was to be the training room.

We placed a blackboard at the front of the room and arranged a collection of chairs and benches in a semicircle facing the trainers. This was less threatening, Maria said, than the usual straight rows placed one behind the other. At the back of the room, trestle tables held tea, sugar, coffee and milk, there was a gas cooker to heat water, and brown-bread sandwiches filled with jam or cold meat. A pile of ELRU *Learning to Play* training manuals, written by Karen van der Merwe, waited on the trainers' table alongside sticks of white chalk and a blackboard duster. The course material was in English, and Maria and Lydia would translate it into Sesotho as they went along. We called them the 'green books' because of their green covers.

Families in the Huntersvlei stad had agreed to host the 14 trainees in their homes. They turned out in force to welcome their guests, who arrived on the back of farm bakkies and tractor-drawn trailers; the taxi industry wasn't as developed as it is today and this was the transport that farmers used. The trainees clutched bulging blue-and-pink plastic shopping bags or cardboard suitcases.

Rebecca's smile was wide. It was a special day, she said, for all of us – the first training of its sort on a Free State farm. Standing next to Rebecca, Maria and Lydia, I felt I'd burst with pride, excitement and plain, terrified nerves. Each of us was breaking new ground and flouting traditional roles. The women, despite their own fears, had stood up to their husbands and they had come. I don't remember what I said to welcome everyone when we were finally seated in the training room, but I do remember it was followed by Lydia saying a prayer and singing a hymn. It didn't take long for everyone to join her. The sound of those women singing followed me all the way home from the stad that day, and has followed me through the years. The clarity and passion of their song reached something deep inside me. Singing is, for me, the sound of Ntataise.

'Hey Mme!'

We had hardly settled in the mottled shade of the now-tall honey locust trees for our post-training indaba when Bonny poured out an indignant torrent of Sesotho and English. 'You promised that all of us who had people to stay would get money for food and accommodation. We didn't get any money. We had to give them our food and we only had enough food for our husbands' skoff tins.' A frown creased her forehead.

My stomach turned into a tight ball. The farmers had given

125

everyone money for their accommodation, but apparently it had never reached their hosts.

'They spent it on other things,' Bonny said. Apart from everything else, there had not been enough room in the already overcrowded houses for these guests. 'It's fine to share with guests for a few days, but for two weeks? We gave them our sheets and blankets, we moved out of our beds for them'.

'But it was your idea, Bonny.'

'I know, but it was a bad idea.'

'Why did everyone agree to it?'

'We wanted the money. And we thought that was what you wanted.'

It *was* what I wanted; none of us had had an alternative, but no one had objected.

('That, my girl, is something you'll have to learn. No one in the stad is going to say no to you.'

'Why on earth not?'

'They're nervous it might impact their jobs,' Anthony said at our own post-training indaba.

'They know that's not so.'

'Don't be in such a rush. You've come a long way with Rebecca. The other women will trust you, but it takes time. And they've told you the mistakes and none of you will make them next time.')

'It wasn't only that.' Maria leaned forward in her chair. 'I might as well have left the green books wrapped in plastic. The women didn't understand me. They talked about the clothes we wore and the different earrings Bonny wore each day. Some of them didn't really know why they were here.'

'But what about the farm meetings?' I said, confused – and, as it turned out, totally naive.

'That was just words. It sounded like something different to do,' Bonny cut in again. 'Some of them thought they were going to be teachers and write things on blackboards. They wanted A E I O U. Now they don't want to be called teachers. They say they aren't teachers – not what they know of as teachers, anyway.'

'What do they want to be called?'

'*Mangwane*,' said Bonny. 'They thought they were going to be *mangwane*.'

'What's a *mangwane*?

'A nanny or an aunty. They say they're not teachers, and you'll have to call us something else.' Bonny was not convinced. She wanted to be called a teacher.

They were all mothers; as far as I was concerned, they were already teachers. They were not being taught to be nannies. We compromised and called our burgeoning nursery-school teachers teacher aides – on paper, at any rate. The women who didn't want to be *mangwane* wanted, Bonny said, to learn to sew or get drivers' licences. 'That's what schools for women do, they teach them to cook and sew.'

Maria stood up, too agitated to sit still any longer. 'Teaching adults is so different from teaching children. I expected them to understand everything all at once – the daily programme, playroom layout, weekly themes, how to talk to children, listen to them and play with them. And there are new concepts which don't have words in SeSotho.' She paused. 'When those women were at school it was either right or wrong. If it was wrong the teacher hit them with a ruler or a wooden stick. They weren't at all convinced about this *papadi* (play). They said schools aren't for playing in. They said real teachers don't play with children. Playing isn't learning, reading and writing is. Teachers, they said, went to the teachers' training college in QwaQwa to learn, not to Huntersvlei.'

Years later, Rebecca told me that they'd all been frightened of not being able to live up to the expectations that came with being a teacher. Teachers and priests were the most respected members of the community. They didn't feel they knew enough to be counted among them. I don't think I ever realised the depth of what I was asking people to do. It was groundbreaking, almost seismic, and it had never occurred to me that we couldn't do it. Was this good or bad? I don't think it was either; it was change.

Maria took the green books away and, shortly after our meeting, started all over again. The trainees came to special workshops and made skipping ropes out of the long, dry grass that grew at the edge of the lands and scraps of material from Alina's sewing group, the way their mothers had made skipping ropes for them when they were children. They sang the songs they knew. They drew in the sand with sticks, modelled small animals out of clay that Maria dug out of the salt pan, and drew on cardboard boxes with pieces of burnt wood. 'That's what they know. That's how they play with their children,' she told me.

Through that first year, the new teachers taught children songs from their own childhood, played games their parents had played with them. They were comfortable with things that were familiar to them. We threw out English nursery rhymes, which were foreign. We re-introduced them years later when Nelson Mandela would sing his 'favourite' nursery rhyme, 'Twinkle, Twinkle, Little Star'. With our small core staff, we relied heavily on expert input from outside, particularly from Denise Parkinson and the ELRU team from Cape Town. Some, like Karen van der Merwe, who had written the green books, were so well loved that her final training session for us would be 35 years later. Once Maria had laid the foundation, the green books became everyone's ECD 'bibles'.

Maria and Lydia were used to teaching or working with adults, and we could not have done without Karen, Ann Short and Denise Parkinson. Karen taught us all 'to praise people. Look at what they're doing right first, then discuss with them what you think they could do better, why you think that and how to correct it'. Among the many things Ann emphasised was to progress from 'the known to the unknown, the concrete to the abstract'. And that was how Maria started to teach the farm nursery-school teachers. She built, little by little, on what they already knew.

Denise Parkinson's arrival at a Huntersvlei training session was greeted with decided suspicion. Who was this woman with her larger-than-life personality? What did she want? As she taught the trainees to make balls out of empty orange sacks stuffed with news-paper, and child-sized furniture out of cardboard boxes and glue, the shy, frightened women came to life. This was something they could do, something they understood: how to make things, use their hands. The Huntersvlei clubhouse buzzed with sound. We pushed the chairs against the walls and spread newspaper on the floor. Denise said there was no right or wrong way and that no one would 'get into trouble'. Why would adult women 'get into trouble?' 'Their only experience of being taught is school and if you didn't get it right, you got smacked, you got into trouble.' Maria translated and everyone got involved in cutting, pasting and painting.

The trainees went home with child-sized chairs, stoves and dolls' beds. They were not yet convinced that children would learn any-thing while they played, but it was a start. It would be part of Maria and Lydia's role to teach all of us – but particularly the teacher aides – how children developed and how they learnt basic concepts – colour, size, shape, in front, behind, large, small, the same, different and so much more – by playing. Making activities to help children learn these concepts appealed to me enormously. Friends, family and acquaintances from Viljoenskroon and Rammulotsi to Johannes-burg were dragooned into collecting different-sized boxes, yoghurt containers, different-coloured bottle tops, empty plastic cold drink bottles, anything that was not torn or soggy, to make activity toys for our learning-through-play programme.

I was at a formal black-tie business dinner with Anthony soon after Denise's visit. A glass bowl of thick chocolate pudding with a coloured-paper umbrella sticking out of the blob of cream in the centre was put in front of each guest.

'They can't let those go to waste,' I whispered to my horrified husband. Before he knew it, I'd stood up and asked in a loud voice, 'Please, may I have the umbrellas for our nursery school?'

Most people laughed; Anthony cringed. Umbrellas, some still sticky with cream, others licked clean, were passed down the tables to me along with business cards. 'Give me a call, I'll try to help with other products,' said several of the 'captains of industry' in the hall that night.

Help they did: 30-year-old sets of red, blue, green and yellow bottle tops, and big, small and medium plastic yoghurt containers, still appear in the 'concept' areas.

20

SUSPICION

What was this nonsense of children playing, she wanted to know. Teachers should write on blackboards, 1 2 3 4.

JANUARY 1981. THE SUPERVISORS visited each of the six farms once a week. Workshops and training sessions were all very well, but our regular follow-up on-site support visits in the Ntataise panel van were crucial to the project. They were what made it work.

We wouldn't realise the full impact of on-site support visits until we stopped doing them, but that was in the future. Each farm was about fifteen to twenty-five kilometres from Huntersvlei, all on dirt roads. When the weather was fine it was easy going, but when it rained, the van, which had 'Ntataise' printed in large blue lettering on its sides, slithered and slipped in the mud. In the back of the van was a specially built wooden fitting with compartments for trans-porting foodstuffs. The paints, crayons, scissors, art equipment and toys were stored in a tin trunk. We gave each school mats for the children to sleep and sit on, mugs, gas cookers, brooms and buckets. Each was given its own wooden blocks, children's books and puzzles, dominoes, matching games, nesting cups, paints, crayons and scissors. Their parents made wire cars, dolls, balls and skipping ropes. They made scoops and watering cans for sandpit and water play out of plastic Coke bottles.

The teachers locked the toys away in cupboards. Maria and Lydia took them out. The teachers packed them away again. 'They don't want the children to break them or dirty them.' Maria and Lydia wanted them set out in the playroom for children to play with. And when the toys were eventually set out to be played with, the children wanted to take them home.

And they did. 'They're not being naughty, they just love the toys,' Maria told me. 'And they don't have toys at home.'

Maria added another verse to the 'packing away' song, which went something like this: 'Now it's time to pack away, pack away, pack away, now it's time to pack away, pack away the toys.' The teachers' voices continued with vigour: 'Now it's time to empty our pockets, empty our pockets, empty our pockets …' Pieces of LEGO would tumble to the floor.

I found that the scene at each new school would be much like opening day at Huntersvlei a few years earlier. The older children tore around with excitement, getting under everyone's feet. The younger children cried and hung on to their grannies or mothers. Lydia and Maria gave the children new pinafores, the teachers and mothers cooked soup and handed out biscuits and oranges. Most farmers added pap, beans and vegetables to the food. I flapped around like the chicken being chased by Rebecca.

The nursery-school buildings were all different. Some were oblong brick structures with concrete floors and corrugated-iron roofs. Others were old sheds with cracked walls and floors. There was even a converted pigsty. The ground around the nursery schools was rough and stony, with scrubby patches of wild grass. There were pit toilets behind each building, all with child-sized seats.

That was in the beginning. Every day, Robyn, her nanny Maria Moloke and I visited the nursery schools to see how things were going and to help where I could. I was happy – and I was also pregnant again. One morning I parked my car next to the Ntataise play van under a row of gum trees, their bark mottled, their grey-green leaves drooping like those on Huntersvlei, only much older. The nursery school on this farm was a sandstone shed that had been around since the Boer War. It was across from the farm workshop, and a good walk from the stad. Outside the shed, there stood a group of very angry women. In their midst was Maria, trying to calm everyone down.

'Hey, Mme,' she said when she saw me. 'These mothers say this woman is their neighbour and that she doesn't know anything about teaching.' Maria pointed to the nursery-school teacher, who stood sullenly beside her, her lip trembling. One mother, angrier than the rest, thrust a sheet of paper covered in rough wax crayon squiggles under the teacher's nose. The teacher swatted it away with her hand. Big tears rolled down her cheeks.

Maria translated the words that poured like water from a broken dam from the irate mother. 'She says we should be teaching her child to write, not draw squiggles. She wants to know about this nonsense of children playing. She says children don't play at school and teachers should write on blackboards, 1 2 3 4.' I'd heard that before. 'I'm not sending my child to this clinic.'

Another woman, dressed in an overall with a blanket tied around her waist, stomped off past the gum trees in the direction of the farm stad, shaking her head and muttering to herself. At that, all the mothers turned and set off after her. We stood there, speechless.

'The children's parents don't know what you're talking about,' Anthony said later.

'But we told them at the farm meetings.'

'Tell them again. Show them. One meeting is not enough. It's all about communication.'

Rebecca agreed with Anthony. 'That woman was right. They don't know about nursery-school teachers. One moment they're their neighbours, talking over the fence, sweeping their yards and cooking for their families, next minute they are nursery school teachers and everyone else is suspicious of them. They don't know what we're trying to do. We've got to keep telling them.'

Anthony was right. I didn't understand the nuances of the different communities. I'd been so busy getting to grips with the contents of the panel van, understanding play activities, collecting usable 'waste', that I'd lost sight of the fact that we were working with people, people who were looking out for their children's best interests and were not convinced by the nursery schools. I had assumed that everyone would be as excited as I was, but we needed to do more to reassure the women that their children would be looked after and learn in safety.

I remembered my father taking Robyn to visit a large Easter bunny at the Sandton City shopping centre. Mothers milled around, pushing their children in front of the bunny with big, floppy ears and falsetto man's voice. He patted each child on the head and gave them an Easter egg. Robyn, however, was terrified, refused the egg and spent the next few weeks sleeping in the passage outside her bedroom, so the 'bunny' wouldn't find her.

We'd presumed it would be a treat.

21

NEW WINGS

The teachers were like butterflies, emerging at last from their cocoons.

I DIDN'T HAVE TIME to tell anyone anything. Claire Elizabeth Evans was born at the Park Lane Clinic in May 1981.

Back on the farm again, Robyn's warm three-year-old body pressed close to mine as we peered at our new baby, asleep in the Evans family crib, with its new turquoise broderie anglaise skirt.

'If she falls out of the crib and breaks will we get another one?' Robyn asked hopefully.

'She mustn't fall out,' I said. Anthony gave her a hug and took his 'big girl' off to look at the new lambs bleating for their mothers in the kraals near the house.

Anthony was a powerful force in all our lives, especially in our children's. Although he wasn't useful when someone was carsick, when the children were small he was there to play with and read to them just about every day. The moment they were old enough, he had them lead calves round the front lawn or play cricket. The farm gave him that freedom. When our children were older, Anthony was always there to advise and – when asked – to guide them. When I look back, my happiest and most secure moments were when we were all at home together, eating together or just being there, secure that we were a family and would look after one another. It gave me a feeling of deep contentment. Anthony was seldom away overnight and we spent few nights apart during our life together. Not that this did not, on occasion, lead to heated arguments, but it brought me closer to another person than I had ever thought possible.

Our expanding family grew alongside Ntataise and soon I was back on the road visiting the nursery schools, this time with Robyn, nanny Maria Moloke and Claire in her carrycot on the back seat of the car. I was carving my own place and was happier than I had been in a long time. Huntersvlei was our children's home and gradually became mine.

Convincing parents of the importance of learning through play for their young children was very much on my mind. I set a date for the first parents' meeting at Huntersvlei.

'Make sure everyone comes?' I begged Rebecca.

'They won't,' she said. 'It's a Saturday morning. Everyone goes shopping on Saturdays.'

So we held parents' meetings on each of the six farms on a week-day after work. Some farmers let everyone off early, some didn't. Tractor drivers and herdsman arrived most reluctantly, it looked to me, in their work clothes. Mothers in their *tjalies* straggled in, chatting in a desultory way. There seemed no sense of urgency to these meetings.

'We're not used to meetings like this,' said Bonny. 'The only meetings we go to are funerals and church meetings. No one worries about time. At funerals the priest waits until enough people have turned up.'

We waited pretty much until everyone had turned up and then Lydia began the meeting with a prayer and a hymn. Maria and Lydia had set up the playroom with all its different art activities, exactly the way they did for the children. There was a table for drawing, another for painting, playdough and clay and, of course, cutting and pasting. Parents sat uncomfortably on the child-height benches and curiously fingered the paper, scissors, paint, crayons, or dough on the tables in front of them.

'They were scared of the paper,' Maria told me later. 'They thought we were going to tell them to write. Many of them can't write.'

We had to convince this rather unwilling gathering that, although their children might not be learning to read and write, they were learning what they needed to help them do so in the future. Words like 'colour', 'size', 'shape' and 'hand–eye coordination' floated round the room. I don't think anyone listened – they were too busy.

The silence in the playroom was broken only by the sound of wax crayons on paper and the swish of paint brushes dipping into yog-hurt containers filled with powder paints of different colours. There were a few coughs and giggles. I too swished paint onto a large sheet of computer paper. An hour or so later, men and women hurried home with their artworks firmly clutched in their hands, to light fires, boil water and make supper. I hoped against fragile hope that we'd persuaded them of the importance of hand–eye coordination, colours, sizes, shapes – and playing. Reading and writing would follow at the primary school, but you couldn't do one without the other. No one, Lydia reported, was totally convinced, but we'd planted a seed and they'd all enjoyed themselves and so had I.

While we were convincing parents about the benefits of early learning, Sister Tseki was on a mission to improve the children's health. All six nursery schools had children with copper-coloured hair, the tell-tale sign of malnutrition. There were children with scabies, runny noses and sore, festering eyes. Sister Tseki's house-to-house visits on the different farms to talk about these issues did not go down well. She was received with great reluctance. 'People don't want her in their homes telling them what to do,' said Rebecca. They don't want to hear what's 'wrong' with the way they're feeding and washing their children, she said. 'They're embarrassed because they're poor. They say there's nothing wrong with the way they look after their children.'

Lydia took over the house-to-house visits and, with her kind voice and manner, she slowly built up the trust we'd been searching for. She held cooking demonstrations using fresh vegetables and wild spinach, which grew easily in the stads. She, like Rebecca before her, arranged small meetings for mothers and grandmothers on each farm. They came out of curiosity. They also came partly, Lydia told me, because of the sandwiches and the cups of tea, and partly to get out of their houses and do something different. Something to eat has become the norm at virtually every meeting or conference I go to, whatever it may be. 'Food is something people know. It makes them feel welcome,' a colleague once said. Apart from nutrition, she talked about cleanliness, about the dangers of food covered in flies, and, while she was about it, the importance of children cleaning their teeth. At the beginning of the year and again at the beginning of each term, she weighed and examined every nursery-school child on each of the six farms. If children were underweight or not gaining weight, she suggested their mothers take them to the clinic in Viljoenskroon.

As the year wore on and the Ntataise van became more familiar, the initial suspicion waned. 'The children love it when we come. They know we are bringing food and toys. They help us unload the panel van,' said Maria, looking far less stressed than during the previous month.

As for me, no one thought I was going to give them an injection any more. Children clung to me, hugged me, pressed my thumb with theirs, chatted away to me – it didn't seem to matter that my Sesotho was still rudimentary.

The end of Ntataise's first year was celebrated by children dressed in red, blue and green pinafores sitting in a semicircle outside the Cottage eating cupcakes (with pink-and-blue icing piled on top), drinking fruit juice and then running in their undies under the sprinklers on the Huntersvlei front lawn, screaming with delight as the cold water sprayed them. This became an annual tradition. The next year, a few children came in bathing costumes, and the next, a few more. The teachers took towels from the pile I'd put on the stoep and dried wet bodies. Sybil joined in for tea and cupcakes on the Cottage stoep with me and the teachers. I never knew whether she was proud or pleased with what the nursery-schools had brought to farm life, but she came to nursery school events and concerts and was a big help with entertaining a number of our visitors. One of my best moments of that first year was watching children in the nursery school playground with toothbrushes in their mouths and toothpaste dribbling onto their hands – a gift from Colgate-Palmolive.

As for the new teachers, they were like butterflies. By the end of that first year they had emerged from their cocoons. Their confidence had grown and their new wings were already taking them to unimaginable heights.

22

TOO MANY QUESTIONS

The trouble with the children, the principal said,
was that they weren't behaving like children.

IT WAS A NEW year: 1982, the 20th anniversary of the arrest of
Nelson Mandela in the Natal midlands. The ANC bombed the
Koeberg Nuclear Power Station. Bombs exploded in government
buildings and offices. The security police bombed the ANC
headquarters in London. FW de Klerk was elected the new leader of
the National Party in the Transvaal. In Viljoenskroon, Maria, Lydia
and I were summoned to the office of Mr Sello, the Huntersvlei
primary-school principal.

The office hadn't changed much since my first visit. Exercise
books were still piled on his desk, papers neatly stacked in the
bookcase behind it. Filing out of their classrooms were girls in too-
large or too-tight school tunics, boys with their hands lost in blazer
sleeves or sticking out like scarecrows. Among the smallest of them
were the first Ntataise children to go to primary school. They gave
us shy smiles. The three of us waited in Mr Sello's office with smiles
of anticipation. He must, we thought, have called us to tell us how
well the nursery-school children were doing.

Mr Sello closed his office door. Mrs Sello, the Grade 1 teacher who was also his wife, sat beside him. Her arms were folded, her mouth serious and unsmiling. 'The nursery-school children,' said Mr Sello, getting straight to the point, 'are badly behaved, noisy, ask too many questions and are uncontrollable.' All in all, they were not doing well. In fact, a number of them had failed. Despite his rather grudgingly adding that they were 'lively, enquiring and freer in expressing themselves' than the non-preschool children, I felt as though someone had kicked me in the stomach. I couldn't understand it. What had they expected? Weren't children meant to ask questions?

'Ai, Mme Jane,' said Maria as we later sat, disconsolate, in my study. 'Mrs Sello feels she's losing control. The way we're taught to teach doesn't allow children to ask questions or give an opinion. She doesn't know what to do if they don't sit still and listen. Children from farms with no nursery schools arrive at primary school totally unprepared for being away from their mothers or grandmothers. A lot of them are hungry and frightened. All they'd heard about school was that there were teachers with rulers that hurt you and if you did get a smack and cried the teacher would smack you again. So they are quiet and don't ask questions.'

'Why don't their parents do something about it?' I asked her.

'If they tell their parents, they smack them too and tell them not to be naughty.'

'That's terrible. Children in smart new school clothes that their families could barely afford, going to school expecting to be smacked. We can't let that happen. How are we going to stop it?'

'Have you seen the farm primary schools?' Maria asked me. 'Some of them are quite good but you should see the rest. They are overcrowded and understaffed. Children in four different grades crammed into one small classroom with one teacher. I don't know how anyone learns.' She drew breath. 'Smacking children with rulers is a way teachers feel they can keep control.' There were no fingers on lips in the nursery schools and certainly no rulers.

'What would you do?' I asked Anthony that evening.

As usual he was reading the news, but stopped to ponder my question. 'I'd involve the primary schools. Tell them the way you do things and why,' he said after a while, pouring us both a glass of wine while he was about it. 'See if that helps.'

I can't say the primary schools were thrilled with the suggestion of workshops with the nursery-school supervisors, but each quarter after that Maria and Lydia ran workshops for Grade 1 and 2 teachers, introducing them to the activities we did with young children, how we did them and why. It was a two-way process.

Just before the Christmas holidays, I watched a solemn line of children walk the couple of hundred yards from the Huntersvlei nursery school to the primary school. They had been invited by Mr Sello to meet the teachers and see where their classrooms would be the following year. Maria smiled at me. The workshops were paying off.

'We must slot in a few more before the schools break up,' I said.

Maria told me I was exhausting her; Rebecca said I should try to do what I was expecting them to do. Children, she said, were not perfect – they didn't do things according to the book. They, the teachers and the trainers were trying to be perfect, but they were not. And nor, from what they said, was I.

'Why don't you calm down?' Anthony said. 'It's been a year of amazing achievements. Tell everyone how well they've done, instead of how much better they should do.'

23

UNEXPECTED PROGRESS

So near yet so far from the dawn of the rainbow, a grapple with age-old attitudes.

I LISTENED WITH DELIGHT and then horror to a request from Van Leer. 'They want us to hold this year's seminar here at Ntataise,' I told Maria and Lydia. Delight, because hosting the sixth Bernard Van Leer South African Early Childhood Development Seminar was a big deal. It said a lot about the work we were doing. Horror, because it was 1983 and I had no idea where everyone would sleep.

It wouldn't, apparently, be at the Mahem Hotel in Viljoenskroon. 'The white people can stay here,' the receptionist told me. 'No blacks, no coloureds and no Indians. Take it or leave it.'

With delegates from Entokozweni in Soweto, the Early Learning Resource Unit, and the Foundation for Community Work from Athlone in the Cape, the Chatsworth Early Learning Centre in Durban and the Zimbabwean projects, we were the rainbow nation. But there was little of a rainbow about South Africa, especially in our neck of the woods.

'Can't help you,' said hotel after hotel. Was I not aware that Indians weren't allowed in the Free State – not overnight, at any rate?

Maria and Lydia seemed resigned. 'That's the way it is,' Maria said to me. No one believed it would ever change.

Finally, a hotel in Potchefstroom, 60 km away and safely out of the Free State, agreed to accommodate all 20 delegates. It was far from ideal, but at least everyone had a bed. We'd prepared gifts for the Van Leer delegates – peanuts from the farm, biltong, lacy doilies crocheted by the children's mothers. Some of the delegates said the gifts were patronising. More than sixty farmers' wives, farm nursery-school teachers and those from the Viljoenskroon nursery schools, farm primary-school principals, teachers and government officials attended the seminars. These were run by Ann Short and each participating organisation. Each showed a different model of early childhood development.

Back then, while the country was experiencing ongoing violence and anti-government demonstrations, we were all grappling with problems on the ground – how to give South African children a chance in life. The seminar bred a sense of camaraderie among us.

But camaraderie was not the norm. On the drive back to Potchefstroom on the second evening, the Van Leer team lost its way. It was a dark night and not particularly pleasant to be stranded in the middle of nowhere. Eventually, someone stopped to help. Their relief was enormous. The man approached and, while they were gabbling their thanks and requests for directions, he switched on his torch and allowed it to play over the occupants of the car. He stepped back, spat: '*Verdomde swartes,*' turned and disappeared into the night. They eventually found their way back and, when I heard of it, I apologised from the bottom of my heart. It wasn't the way I'd hoped the conference would end, and I waited anxiously for Ann's report.

In the event, she wrote: 'Unexpected progress has been made in this largely rural region. The Bernard van Leer Foundation has funded this experimental farm project Ntataise in Viljoenskroon for

the past three years. It has received close guidance from ELRU ...'
Why had it been unexpected? Ann would never tell me.

The Free State and Northern Cape Regional Welfare Board were,
on the other hand, enthralled by our conference. 'Mevrou Evans,
will you run a workshop on early childhood development for us?
There are nursery schools springing up all over the place but there is
nowhere to train the teachers.' The workshop was to be in Bloemfontein, some 300 kilometres away, for 80 fledgling preschool
teachers and their management committees.

'They were like sponges,' Maria reported on her return. 'They
soaked in everything we told them.'

Nursery schools – or early learning centres, as they had come
to be called – mushroomed in small rural townships throughout
the Free State. They had no daily programmes, no equipment,
and unqualified, untrained teachers. No sooner was the workshop
finished than the Welfare Board asked us to help them set up a
training programme. In between all this, Maria and Lydia continued
their own training with ELRU in Cape Town. ELRU trainers Karen
van der Merwe, Ann Short and Welekazi Dlova were regularly at
Huntersvlei, visiting the nursery schools and running workshops for
the teachers. Lydia started a structured mother-and-child playgroup
programme.

Maria and I drew up a programme for the Welfare Board, but it
was getting too much for all of us and our own nursery schools were
suffering. We were spreading ourselves too thin. 'Is this what we
want?' I asked Maria. 'There might be more and more preschools,
but what about the quality?'

If we weren't careful, quantity would win over quality. 'That's
not what we want,' said Maria.

At the end of 1983, our first grant from the Bernard van Leer
Foundation was to come to an end. The Foundation would renew
the grant, but only once, I was told. I should begin to look for other

funders. I felt the first stirrings of panic. What would we do if we couldn't get funds? The farmers would not be too pleased about taking over the salaries of the teachers, and the parents could pay only minimal fees. It was time the government started providing funding.

The Department of Education and Training in Kroonstad and I were no strangers. My contact palpably cringed when he saw me at his door. I told him we wanted the farm nursery schools to be registered and that we wanted subsidies. He shrugged. 'I'll see what I can do, Mrs Evans.' We weren't very hopeful.

The Van Leer Foundation agreed to fund a second three-year term but it wanted to know what difference we were making to children's performance in primary school and how we were going to disseminate our work; they wanted quality and quantity. We felt we were making a difference. The report-backs we received from primary schools had swung around from the children being naughty to the children being easier to teach, and I received many requests from primary-school principals to allow all potential Grade 1 children to come to the nursery schools. The South African Human Sciences Research Council (HSRC) had already embarked on a study to assess the preschool programme in promoting school readiness among the children with whom we worked. They were doing this by testing Grade 1 pupils at the Rammulotsi primary schools who had not been to nursery school, and comparing these results to those of children at farm primary schools who had been to a Ntataise farm nursery school. It was a huge blow when I received a call from the HSRC to tell me it had run out of funds for this particular project and was not able to finish it. It was some years before we were able to carry out a scientific assessment of our impact.

If Ann Short had taught me nothing else, she'd taught me the value of observation, and it was with great confidence that I told the Van Leer Foundation how our pilot project had transformed the new teachers. I had watched them, over the three years, change from women who felt they couldn't to women who knew they could. Women with no confidence and no prospect of a career beyond running a home or working on the lands became confident, outspoken, often leaders in their communities, women with jobs and futures. They may not have been be running a full educational programme yet, but they were well beyond offering only care to the children in their playrooms. Maria and Lydia felt more comfortable working with the women and children than they had in the previous three years. They were confident in themselves, experienced and knew what to do.

There had been changes in the preschools themselves too. The Makvoël preschool had started in a room attached to the farm workshop. Grease, tractor parts, chains, spanners and nails had lain on the ground. It was hardly a nursery-school environment. The room had a gaping front with no door or wall. It was cold in winter, noisy all the time and not safe for children. Some months later, the supervisors arrived there for their weekly visit to find that a brand new school had been built in the Makvoël farm village. The walls had been painted and the floor cemented. There were small benches and tables, and big child-friendly windows.

As for me, I loved being part of a team with Maria and Lydia. I had a whole new group of women to talk to and work with. We became good friends and shared many special occasions.

24

THE DO-GOODER

As the drought breaks, a little too late, a
visitor from abroad casts new light on what
it means to do good.

'MY MOTHER,' ANTHONY SAID, 'has suggested we swap houses.'

With our third baby on the way, we, like the nursery school, needed extra space. Plans to extend our 'two-pitch *pondok*' were spread on the table in front of me one afternoon when Anthony arrived home early. He was flustered and wouldn't sit down.

'Why would she want to move out of her lovely big house with all her things, all her memories?' I turned to look at him.

'Because it's big. It's hard for her, but I suppose it's the right thing to do,' he said.

I was excited about the move, not because the house was big but because it was beautiful. The wood-panelled rooms, the wooden beams in the dining and sitting rooms, and the fireplaces were charming. That the house was so big – and that the Cottage, the separate building with its Dutch gables, where Anthony and I had stayed until our own house had been built, was some 100 metres from the house with its vast downstairs entertainment room and upstairs en suite accommodation – was a plus. Ntataise was increasingly being called upon to host visitors to the nursery school. Farmers' wives, farmworkers' wives, schoolteachers, university lecturers – the list grew. This would give me the space we needed to invite a good number of people to a meal and to spend a night.

'First,' said Anthony 'before you think of entertaining, we'd better move in, and from the look of you we'd better do it soon.'

Boxes and crates filled all the available floor space. Cupboards lay open as Monica Masukela, Maria Moloke and I reached and packed, reached and packed. One morning I leaned forward to lift a plate. It was heavy and I rocked back on my knees. An excruciating pain tore through me. I dropped the plate and phoned Anthony in a panic.

Three hours later I was in Johannesburg, in the gynaecologist's consulting room. But this time, there was no miscarriage. I simply had to take things easy, he told me. That was not going to be easy. Robyn and Claire, now five and two, tore round the 'big' house in excitement, settled into their new bedrooms and made sure the new baby's crib was waiting in the baby's bedroom. Robyn was of the opinion that the four of us were enough in our family; when Sally Margaret Evans was born two months later, her two sisters peered into the Evans crib, not entirely convinced about the joy of our cuddly new baby.

I'd moved into the 'big' house with some trepidation – I wondered whether it would ever really be my house. The newly painted walls enclosed so many of Sybil's memories, I thought. 'We'll make our own memories,' said Anthony. But I didn't feel the house would ever really be mine. As my sister-in-law Wendy put it, 'You've been a good custodian,' referring to the house. She was right; it was a family home, and belonged to all of us. But later, when Anthony died, the house would become mine as never before. I'd cling to it and the memories it held. The memories and traditions that permeated the house and the Cottage became mine and our four children's; I no longer felt on the periphery.

While we and our three little daughters set about making those memories, white puffs of cloud built up in the west, merged, darkened … and scattered.

'We won't get a crop this year if it doesn't rain soon.' Anthony frowned at the sky.

Women from the stad held a prayer meeting in the dry pan close to the main road. They danced on the brown, cracked soil, holding in their hands brittle twigs with crisp, dead leaves clinging tenuously to them, praying for water to make them grow. We watched the strong maize plants slowly wilt. The shiny green leaves dried and curled into themselves. No cobs formed. Without rain, there was no pollen to fertilise the plants. Day after day the clouds built up. Day after day they evaporated into the sky's infinite blue. The sun sapped every drop of moisture from the ground. Anthony's face was lined with worry.

Our nursery schools were hanging on, but the farmers were struggling without an income. The nursery schools were not their top priority. Finally, when we had all but given up, streaks of lightning rent the air. Thunder crashed around us. Angry purple clouds built up and rain fell. Drops turned to grey sheets of water. The gum trees near the house moaned as the wind howled through them. When the skies cleared we walked through the lands, our black gumboots growing heavy with mud. Robyn and Claire jumped in puddles and squished the unfamiliar thick brown mud through their fingers. It was too late for that year's crop, but at least the drought had broken. However worried Anthony was, he had an extraordinary ability to remain outwardly composed. The government of the day made financial help available to farms that had suffered badly in the drought. At Huntersvlei, all unnecessary expenditure was cut back. The accountant suggested we cut salaries, until he understood that would include his. Money for workers' salaries came from the government support. Everybody had food to eat and money to take home. But it brought home to everyone how risky a business crop farming was, especially when one depended on the rain.

The day after the drought broke, a letter arrived for me. I opened it distractedly, worrying about Anthony and the farms. I read it once, without taking in the contents. Then I read it again. I tore yet again across to Anthony's office, waving the letter in the air. 'Can you believe it?' I arrived at his office, puffing. 'All six original farm nursery schools have been registered with the Department of Education and Training. The new nursery schools will follow. And they will all receive a subsidy!'

Originally, this amounted to R25 a term for every five- and six-year-old, but the amount increased to R3 000 a year for a registered farm preschool with a minimum of 15 children and a maximum of 30. It included three- and four-year-olds. The department would accept pit toilets with child-sized seats and outdoor hand-washing facilities as sufficient to allow for registration. It wasn't much money, but it was groundbreaking – the first farm nursery schools, certainly in our province, to be registered and subsidised by a government department.

'You should be proud of yourself,' said Anthony. 'I am proud of you.'

Anthony might have been proud of me, but not everyone was. I wasn't at the annual Van Leer Conference that year, held at the Van Leer-funded Entokozweni project in Soweto, which was just as well. It was bad enough hearing Maria and Lydia tell me, on their return, that one of the main speakers had labelled Ntataise's work 'patronising' and had said that the Ntataise director was a 'white do-gooder'.

'We told him you weren't anything like that, but he wouldn't listen.'

I had never met Dr Walter Barker. He was director of a Van Leer-funded project in the United Kingdom. He too was white, and I was livid. 'What does he mean by 'patronising'? Do I talk down to people? Treat them like children? Tell me, honestly.'

'You get cross if everything isn't perfect but we all work as equals. You are not patronising,' said Maria.

'He said I was a do-gooder.' The words burst out of me that evening.

'Calm down, my girl,' said Anthony. 'He's never met you.'

I didn't want to be seen as doing things I thought were good for people. This was obviously how some people saw me – a white girl, living in a big house, lording it over poor, black people. I decided this unknown Dr Barker should come and visit us.

Being a do-gooder in South Africa of the 1980s meant, as I inter-pret it, being a well-meaning white person doing what he or she thought was good for someone of another colour. The recipient often wasn't consulted, was presented with a fait accompli and didn't find the intervention particularly helpful. Local farmers' attempts to 'help' people in the different farm stads in our organisation live 'better' lives by running garden competitions and holding sports days to keep children busy in the holidays was what do-gooders did. The activities had no impetus of their own. To keep going, to be sustained, they would have to be driven by the people concerned. It was patronising in the extreme to imagine that people didn't have their own pursuits.

In the early days, the nursery school may have been seen as a 'good-for-children' initiative, but it is 40 years on and the Huntersvlei nursery school has led to the development of Ntataise, an NGO that generates its own energy and is led by amazing black and white women, filled with the same passion as I was all those years ago.

Mapitso Malepa, director of the Van Leer-funded Entokozweni early learning centre in Soweto, got in first. 'Dr Barker,' her voice crackled down the party line, 'wants to visit Ntataise.'

'That's exactly what I was thinking. When would he like to visit?'

We worked out the logistics. 'Let me give you some advice,' Mapitso said. 'Let him see Ntataise is not only a white-run project. Make sure he spends the day with Maria and Lydia and has lunch with one of your trustees, one he couldn't even vaguely think of as being a white do-gooder.'

Dr Barker arrived a week later and was met at the nursery school by Rebecca, the teachers, and Maria and Lydia. He spent the day with Maria and Lydia and had lunch in a farm village with Abel Dlamini, a Ntataise trustee and principal of a neighbouring farm primary school, and Abel's charming wife Mary. He arrived on a glorious Free State evening to spend the night with Anthony and me at Huntersvlei. The air was still, the sky a clear, inky blue and the stars, with no city lights to hide them, a myriad of fairy lights. This man, whose remarks had so stung me, sat with us on the stoep and talked with us. I found it difficult to equate this gentle soul with the man I'd been expecting.

He told us of his work with 'travellers' in the United Kingdom and explained that he'd left South Africa to marry a Chinese woman, a relationship forbidden under apartheid laws. He'd left the country with hate and sadness in his heart. We spent most of the evening discussing the healing qualities of zinc in food and on the maize crop. No mention was made of white do-gooders.

Soon after this, a group of farmers' wives from Ventersdorp, the heart of right-wing Afrikanerdom, visited the farm nursery school. We wanted nursery schools on as many South African farms as possible, so we welcomed them. The leader of the group worked for an organisation called the Landelike Stigting, or Rural Foundation, which they said had been set up by farmers in the Western Cape to upgrade living conditions for farmworkers. I had never heard of the Foundation, but if it was working on farms it seemed I should find out more about it before it started to reinvent the wheel as far as farm nursery schools were concerned.

25

SOWING THE SEEDS

*'Is that the nursery school?' asked callers
from across the country, reaching what was
once known simply as a farm.*

THE RURAL FOUNDATION'S SPACIOUS offices were in the heart
of the Cape winelands. The tall and craggy-looking director, Okkie
Bosman, was as curious about me and our work as I was about him
and his. He talked about the Rural Foundation. I talked about
Ntataise. We both talked about rural development. He asked what I
wanted from him. I told him I wanted to spread the idea of nursery
schools on South African farms, and he had access to many of them.
I wanted that access and I wanted to see if our organisations could
somehow work together so as not to reinvent the wheel.

The newly established Rural Foundation concentrated on training workers' wives to be '*Nompilos*', or health workers, he told me.
Farmers in South Africa at that time were all white. Many were not
known for their good labour relations. Working and living conditions on many farms were hard: many farmworkers' homes had no
water and poor sanitation, and salaries were low. Farmworkers

ranked among the poorest of South Africa's poor. The Rural Foundation developers were, in the main, white, Afrikaans-speaking men and women. I flew back to Johannesburg wondering if the Rural Foundation was really addressing the needs of workers – or those of farmers.

Despite my misgivings, Okkie Bosman spread the word. His support coincided with an article in Johannesburg's *The Star* newspaper, headlined 'Ntataise – the first organisation in South Africa to promote preschool education for the children of farmworkers', along with photographs of Maria, Rebecca and me throwing balls to children, and children eating sandwiches and drinking milk. And this was not all.

It took two days to shoot the TV feature on Ntataise. Usually articulate trainers became tongue-tied. People from the stad lined the nursery-school fence, fascinated by the cameramen and their equipment. The children were out of control with excitement, gathering in front of the camera, asking to be photographed. My children were not about to be left out – they wanted their pictures taken too.

The feature was screened on a Tuesday night on the SABC TV magazine programme *Network*, directly after *Dallas*, the most popular soapie on TV at the time. Robyn and Claire sat on the carpet, Anthony and I leaned forward on the well-worn red leather chairs. I was jumpy with anticipation. We all stared at the television while the urbane announcer Tim Modise introduced Ntataise to South Africa. Hardly had the feature ended than the phone rang and, for the next few weeks, it never seemed to stop.

'Is that the nursery school?' voices demanded over the phone at all hours.

'I suppose it is,' said Anthony with a sigh, a happy one or not I wasn't sure.

Whatever the time of day or night, Ntataise and my family

were one. It wasn't a job, it was part of my life – and none of us could get away from it, even if we wanted to. Requests to visit the Huntersvlei preschool came from women in places Maria, Lydia and I had never heard of – Koppies, Bothaville, Koster, Boons, Derby, Bethlehem, Haenertsburg – some places close by, others hundreds of kilometres away. They turned 1985 into a year of totally unexpected expansion; we had achieved our dissemination. While I was swamped with requests from farmers' wives wanting to visit the Huntersvlei nursery school, Maria and Lydia were swamped with requests from women who wanted to be trained so their children could attend a nursery school. This incredible reaction was almost too much for us. Carloads of Rural Foundation developers, farmers' wives, farmworkers' wives, social workers and government officials from towns such as Clarens, Reitz and Harrismith in the Eastern Free State, and Devon, Setlegoli, Rustenburg and Carolina in the Transvaal, came to see the Huntersvlei nursery school. An inquiry even came from far-off Tzaneen.

We made pots of tea and our usual plates of sandwiches. The nursery-school children thrived, loved the attention, kicked balls, dug in the sandpit, sang songs and generally showed off. I was invited to address countless groups of farmers' wives. Sometimes Maria came with me, sometimes I went on my own. We were still deep in the apartheid era. At first I found myself talking to community and church halls filled with white women. I asked that workers' wives also be invited to attend.

'They'll never let them come,' said a colleague. 'Not in those communities. I'd be petrified of talking to all those people. Don't you get nervous?' she asked.

'I do get nervous, but I love public speaking, I'd much prefer to face a hall full of people than a small group asking me personal questions – or, even worse, a social function where I don't know what to say to anyone.'

Despite my colleague's cynicism, farmworkers' wives joined us and the number of our speaking engagements got out of hand. 'I can't believe so many people are interested in early learning for children on the farms. They are such conservative communities,' I said to Anthony.

'Farmers are seeing nursery schools on their farms as a way of attracting and keeping workers and, from what I can gather from our farm, farmworkers see them as a way of ensuring food and safety for their children. I know they don't get the learning part, but that's where you come in,' he said.

'Okkie Bosman of the Rural Foundation told me he thought that farm nursery schools were becoming a major growth industry.'

'They are: there is more goodwill around than farmers are credited with, because parents want the best for their children and because you and Maria and Lydia are driving the issue, and offering to help people establish nursery schools,' said Anthony. 'You are laying yourselves open to a lot of work.'

Anthony didn't tell me often how proud he was of my achievements, but I knew he was. I could not have done it without him. Apart from his helping to edit funding proposals and entertaining a seemingly endless stream of visitors to the nursery school and overnight at Huntersvlei, he was my sounding board and constant support, whatever the issue.

'It's too much. We need a break,' said Maria. 'I don't think I could drive another kilometre, or give another speech.'

She and Lydia, like me, found the unexpected onslaught of interest overwhelming.

'Why don't you write it all down?' Anthony asked. 'Then none of you will have to travel and talk so much.'

It was the obvious next step. I began work on a booklet almost immediately and Anthony came home each day to find me submerged beneath piles of notes and reference books scattered over the dining room table. Eventually, he could stand it no longer. 'What a mess,' he said.

Ntataise had outgrown the dining room table. We turned a garage into the Ntataise office. Workmen carried away the heavy roll-down metal doors and replaced them with a whitewashed wall and wooden door. A large window overlooked the rondavel and the backyard of the main house. We added a hard-wearing carpet, blue curtains, a new phone and two desks, one for me and one for a new secretary and bookkeeper, who could type and understand the vagaries of computers. It felt very grown up.

I transferred the 'mess' from the dining room table to my new desk and began to write the answers to the queries we most frequently received: Could a mud hut be used as a playroom? What sort of timetable should be followed? What food should the children be given? Which activities? How did they make toys? Who could be teachers? Who'd teach them?

Writing the book was one thing. I was enjoying it – but who was going to illustrate it? It had to have illustrations to back up visually what I'd written.

'I'll illustrate it,' said Bonny.

'Can you draw?' I asked.

'I don't know, I've never tried.'

'In fact,' Bonny told me once the book was finished, 'I've never drawn in my life before, but I reckoned it couldn't be that difficult and I wanted to do it.'

It wasn't as easy as Bonny had imagined. Perspective seemed to baffle both her and me. It was only when the floor was littered with crumpled balls of paper that we literally begged for help.

'I'll help her,' said trustee Sandra Botha. 'It's not difficult.' And when you knew what to do, it wasn't. Not everyone was enthralled with the two-dimensional drawings, but Bonny and I were delighted with ourselves. We printed 700 copies of *A Farm Nurs[ery]*, illustrated with Bonny's figures. We sold them from our off[ice], packed and posted them. Nursery schools and women looking [after] children bought them, and by year-end we were sold out. I had t[he] booklet translated into Afrikaans, Sesotho, isiZulu and isiXhosa. We've since printed thousands more.

While I was writing *A Farm Nursery School*, Maria wrote Ntataise's first training programme, a two-week preschool introductory course on early childhood development. She put the completed work, contained in a large, mottled-grey cardboard file, on my desk with almost reverential care. 'I designed it specifically for women on farms and in rural areas, women who live a long way from towns, who work in sheds, converted pigsties, corners of packing sheds and buildings that were never designed to be nursery schools,' said Maria, sitting in the blue upholstered chair opposite me. 'These women have limited resources, they have no transport, pretty low levels of education and work in real isolation. Apart from anything else, the rural conditions are so different from towns. I've learnt so much about it in the last couple of years. I hope the course helps.'

Maria drew her breath. I picked up the typed pages. Before I could say a word, she continued, 'I didn't want to show you until I'd gone through it with our Viljoenskroon farm nursery-school teachers. I couldn't finish it without their help. I had to know if what I'd written worked for them or not. I like working this way. It is much easier working with a small group of people. We can go big later.'

Go big we did – but it wasn't later. This course, along with later adaptations and extensions from Ann Short, became the basis of one of the earliest ECD short courses designed specifically for people living in rural South Africa.

Maria hadn't finished talking. 'I will train women on farms in other parts of the country, but I can't train the Viljoenskroon women too. I can't do both. It's getting too big for me.'

by now assistant trainers doing on-site
oenskroon farm nursery schools. In
rammes they'd attended at ELRU,
g' at the well-developed African Self
Soweto. These visits had more than

so pleased we went, Jane. We could put what we learnt at
ELRU into practice. The theory suddenly made sense. I have a much
better idea of what a nursery-school play area should look like,'
Bonny had told me.

'We have a much better understanding of what and how children
could learn through their play,' Rebecca added on their return to the
farm.

'Gosh, Maria, a new member of staff means more funds – and
where are we going to find a trainer?' We agreed that, if I raised the
funds, Maria would find a trainer. Feeling shaky around the knees
and trying to sound confident all at the same time, I phoned Edzo
Tonkes at the Van Leer Foundation in The Hague. I asked if the
Foundation would come to the rescue. An answer wasn't immediately forthcoming; after the rather heavy silence, I wasn't holding
my breath.

The answer came a few days later. 'We'll do it, Jane. We'll fund an
expanded Ntataise programme. You are disseminating the work, but
you must not become financially dependent on us.'

Maria brought Alice Ntisa, a primary-school teacher from
Rammulotsi, to meet me. Her brother, Joseph Chomane, had
become headmaster of our farm primary school when Mr Sello had
retired; Alice was no stranger to Huntersvlei. She joined us in August
of that year. She went straight to the ELRU in Cape Town to start
her training and, above all, to learn how to teach adults.

'It is so different from teaching seven- and eight-year-olds,' she
said to me when she got home. 'I had to learn how to talk to adults,

how to get them to trust me and like me before they'd be prepared to learn from me.'

Even with the booklet finished, I began to understand how Maria sometimes felt: swamped. I would drive to town to buy Bertha needles and thread to mend torn overalls, only to get back to the farm and turn right around again because Rebecca had run out of soup powder. No sooner was I back than Bonny would say, 'I need Koki pens.'

'Can't you get them yourself?' I exploded one morning, unfairly. Bonny looked hurt. There was often farm transport to town – but often there was not. Ntataise may have been one of my priorities, but it wasn't necessarily everyone else's – and it certainly wasn't the farm's, especially during planting and harvesting.

Of the Ntataise team, only Maria and I had driver's licences. 'We need another driver,' Maria said.

'I agree. But who?'

A thought crossed my mind: if she could draw, why shouldn't she drive?

'Not that one thing has anything to do with the other,' said Anthony when I told him my plan.

This did not deter me. 'Would you like to learn to drive?' I asked Bonny.

'Me, drive?' Bonny was amazed. 'Of course.' Her pretty face lit up.

'This is much harder than drawing. I failed my test,' a despondent Bonny told me a couple of months later.

'Keep trying, you'll get it'.

Weekend after weekend, Moses taught Bonny to drive in a farm *trokkie* until the engine didn't stall and the brakes didn't squeal. Eventually, one morning there was a determined knock on the door. Bonny peered through the glass panels on either side of it. Her mother Miriam stood next to her.

'That's a nice surprise.' I stood back to let them in.

We had barely walked into the study when Bonny said, 'These are for you,' and thrust a posy of pink flowers into my hands. 'And this,' she said, 'is guess what?'

'Your driver's licence? Bonny, that's fantastic! Well done.'

Miriam, by now ensconced in a deep, red leather chair, fanned herself with her hand. 'Mrs Evans, thank you for helping this child of mine.'

Bonny's huge grin was all the thanks anyone needed. I didn't need thanks – I thanked Bonny. I, and Ntataise, needed Bonny and her driver's licence: I was pregnant with our fourth child. This time there was no nausea, no dashing to the bathroom. I didn't have time to feel sick. Every day, the green canvas bag we used to collect our post from the post office was full. Letters in blue ballpoint pen on lined sheets of thin white, green and pale-blue paper all ended up in my in-tray. Each letter was a request for help from someone who was setting up a nursery school and needed training or advice.

We decided to set aside the first two weeks of each term for training. Sixty-eight women from the Free State and the Eastern Transvaal (now Mpumalanga) attended training at Huntersvlei that year.

'Do you give recognised qualifications?' aspiring nursery-school teachers asked me time and again.

'No, we don't. There aren't any government-recognised qualifications to give. But everyone who completes the course gets a certificate of attendance.'

Families in the Huntersvlei stad still hosted trainees. But by now, we had watertight agreements on fees for accommodating and feeding the trainees. All seemed to have settled down – or so I thought.

Autumn had set in and the leaves on the trees were turning yellow. There was a chill in the air the evening I was summoned to the clubhouse. Nineteen trainees waited for me, seated in the usual semicircle, without smiles. Some looked at me, others at the floor. Our discussion was like peeling an onion, removing one layer at a time until we got to the heart of the matter.

It was the same problem: food. 'We are not getting enough to eat. We want pap and we want more meat.' The spokesman appointed by the irritated trainees pointed hopefully at Anthony's prize Sussex cattle grazing in a camp outside. 'There's lots of meat there.'

Everyone laughed. I could imagine what Anthony would say to one of these prize specimens landing up in an Ntataise cooking pot.

'What did you decide in the end?' he asked me when I told him of the bull's narrow escape.

'We agreed that trainees' hosts would give their guests breakfast and supper, and Ntataise would cook the midday meal.' To cook a midday meal for some 19 people every day meant a kitchen to cook it in. There was no such thing in the stad. 'I said we'd cook the midday meal in our kitchen.'

'Good luck,' said Anthony.

Monica Masukela glowered at me when I offloaded large stainless steel cooking pots and packets of provisions in our kitchen. For the next two weeks she would be cooking for 19 people once a day – a beef stew, roast chicken pieces or chicken pies, accompanied by a big green salad. Pudding was easy: we served fresh or tinned fruit and custard.

'Mrs Evans, you are giving me too much to do. I can't cook for the household and the training,' Monica said. 'I need someone to help me.'

That wasn't the end of the problem. The trainees included rural and urban women. 'They do not like to eat the same things. Their tastes are different. The farm women don't want pies and nobody wants a big green salad,' Maria told me.

Every day was a minefield, with everyone wanting something

different to eat and Anthony roaring with laughter and reminding me that not everyone liked the insubstantial, dainty food I'd chosen for the menus. 'Who,' he said, 'wants to eat lettuce leaves?'

Clearly not our trainees. Monica made suggestions for a change in the menu. Maria and Lydia asked the trainees what they liked to eat. We eventually got the menus right, and someone to help Monica.

'Thank goodness for that,' said Anthony. 'Now maybe I'll also get lunch.'

26

A WARNING

In a climate of chaos and anger comes a sinister warning from the security police.

IT WAS 30 JANUARY 1986. Men in khaki shorts and shirts patrolled the grassy verges outside the Salomon Senekal Primêre Skool in Viljoenskroon. Pistols bulged on their belts. Their faces looked grim.

'Stay in the car,' I said to Robyn, who pressed her nose against the window, peering at the menacing men outside.

'Why? What's wrong?'

'That's what I'm going to find out.' I walked up to one of the parading men. 'What's going on?'

'There's revolution in the township. The children are marching on the administration office. They've burnt down councillors' houses. We're frightened they might come here,' he replied.

'Stay where you are. We're going home,' I told Robyn.

I parked my car under the syringa tree. Maria Moloke ran out of the house, wringing her hands and crying uncontrollably. 'They killed him! They killed him!'

I steered her into my study and she collapsed into a chair. She was in shock. 'Who killed who?'

'They killed Letshabo. They shot him.'

I scrabbled in my handbag and gave her a crumpled tissue. Tears pouring down her face, Maria Moloke told me that the schoolchildren in the township had had enough. They were sick of how the municipality treated their parents. They wanted water, they wanted tarred roads. Nobody would listen to them, so they had marched to the administration offices to give the township manager a petition.

Officials, she told me, had closed the imposing gates that guarded the administration's Rammulotsi offices. Outside the gates, school boys had sung and thrown stones. They'd broken through the fence and marched inside the building and started to burn papers. The officials had shot at them and Letshabo Nthethe, Moses's nephew, had been killed. Others had been arrested and locked up.

We were interrupted by the phone. It was Lydia. 'I'm in the Ntataise office. Come quickly.' I left Monica giving Maria Moloke very sweet tea to drink, and ran outside to our office. 'The Comrades ordered people in the township not to come to work today, but I wanted to tell you what was going on. None of us slept last night. There was an all-night vigil. The Comrades made us dance, they said they would whip our feet if we stopped dancing.' Lydia buried her head in her hands.

I put my arm around her heaving shoulders. 'I'll take you home.'

'No, don't go near the township, no one must see me. Go along the main road to Parys then drop me near the lands. I'll crawl back through the mealies.'

'You can't do that. Let me take you home,' I said, horrified.

'No,' Lydia implored. 'You mustn't, they'll whip me.'

I was shaken at seeing Lydia creep through the maize plants, her clothes a flash of blue between the thick green mealie plants. At home I found Bonny waiting for me with Maria Moloke.

'Hey Mme, everyone in the stad is so frightened. Our children came home from school in Rammulotsi. They were terrified. They were forced out of the buses this morning by the Comrades who said they must join them. The only way not to was to get away and run home.'

'It's time we talked and listened to each other,' said Anthony after he had met with the liaison committee that afternoon. Sitting on the Huntersvlei stoep in the cool evening air, listening to crickets a few nights later, it seemed impossible to believe that we were just six kilometres from the smouldering township. Ishmael Mabitle, Andries and Sandra Botha, and the leader of the Comrades, Smanga Toli, had accepted our invitation to talk. Smanga Toli sat ramrod straight. His short, wiry body quivered. In front of him he held a piece of paper from which he read the Comrades' 'demands'. The Comrades wanted the township councillors to resign. They were, he said, 'apartheid puppets'. The Comrades further demanded tarred roads and running water. They wanted high-school classes to be extended beyond Standard 8. There was nothing unreasonable in what these young men were demanding; they were simply insisting on what should by any human right be theirs. I hadn't met Smanga before but I knew his father, a kind, gentle man who worked at the Standard Bank in the dorp and would always stop me to say hello when he saw me.

We ate dinner in the dining room. Its panelled walls, and the roast beef and vegetables, were such a stark contrast to the poverty in Rammulotsi just a few kilometres away. I felt incredibly uncomfortable. I wondered what Smanga thought of us. He's never told me, but we've remained friends since that day.

The next day a delegation of Comrades visited Anthony in his office. They needed money to get their colleagues out of jail. They were casting around for help, for someone to hear them. They sprawled in the worn leather chair, sat upright on wooden stools, stood or paced about the room. But they all poured out their problems. Anthony gave them money. Today one of those young Comrades is an ANC member of Parliament; another has served a term as the mayor of Rammulotsi.

While Anthony was talking to the Comrades, the police were pestering Ishmael Mabitle. They wanted to know what he had been doing eating at a 'white man's house'.

'For God's sake,' Anthony told the station commander later. 'Ishmael Mabitle's our friend. He and Smanga were our guests. We'll invite whoever we like to our house.'

Back on the farm, members of the men's committee pounded on Anthony's door. 'If any black farm people shop in the white shops in Viljoenskroon over the weekend, the Comrades say they will cut off our ears,' they told him. Transport to town was laid on as usual, but only a few hardy souls went to shop. A pall of fear hung over Rammulotsi and Viljoenskroon. Young black men were in jail; white men continued to patrol the streets of the white town, holsters on their hips, hands on their guns. The men on the farm respected Anthony and trusted him. This gave weight to their open interaction with him, which was vital, especially in times of crisis. It also gave a sense of security to both the workforce and their families, and to us and ours.

In the middle of all this anger and fear I received a phone call from a Willemien le Roux, who said she was starting a preschool project called Khuru near the town of Ghanzi in Botswana, to be funded by the Van Leer Foundation. 'Would Ntataise help train their teachers?' she asked.

'I've been to Ghanzi.' I said. 'When I was a university student, I was a member of the South African Voluntary Service. We built a schoolroom for San children on a farm not far from the town.' As I told her of my experience there, over a line that crackled and echoed,

I could almost feel the grassy, slimy mixture of dung and mud squelching through my fingers, smell the hunk of goat I'd been given to cook for supper.

When I told her this, there was a momentary silence. 'That school was on my parents' farm. I was a little girl but I remember the South Africans making bricks and building a schoolroom for the San children on our farm. What a coincidence.'

It was a moment of pure serendipity and we both felt quite emotional. Lydia said she wanted to go and do the training. Wilhemien and her husband fetched Lydia from Viljoenskroon. It was a long journey through kilometre upon kilometre of desert, bush and scrub. Lydia, who was getting older, felt every bump.

'It's so remote,' she said when she returned. 'Those women know nothing about preschools the way we do it.' The Khuru project wanted her back and she wanted to go. She'd hardly returned from the second visit when the police accosted her in her Rammulotsi house, wanting to know what she'd been doing in Botswana, what sort of training she was giving. 'They said they'd be back.' Lydia sat in my study trembling, clutching a mug of hot tea. I phoned the local chief of police, incensed. I told him Lydia had been in Botswana at Khuru's invitation, teaching San women how to make toys out of toilet rolls and empty cardboard egg boxes. I asked him to please stop harassing her, or any of us, for that matter.

'Ja, Mrs Evans, but her training could still be subversive.' How on earth the training we'd been offering could be subversive I didn't know. I have never looked at toilet rolls and egg boxes in quite the same way since. Nonetheless, neither the police nor the security police bothered Lydia or Ntataise again.

27

DRUMBEATS

Sleepless nights on the farm, and not just because of the brand-new baby.

IN OCTOBER 1986 I went into labour and, this time, asked for an epidural. I was relaxing into a pleasant sense of numbness when the sister's harsh voice filled the theatre.

'This baby is in distress.' I tensed, wanting to be sick.

'Relax,' they told me, slipping oxygen tubes into my nose. Anthony stood in the background, looking uncomfortable in his green theatre gown.

I waited in almost as much distress as the baby to hear the word 'Caesar' but it didn't come. Instead the doctor said, 'It's a boy!', and David Rhys Evans's wails filled the theatre.

Later, his sisters looked at him in his tiny hospital trolley through the wide nursery window.

'He looks scrawny,' said Robyn.

'He has legs like a chicken,' said Claire.

'I want to hold him,' said Sally, standing on tippy toes and pressing her two-year-old fingers against the glass.

The news spread fast: Jane had had a boy. Anthony said there was going to be a *mokete*, a celebration, on each farm. They would slaughter an animal in honour of the boy.

'Did you slaughter an animal when we were born?' Robyn stood beside her father, a miniature Anthony, all seven determined years of her.

'No,' said Anthony, 'but we celebrated just as much.'

'But why are animals slaughtered for David?'

'He's a boy. It's tradition. Everyone on the farm feels a boy means that there is someone to carry on with the farm when I grow old.'

'You mustn't grow old. You must carry on with the farm.' Robyn wrapped her fingers around her father's hand.

Between the sleepless nights, three little girls who needed me and a baby boy who constantly had to be fed, I felt like a well-kneaded lump of playdough. This, however, did not stop people from phoning me, or stop me from taking the calls.

'You can't mean it,' I said to the Department official, absolutely horrified. New nursery schools, he had just told me over our as-always crackling phone line, would no longer receive subsidies. There were no funds, and the best he could do was to put their names on a waiting list. It was the start of 1987. There were now 16 farm nursery schools in Viljoenskroon, 30 teachers and some 360 children. It was, as Maria said some 11 months later, a very exciting year. Interest in establishing nursery schools on farms in other parts of South Africa was growing and everyone wanted to know how they could get a state subsidy.

While we worked well with the local education inspectorate, the national inspectorate was entirely unhelpful. I implored Nita Geach, chief nursery school planner with the Department of Education and Training, to help. She was impressed with the project and said she'd do whatever she could, but it seemed that state support for farm nursery schools would not be readily available in the future. In fact, it might be stopped altogether. The demand for training, however, did not end – its sheer volume was creating its own problems. At Huntersvlei we nearly had a rebellion on our hands. A total of 180 visiting trainees would need accommodation on the farm that year.

'There are too many people,' the liaison committee told Anthony. 'Huntersvlei families can't put them up any more.'

'We'd prefer to sleep in the clubhouse on the children's mats,' the trainees said.

And Monica Masukela was quite clear: 'I can't cook any more for these people and still do my other work for you, even with help.'

Besides the perennial problem of accommodation and food, women on the current course didn't speak Sesotho and Maria didn't speak isiXhosa. There was total uproar. I don't know how we'd not picked that up beforehand. A teacher at the Hebron nursery school who spoke isiXhosa volunteered to help. Before she could even think about it, she found herself in a training session, translating.

But language was only half of it. Women from farms and women from towns still didn't mix. They ate differently and the town women quite overshadowed the farm women in training sessions. 'The urban women are better educated. They're more relaxed and outspoken,' Maria said. 'The farm women have a very low standard of education and they are shy and withdrawn. I suggest we split the groups – farm women at the beginning of each term, town women at the end.'

And, we agreed, there would be no more than two languages per course.

It was at about that time that we managed to double-book a training session. Nothing I did or said would convince the twenty or so women scheduled for two weeks later, sitting expectantly with their suitcases and plastic bags next to them, having been given the wrong starting date, to leave. They cried, pressed wet handkerchiefs to their eyes, sat firmly on the benches. In the end we paid for their trips home, sent boxes of biscuits to say we were sorry, and rebooked their training.

In between all of this, two things happened. Ten of our first teacher aides completed the *Learning Through Play* ELRU green-book programme, along with Maria's two-week programme, and received their certificates of attendance. This was a huge step, and a far cry from backbreaking work in the dusty, thorn-filled lands or sitting at home unemployed. There were many tears when we presented the women with their smartly typed blue cardboard certificates with the Ntataise logo at the head of the page. Not only from the teacher aides: I too cried with the sheer joy of it all. We promoted Bonny and Rebecca, their certificates already framed and proudly hung on their bedroom walls, to trainers. Like we'd done for others before them, we waved them on their way to Cape Town for further training as they clambered onto the daily train at the Klerksdorp station.

We received a well-timed visit from Jane Hofmeyr of the Mobil Education Trust. I had sent the trust a request for a large sum of money; she had come to suss us out. If the trust approved our request, it would be a godsend and solve many of our training problems – like where trainees should sleep and where their meals would be cooked. In time, I'd come know Jane in her role as head of the Independent Schools Association of South Africa. Like Ann Short, she was a woman of formidable intellect and she gave us a thorough grilling. I had no idea whether we had managed to impress her. I'd tear open the mail each day, but there was nothing. I had grown no more patient with the years. The wait was agonising. I couldn't bear it when anyone turned us down. I never quite understood how they could.

At last the letter came. The grant had been approved.

It transformed our training operation. It bought a new Ford Husky for the farm visits and built a training centre right next to the Huntersvlei nursery school. There was a training room, a kitchen with a large industrial stove and oven, a dining room with four wooden tables covered in bright, orange-and-red plastic tablecloths, and three dormitories: a blue room, a red room and a green room. Red, blue and green curtains swelled with each passing breeze. I ruffled my fingers through the matching candlewick bedspreads; they felt soft. Each bed had its own mat and its own wooden bedside cabinet. We built the showers and toilets at the far end of the building.

The Mobil Trust project officer I worked with was Trevor Manuel, who would later become Minister of Finance in the country's new government. I'd just turned 40 in early March 1988 when Dr Ken Hartshorne, a controversial and well-known educationist, opened the new Ntataise Training Centre. Mobil, other funders, Ntataise staff, trustees, family, government officials, farmworkers, farmers, nursery-school teachers and children stood on the Huntersvlei nursery-school playground, which was by now covered in thick, green kikuyu grass. Song melded the gathering, for that short time, into the country we could become. Dr Hartshorne told the gathering that the strength of early childhood development for black children at that time was that there was no government interference in it, and that its strength came from the informal sector. And he was right. We kept the Department in Kroonstad in the loop, but could do pretty much as we liked.

A local municipal dignitary clasped my hand with fervour. 'It's a great day for Viljoenskroon, Mevrou Evans,' he said.

A nursery-school teacher from nearby Bothaville stopped me and said, 'You know, when I was a child we went away from the farms to learn. Now we come back to the farm to learn.'

We were beyond proud of what we had managed to achieve here in the rural Free State. The training centre was to be the hub of a wheel, its spokes reaching out to other emerging centres. It was a wheel that must keep turning to serve the increasing number of rural women who, through the nursery schools, were being given the chance for a life beyond hoeing or working in a packing shed. Whatever the future would bring, everyone was in the mood to celebrate that day, and the haunting sound of drums and excited voices carried on until late that night.

28

FAR AND AWAY

*The message of Ntataise takes to the road,
but the road is long and hard.*

'HAI, HAI, STOP, STOP!' Bonny pounded the cream-coloured bakkie's roof. But it was too late. Cardboard stoves, homemade books and puzzles flew off the back of the bakkie and landed in muddy pools at the side of the great north road. The teaching materials that trainers Bonny and Maria had so carefully made for this first training visit to Vaalwater, a tobacco-growing area some five hours north of Viljoenskroon, turned to soggy brown pulp.

I watched Maria and Bonny go through endless difficulties in those early years, travelling vast distances in mainly the Free State, the Eastern Transvaal (Mpumalanga as we know it today) and the northern parts of South Africa to offer training in early childhood development to farmworkers' wives or daughters in all sorts of conditions.

Nearly all the requests came as a result of Ntataise's exposure in magazines, newspapers and on national TV, and my visit to Okkie Bosman. The need was tremendous and so was the demand. An amazing number of farmers were prepared to fund nursery schools.

In Vaalwater, north of Johannesburg, Maria and Bonny were pioneers, the first people to offer training in ECD in that part of the world. They were also, Bonny informed me, the first people from the Free State to eat what she described as 'bits of different wild animals'.

'Mopani worms,' she said. 'They were alive and they just put them in a pan and fried them in oil then added tomatoes and onion. I couldn't eat it, but the course participants loved it.'

Sleeping arrangements were such that Bonny and Maria found themselves sharing a bed. 'Don't fuss, Mme Jane,' Maria told me over the phone. The Rural Foundation developer who had arranged the training course scurried around until there was food that both our trainers could eat and beds for them to sleep in.

The message must have spread. Maria and Bonny's next training trip was to Malelane, a small Lowveld farming town seven hours from home near the Mozambique border. The Rural Foundation developer in that area promised me they would be well looked after. They stayed in the comfortable Malelane Hotel and were taken to the Kruger National Park for the weekend.

'I saw an elephant!' Bonny yelled down the crackly landline. 'I've never seen one before.'

Maria took the phone: 'Every day farmers' wives come in with waste material for our toy-making sessions and just to see what we are doing. And they bring us all special food to eat, a treat,' she told me.

And yet, despite the problems with their living conditions, Maria and Bonny had found the Vaalwater women much easier to train. 'The Malelane training was heavy going. The Vaalwater women were better educated than most of the women we work with. They'd all reached Standard 8. The 25 frightened women on the Malelane course had firstly been chosen by the farmers and didn't know what they were going to be trained to do, and they had far less schooling and were shy and wouldn't talk for the first few days, at least not to us. Most of them couldn't read or write,' said Maria. 'And we don't speak siSwati but we managed to understand each other in isiZulu.'

'What did you do?' I asked her.

'We scrapped our written material and used crayons, blocks, whatever we could find to show them what we were talking about. At the end of the course, the most frightened of the women stood up and thanked us on behalf of the group. It made it all worthwhile,' said Maria. 'But,' she added, 'this is just the beginning, these women are going to need constant assistance in implementing what we taught them. I struggled to understand it all and I'd been a primary school teacher. They've been working in the fields and suddenly they're expected to run nursery schools.'

The Rural Foundation developer was full of praise for Maria and Bonny. 'Jane, you will never understand exactly what the course has done for these farm women. No black women in this farming community have ever been exposed to this type of training and the status and confidence it brings with it.'

While we visited the Viljoenskroon nursery schools regularly and frequently after training courses, we weren't doing the same for the new schools that were springing up in other parts of the country, as Maria had advised. If they were to flourish and Ntataise was to give them effective support, we had to know what their specific needs and problems were. Early one morning Maria and I set off on a day trip to Bethlehem in the eastern Free State, not far from the Lesotho border. Anthony and Maria Moloke were left looking after our children. In the early light, the flat maize fields gave way to rolling green plains framed by table-top mountains. Rough clumps of bush dotted the hillside.

The sign 'Ntataise' at the gate told us some three hours later that we had arrived. Age-old rocks streaked with black watermarks balanced precariously on top of one another and a cowshed converted to a nursery school stood in their shadow. Inside, a hard, brown dung floor was covered with a faded rug, its fringe long gone – but it was warm. A pile of scuffed shoes and socks stood near the door. Weather charts and posters with pictures of the parts of the body were stuck to the wall alongside roughly torn pieces of computer paper covered in scrawls of wax crayon and water paint. Light struggled to filter in through small windows.

Rosina, the teacher, flung her arms around Maria. She showed us her playroom. There were a few children's storybooks stacked on a cardboard box, and piles of *Landbouweekblad* magazines for children to cut pictures from in the art area. A few puzzles and homemade blocks were laid out exactly the way Maria had taught her. Ragdolls were tied to the backs of both boys and girls, and an animated tea party was taking place around the papier-mâché tables and chairs Rosina had made at the Huntersvlei training course. The nursery school had a basic framework, but as I sat and watched and listened to Rosina interact with the children, I felt a knot of excitement mixed with disappointment. It was a start, but it had to be better. Much better.

The farmer's wife hurried out of the sprawling sandstone farmhouse when our visit to the nursery school was over. She'd invited us to lunch. Bethlehem is one of the coldest places in South Africa. Inside the spacious entrance hall a fire blazed in the grate. Over welcome plates of hot beef and vegetables, we told her the nursery-school teachers were doing well, but as I ate I knew that we had a long way to go. Our next exploratory trip was to the Eastern Transvaal (Mpumalanga). The Lowveld air was hot and humid, so different from the harsh, dry Free State. I loved the heat, the incessant screech of tropical insects and the sweet smell of orange blossom. Bougainvillea flowers – shocking purples, pinks and yellowy white – tumbled down walls and fell over high fences. Maria and I drove over gravel roads that wound their way through fields of thick, green sugar cane and hectares of shiny-leafed citrus trees. Oranges hung from their laden branches like golden balls.

Neat rows of small brick houses surrounded the nursery school we were to visit. It was in the middle of the farm village. A woman stirring a three-legged pot stopped and waved. Children in overalls of different colours stood in two lines, one on each side of the entrance to the nursery school, whispering to one another, pushing, laughing and pointing at our car. Maria disappeared into the teachers' waiting arms. They had attended her Malelane training programme and she hadn't seen them since. They stood back rather more shyly when I was introduced.

The school was built of wood. An office, a storeroom and a small kitchen formed the backdrop to the large playroom, which was covered with precisely laid thatch but open at the sides. 'It gets so hot here we have to have a through-draft,' the farmer's wife told us. Most of the nursery schools in the Lowveld were built with three open sides. The concrete floor was covered with mats and each activity area had been neatly demarcated and labelled. But puzzles had pieces missing, a lonely doll had one arm, crayons were broken and the pencils had no points. There was no story time and, to my horror, the teacher aide was writing with grim determination the letters 'a', 'e', 'i', 'o' and 'u' on a tatty blackboard.

After yet another field visit to the Eastern Free State, this time to the town of Ficksburg with its asparagus plants and cherry trees, Maria found the nursery schools in no better state than those in the Lowveld. There was something we were not getting right. Maria had identified the problem; these visits just reinforced it. 'We train people and we leave. No one really knows what to do. They've learnt a little but there's no one there to help them learn more. There's no one to guide them. One moment those women are working in the mealie fields or picking oranges or asparagus, the next they're expected to be nursery-school teachers.' Where a farmer's wife helped, things tended to improve, but on farms where she was not involved, not much happened. We were expecting far too much from the women after their few weeks of training. A well-qualified nursery-school teacher in the white areas had at least three years at a teachers training college and ongoing support. The women we were training had so much to catch up in their basic education before they could even begin to implement or really understand what we were teaching them.

The 'away' nursery schools were simply not good enough. They were providing the children with care but not much else. 'Don't worry,' said Anthony. 'You've laid the foundations. It's a good start. You'll sort it out.'

But how? Our trainers were already spending weeks away from home conducting training courses. They had a full programme. I couldn't ask them to be away from home for longer than they already were.

29

PATIENCE

*Her hair was squashed under a doek. She
wore flat shoes, an overall and no make-up.
'Do I look too sophisticated now?' she asked.*

'THEY WON'T DRAW.' THE young woman, her doek pulled low over her eyes, took a swipe at a young boy who was carefully aiming wax crayons at a little girl's back. 'They never listen to me.' Tears rolled down her cheeks.

My heart went out to her. She had an impossible job, a playground full of children and not the first idea of how to play with them or keep them busy. We had been called in, at the request of the Bernard van Leer Foundation, to extend Ntataise's reach to the Western Cape. The Rural Foundation's community development project had set up nursery schools on numerous Western Cape farms, but the teachers were completely untrained. They were basically running what Rhys had predicted – a nannying service.

The nursery schools were spread far and wide and we drove deep into the hinterland in the week I went to visit, through valleys of neatly laid-out vineyards laden with bunches of purple grapes, to reach this nursery school. I looked at what the teacher was trying to make the children do. Three- and four-year-old children couldn't possibly draw the vase of flowers that she had hopefully placed on a table for them to copy. There were no toys, nothing for the children to do. Later that day, surrounded by the yeasty smell of wine vats, I gave a presentation on how to start a farm nursery school to a group of developers – who told me that, between them, they worked on 250 farms, all of which wanted nursery schools.

Susan Sedigo, a Rural Foundation developer based in the Western Cape, was seconded to Ntataise. She came to Huntersvlei so she and I could spend time working out a plan for her new venture. We looked at the scope of what she would be expected to do.

'It's just not possible for one person to visit that many nursery schools,' I told her. We were sprawled on my study floor, looking at maps of the Western Cape.

'We'll manage.'

'I don't think so ...'

'Let me try.'

My fears had been well-founded. Only months later, Susan resigned. The job was just too big for one person and the Western Cape, at the southern end of South Africa, was too far from Ntataise – over 1 200 kilometres away – for me to manage the project. Very reluctantly, I realised that there was only so much we could do. There were limits to our capacity; we couldn't offer effective training, let alone support, to the Western Cape. Between ELRU and an organisation called Grassroots, there was excellent support for those Western Cape farm nursery schools in Cape Town, right on their doorsteps.

Nervously I dialled the Van Leer Foundation phone number in The Hague. I had to tell Nico van Oudenhoven that there would be no Western Cape project despite the fact that the Van Leer grant was already in our bank account. With a considerable amount of cheek and my body pumping with adrenaline, I asked, 'May we use those funds to better our training services to nursery schools on farms in the Eastern Transvaal and Eastern Free State? There are about seventy of them.'

The silence flowed almost deafeningly through the line from The Hague to Viljoenskroon.

'Okay, Jane, but this is the last time. The Foundation cannot carry Ntataise indefinitely.'

I would have to work hard to raise funds in the longer term, but I wasn't going to stress about that then. We could now appoint full-time Ntataise trainers to be based in both the Lowveld and the Eastern Free State. Viljoenskroon to Nelspruit was a good six-hour drive. Try as I might, it wasn't any more feasible for me to manage the trainers who'd be working in those far-flung nursery schools than it had been for me to manage a project in the Western Cape, even further away.

Anthony rolled his eyes in horror when I even suggested it. 'You must get managers,' he said.

I began the search for people living in those two areas who would work with Ntataise and manage the burgeoning nursery schools and the Ntataise training projects. I couldn't even say 'suitable' people, because I didn't know who we were looking for until I found them. As it turned out, it was serendipity all over again.

Some months earlier I'd received a phone call from a woman who said her name was Margaret Solomon, the wife of Dennis Solomon, a leading South African citrus farmer. She wanted to start a nursery school on their farm, but wanted to see ours first. A mover and shaker, Margaret Solomon had helped establish nursery schools in Kanyamazane – a vast, ever-growing township bordering Nelspruit in the northeastern part of South Africa, on the Crocodile River. She duly arrived to visit Huntersvlei, and the seeds of a firm friendship and a major nursery-school movement were sown.

Margaret accepted with alacrity when I asked her, some time later, if she'd help Ntataise establish and manage a farm nursery-school training organisation in her area. That is how she became the director of what in time would come to be called Ntataise Lowveld.

Our regular Friday telephonic 'management meeting' became deeply entrenched in the Ntataise psyche. Woe betide anyone who was on the phone at nine o'clock on Friday mornings when Mrs Solomon, with a temper to match her red hair – quite out of keeping with her diminutive frame – was scheduled to talk to me. Her dedication and commitment never wavered through the more than twenty years for which she ran Ntataise in the region.

We advertised for a Ntataise Lowveld trainer by word of mouth, much like in Viljoenskroon, through clinics, nursery schools, primary schools, churches. On a day Margaret and I settled in the cane chairs on the patio of her home on their farm, Crocodile Valley Citrus Estates, a few kilometres outside Nelspruit – one of the most progressive farms in terms of labour relations and education for workers and their children in the country. We interviewed a stream of young women. We wanted someone very particular: someone with a driver's licence, someone who could speak isiNdebele and isiZulu, the languages of the area, and understood local customs. Besides all that, we were looking for a qualified nurse or social worker – or, best of all, an experienced primary-school teacher.

'I don't think we are going to find the right person.' Margaret stood up to clip a dead flower off a rose bush when in walked Winnie Mashaba. A primary-school teacher from nearby Kanyamazane, this articulate and good-looking young woman met all the requirements and more. Without much ado we offered her the new post, and she accepted. She set off almost immediately to Ntataise in Viljoenskroon and ELRU in Cape Town for training in early childhood development.

Lynette le Roux, the competent and self-effacing wife of Paul le Roux – the Rural Foundation developer in the Bethlehem–Clarens area of the eastern Free State – was more reluctant to take on the task of managing the Ntataise programme in their area. She was uncertain about her ability to manage people and what my expectations of her would be. The Le Roux's farm, Spes Bona, lay enfolded in the foothills of the Maluti mountains a few kilometres from the picturesque town of Clarens. In winter the icy weather crawled under coats and jerseys, and in summer the sun drenched the widespread farms with relentless heat.

Finally, over tea and homemade rusks on the long, enclosed stoep that ran the length of her weathered stone house, Lynette agreed to manage what, in years to come, would come to be known as Tshepang. In those days, it was Ntataise Eastern Free State. I promised to support her with regular visits and a weekly phone call.

We followed much the same word-of-mouth advertising for our Eastern Free State trainer, and appointed a qualified social worker to the position. Neither Margaret nor Lynette, nor the other 'Ntataise advisors' who would follow them in other areas of the country, were formally employed by Ntataise. Their work was voluntary. It wasn't an easy job; the farms were far apart and the nursery schools were heavily dependent on the farmers' goodwill. Each of the farms that joined the Ntataise programme agreed to make a building available to house its nursery school. These varied widely from mud houses to sheds, to new brick or wooden structures. The farmers agreed to pay the salaries of the women appointed as nursery-school teachers. They agreed to provide food for the children and transport for the trainee teachers to training sessions and workshops. In theory, this was all good. In practice, it didn't always work that way. Many a trainee arrived halfway through a workshop or found herself standing forlornly on a muddy farm road in the descending evening gloom, waiting for a bakkie to fetch her and take her home.

One day the newly appointed Eastern Free State trainer drove 140 kilometres on lonely country dirt roads on a scheduled visit, only to find the teacher working in the fields, the children at home and the nursery school closed. 'It's harvesting time – what did you expect?' boomed the furious farmer when we confronted him and asked where on earth the teacher had been. Many of them still saw it as that nannying service, a way of keeping the children looked after and fed while their mothers worked in the fields. But in planting season everybody worked, even the nursery-school teacher. Grandmothers looked after the children. Soon after that abortive visit, the Eastern Free State trainer crashed the Ntataise car. She emerged unscathed, but promptly resigned.

It was back to the drawing board. In response to our announcement, a young woman I regarded as glamorous arrived at Huntersvlei for an interview. She wore a tailored suit and high-heeled shoes, and wore her hair in a bouffant style. 'My name,' she said as she sat down, 'is Patience Ntsoane.'

She radiated warmth and confidence and I liked her immediately. 'I can't offer you the post, though,' I said regretfully, after our interview and copious cups of tea. 'You're just too sophisticated for us. The rural women won't accept you and I'm not sure you'd manage there.'

'Nonsense,' she said. 'Give me another chance. I'll be back tomorrow.'

I hardly recognised the woman who knocked on the office door the next morning. Her hair was firmly squashed under a doek. She wore flat shoes and an overall, had no make-up on, and looked demurely at the floor. 'Do I look too sophisticated now?' She looked up at me.

Patience joined the Ntataise training team and stayed with us for well over twenty years.

30

THE AMBASSADOR

In the aftermath of tragedy, an official visit brings hope for positive change to a broken system.

IT WAS ALICE NTISA who answered Alina Marumele's frantic cries for help. Her 16-year-old grandson, who should have progressed to high school three years before but was still at the Huntersvlei primary school, had hanged himself in her house in the stad. He couldn't take the teasing and the humiliation of sitting with children three, four and five years younger than him any more.

Alice helped cut him down.

We were all shaken to the core. It took this tragedy to reinforce our own belief in the importance of the work we were doing. As increasing numbers of black primary- and high-school children failed their exams, international research pointed to the positive effects of early interventions, especially for children from poor backgrounds, deprived of food, healthcare and stimulating play.

In the early 1980s, in the wake of the 1976 Soweto uprising, at the government of the day's request the Human Sciences Research

Council conducted research into the state of education in South Africa and came up with suggestions for how to reform it. The commission to carry out this work was set up under the chairmanship of JP de Lange, a leading South African educationist. The resulting De Lange report was scorned by many as perpetuating segregation. Although the report said, in essence, that all South African children, irrespective of race, sex or religious beliefs, should have equal standards of education, it did not make it clear whether this was to happen in an equal and integrated way.

Among other things, the report recommended the introduction of preschool education, especially for children from disadvantaged backgrounds. No funding was to be made available for the introduction of this early learning on a broad scale, however. Once again, only those who could afford it could have it – and black children growing up in poverty continued to be marginalised. They were reliant on gutsy women from the communities they lived in – and organisations like Ntataise, with financial backing from big business, overseas foundations, individuals and, in our case, the farmers – to make early learning happen. Even then, it happened for only a few.

While our focus was on farms and farmworkers' children, nearby township nursery-school teachers begged to attend training sessions – and asked whether they could bring children from their nursery schools to visit the farm. And so, children who had never been on a farm before visited Huntersvlei, arriving in big buses. When everyone had watched cows being milked and newborn calves suckling from their mothers, dug up peanut plants and seen how mealies grew, they ate sticky buns and drank mugs of orange juice at the Ntataise centre while their teachers walked around the playrooms and chatted to the Huntersvlei nursery-school teachers.

In addition to these young visitors, the Ntataise trustees, Anthony and I entertained funders and potential funders, welcomed them to the project and invited them to stay over. Among them were the

British ambassador Robin Renwick and his wife Annie. As we walked them over to our guest cottage, where they were to spend the night, the ambassador – later to become Sir Robin, then Lord Renwick of Clifton – ran his hand through our Labrador's golden coat. The dog was promptly sick all over his shoes.

This was not an auspicious introduction to Ntataise. But it didn't seem to deter the Renwicks, and Maria and I gave them a full tour of the Ntataise Centre and nursery schools the next day.

In the midst of all this I was informed that it was once again Ntataise's turn to host the Van Leer conference, five years since the last. 'We are not staying in Potchefstroom this time,' said Ann Short. And they didn't have to. Between Huntersvlei and our friends, we found plenty of Viljoenskroon beds to give all the delegates a comfortable night's sleep.

The accommodation problem may have been solved, but the conference was not without other hitches. On the last night of the conference, Anthony and I had pushed tables together in the Huntersvlei dining room to make room for 26 people to eat. It was to be a special evening, around a table set with glasses that shone in the flickering candlelight. I was so proud to have my colleagues in our home, and so pleased that they wanted to be there.

This, of course, did not stop me from putting my foot right in it, not causing hurt as much as incredulity. I was sitting beside Ishmael Mabitle, who had arrived on time, on the soft, gold-patterned couch in our sitting room. I glanced at my watch. 'I wonder why everyone is late?'

Ishmael looked me in the eye and said, 'Jane, you whites are funny. You expect people to arrive on time, smelling clean and dressed in pressed clothes. There is hardly any water in Rammulotsi, there is no transport and there is no electricity. I think it is amazing that anyone arrives at all.'

They did arrive, and we sat down to a dinner of chargrilled steaks which had, with their tantalising smell, been cooking on the braai fires set up in the garden outside the dining room. I cut into one of them and remarked to Rose, the delegate from the excruciatingly poor Alexandra township in Johannesburg, 'Gosh, this is tough.'

She put down her knife. 'This piece of meat, Jane,' she jabbed the steak with a fork, 'would feed an entire family in Alex for a week. It is delicious meat.'

Ishmael's and Rose's words bounced inside my head until the early hours of the morning, when I eventually fell asleep. I didn't feel so much chastened as ashamed of myself.

We'd hardly started the new year when Maria, settled in my study for our usual Friday meeting, said, 'Our trainees need to see a first-class nursery school. The Huntersvlei nursery school is good, it's well laid out, it's got the necessary equipment, but it's a work in progress.'

I was momentarily stung, but I had to agree with her. We knew the difference we were making – we could compare it to what there had been when we started. But trainees found it difficult to visualise the standards that Maria was talking about and how they were expected to interact with the children, listening and not just telling. Learning meant desks in a row, fingers on lips, doing what the teacher said.

I explained the problem to the principal of the 'white' nursery school in Viljoenskroon and asked if we could bring groups of trainees to get first-hand experience of a well-functioning preschool.

'You are welcome, Jane, in the afternoon, when the children have gone home.'

'How will that help us?' I asked her.

'Well, Jane, you know they are black women. They can't come when there are white children here.'

'I could hardly believe what I was hearing,' I said to Anthony. 'I'm not going to be beaten by a narrow-minded nursery-school teacher.'

Robin Renwick and the British Council came to the rescue with funding to allow us to hire a professional producer, lovely Ailsa Tulloch, to make our initial series of Ntataise training videos.

I worked with a professional scriptwriter to complete the scripts. I found it agonising work. I wanted every word to be perfect, which took time and patience from the scriptwriter. The actors were our trainers, nursery-school teachers, parents and, of course, the children. The playrooms in which the videos were shot were our own, immaculately laid out, the activities and play equipment as good as any nursery school could provide – including our homemade learning materials. The videos were simple, bright and colourful, and painted a clear picture of hope for all the people who watched them.

'How on earth are you going to show them to people? You work in such isolated places. Where are you going to get electricity from?' said Anthony after oohing and ahhing at the videos, their quality, and so on.

We weren't going to let something this small get the better of us. Along with the videos, the British Council gave us funds to buy portable TVs combined with video cassette players for every Ntataise field trainer. The trainers plugged them into the lighter sockets in their cars, turned the engines on, and we had action. They worked anywhere, under a tree or in the open veld.

At last, our trainers could show the trainees examples of the quality we were hoping they would achieve.

31

WOMAN OF THE YEAR

The triumph and the honour were
mine to share.

MY HEART WAS BEATING like a million birds' wings. I had just put
the phone down from a call from Marika Sboros, editor of the *The
Star*'s women's pages. 'You've been nominated for the Woman of
the Year,' she'd said.

'Please don't ask me to accept it,' I said. I wanted the nomination.
I wanted it more than anything, but I didn't think I had a hope of
winning and couldn't bear to lose.

'Think of what it will do for early childhood development. You
have to accept the nomination.'

There were 14 candidates. Robyn counted our photographs in
The Star. I read the descriptions of the other nominees. My chances
receded with every name. Harriet Ngubane, first black full professor
at the University of Cape Town, PhD from Cambridge, head of the
Department of Anthropology; Mmapula Makgoba Helen Sebidi,
former domestic worker, awarded a Fulbright scholarship to exhibit
at the Worldwide Economic Contemporary Artists' Fund Exhibition
in the USA; Sonja Laxton, triple Springbok, award-winning

marathon, cross-country and track athlete; Shaleen Surtie-Richards, award-winning actress …

'It doesn't matter about winning,' said Anthony. 'It's fantastic to have been nominated. Don't expect to win, just enjoy yourself.'

Enjoying myself was not so easy. My mother, my guest for the day, and I pushed our way to the registration table through what seemed like hundreds of milling women, all drinking tea and coffee and eating egg and cucumber sandwiches in the glitzy Carlton Hotel in downtown Johannesburg. How could they eat anything? I felt quite sick with nerves. Sweat trickled down my back. My smart cerise outfit clung to me. It was agony waiting for the awards ceremony, which would take place later in the day.

It was the eve of the new South Africa. My fellow finalists included brave black South African women recognised for the part they had played in the struggle. During the morning, each of the finalists was assigned a different room to tell delegates what we'd done to achieve our nomination. I felt quite unreal talking about Ntataise to the women sitting in front of me. The whole day felt dreamlike.

As I walked out of the ladies' room before lunch, I bumped into Rex Gibson, editor of the *Rand Daily Mail*. He grinned at me. 'You do know who the winner is, don't you?' I just stared at him. 'Well, good luck,' he added.

The ballroom doors opened. Round tables draped in starched, floor-length cloths filled the room's considerable space. In the centre of each table was a bowl of summer flowers, whites, blues and pinks. It was like being back in high school waiting in assembly, hardly breathing, for the headmistress to announce the new prefects, of which I was never one. I wanted to win for Ntataise. I wanted us to be acknowledged as players in the struggle for education in South Africa and I wanted people to understand that what we were doing was real and important. It wasn't a nannying service – it was the foundation of a child's education.

A waiter cleared my untouched lunch plate. The huge glass chandeliers dimmed. Harsh white light from TV cameras drowned the stage at the front of the ballroom. I sat, not moving a muscle, while the editor of *The Star*, Harvey Tyson, handed out awards to the 'Unsung Heroine' and the 'Rising Star'.

'And now,' said the master of ceremonies, 'the moment we've been waiting for.'

My mother, sitting across the table from me, mouthed 'good luck'. Harvey Tyson shuffled through his notes, sipped some water. Hurry up, please hurry up.

At last, he bent close to the microphone. 'And now it's time for this year's Woman of the Year. The winner moved from the town to the country, from a career in journalism to a career in ...'

My gaze followed his. Who was he looking at?

'*The Star* Woman of the Year for 1988 is ...' He paused. I stopped breathing. 'Jane Evans.'

The room spun. I heard a huge cheer. I had won! I was the Woman of the Year.

The Star carried a half-page picture of me right on the front page. Posters pasted to trees and lampposts told everyone: 'Farmer's wife is Woman of the Year.' I was buried in a welter of arms. That evening, I was on national TV news. What a fabulous thing for Ntataise – and, of course, for me. I was beside myself with excitement. There were articles about Ntataise and the importance of early learning, especially for disadvantaged children from farms and isolated rural areas, in an ever-growing number of newspapers and magazines. There were programmes about us on television. We talked about the importance of care, but also education, for young children. We talked about the Ntataise model and how poorly educated farmworkers' wives and daughters, operating in the most basic of circumstances, were, with good-quality training and ongoing support, making a marked difference to themselves and the children on a growing number of South African farms. Our work had never been done before on South African farms; civil society was taking matters into its own hands.

Unashamedly, I took full advantage of the exposure the Woman of the Year award had brought us. Doing so was hard work, but we needed it. Van Leer's words were never far from my mind: we needed funding and we wanted early learning for children on farms and in rural areas to grow.

Apart from the media, I was invited to give talks at school speech days, township celebrations and business gatherings. It was a heady time. Shortly after the awards ceremony, Dr Ellen Kuzwayo, the fiery and well-loved South African author and anti-apartheid activist, visited Ntataise. I had met her earlier in the year at the American consul general's fourth of July party in Johannesburg. Surrounded by the Stars and Stripes, she had told me that she found it hard to believe a white woman had started nursery schools for black children.

'Come and see,' I'd said.

'I will,' she'd replied.

The children sang 'Nkosi Sikelel' iAfrika', their voices cutting through the still, dry air on the day Dr Kuzwayo came to Huntersvlei. She smiled and touched their heads. The teachers, almost overcome by her visit, showed her the playroom and told her about their work.

'I can't believe she came all the way to Viljoenskroon to see us,' Maria said after we'd all finished lunch and waved Dr Kuzwayo and her companion for the day, Robyn Raphael from the US embassy, on their way.

At about the same time, we had another visitor – this one unexpected. It took a minute for us to recognise the upright, confident man who walked across the lawn towards us, put out his hand and said, 'I'm Terror. Robin Renwick said I should meet you.'

It was indeed Terror Mosiuoa Lekota, recently released from his prison sentence on Robben Island for his role in the struggle. He, Anthony and I talked late into the night. He was the first member of the ANC we had spoken to in depth. His was a world we had only read about, yet our hopes for South Africa were the same. One night, a few weeks later, he and some of his struggle colleagues came back to Huntersvlei, this time for a dinner attended by Ntataise trainers and Viljoenskroon farmers. We ate at the long table in the guest cottage. The silence felt like a velvet curtain as we listened to Terror talk about what it felt like to stand in the dock waiting to be sentenced for activities he did not regard as criminal.

Most of the guests would not see Terror again, but we did, many times over the years. He has remained a good friend.

32

FLYING THE COOP

*It's harder to lead a young child by the
hand, when the child is your own.*

'I AM NOT SENDING any child of mine to boarding school.' This
was something of a contradiction on my part. I'd always known our
children would have to go away, but somehow I hadn't thought the
day would ever come. Those tiny little babies who'd nuzzled so
warmly into my neck were growing up.

Our four children were asleep in their beds. I forgot about
whatever I'd been stirring on the stove for our dinner, and waved a
wooden spoon in agitation. Anthony took the spoon from me. The
kitchen filled with smoke. He opened the windows to let the grey
curls out. 'How do you propose to educate them? Keep them here at
a school that won't let a black child onto the grounds?'

I sighed miserably. I was too choked up to talk.

'Don't be so silly.' Anthony put his arm around my shoulders. 'I
went to boarding school when I was eight, on the train from Kroonstad to Pietermaritzburg. I've turned out okay.'

The mention of Pietermaritzburg made it even worse. 'She's not
going to Natal – that's six hours away!'

There was some compromise, and the beginning of 1990 saw ten-year-old Robyn packed and ready to be a weekly boarder at St Andrew's School for Girls in Johannesburg.

Dressed in her brown school tunic, a turquoise smocked blouse peeping out of the round neckline, Robyn looked so small and skinny.

'Time to go.' Anthony lifted her bulging suitcase off the grass outside the back door and put it into the boot of his car. Robyn held her small, brown, everyday school case in her hand.

'Good luck, Robs. See you on Friday.' Claire, barefoot, in shorts and T-shirt, hugged her big sister.

'Why must you go away?' Sally started to cry.

This set us off. David wrapped his arms around Robyn's waist and clung to her. Anthony wiped his eyes. I swallowed hard and climbed into the front seat of the car. Sybil herded the other children into the house, then turned and waved us goodbye.

The drive from Huntersvlei to St Andrew's in Bedfordview, Johannesburg, took just over two hours. Anthony and I made aimless conversation. Robyn got progressively quieter.

'It looks like Huntersvlei,' I said inanely. 'A bit, anyway.'

The clear, blue Johannesburg sky framed the school's white gables. Wooden window frames and grassy courtyards broke the glare of sunlight that bounced off the white walls. Robyn was one of four new primary-school boarders that year. We all gathered on the lawn to drink tea and meet the other parents and girls. When our cups were empty, and I couldn't squeeze another drop out of the pot, Anthony said he thought it was time we left.

'We'll look after her,' the primary-school headmistress promised.

I knelt down and gave Robyn a big and anguished hug, holding her rigid little body tight, then headed for the car. We drove the whole way home in virtual silence.

'If I talk I'll cry,' I gulped somewhere near Parys.

'Me too,' my strong husband said. He held my hand – tight.

Our first baby had flown the coop. Little did we know, as we drove home that day that, as a new era began in our lives, so a new one would begin in South Africa.

The second of February 1990 was the last day of Ntataise's first introductory training course of the year, and the last day of the South Africa I'd be born into. I fastened my seat belt, turned on the car radio to listen to the president's address as he opened Parliament, and reversed out of the garage to drive to the stad and the training centre. State President FW de Klerk's voice sounded determined and clear. I couldn't believe what I was hearing. I drove as fast as I could on the dirt road, stopped the car outside the training centre and turned up the sound. I flung the door open.

People gathered around in time to hear him say, 'The prohibition of the African National Congress, the Pan African Congress, the South African Communist Party and a number of subsidiary organ- isations is being rescinded ... I wish to put it plainly that the govern- ment has taken a firm decision to release Mr Nelson Mandela unconditionally.'

The stunned silence turned into an incredulous roar.

'I don't believe it, I just don't believe it,' a woman whispered and clasped her hands around her head.

'It's too big to believe,' said another.

Cries of 'amandla' echoed around the training centre. 'Awethu,' came the replies. Trainers and course participants grabbed my hands and said a prayer of thanks for Mr Mandela's release. I remember thinking that there was nowhere else I would rather have been to have heard this momentous news than with my Ntataise colleagues and friends.

The 11th of February 1990 was another day millions of South Africans thought they would never see. Maria Moloke, Monica Masukela, Moses Nthethe and I crowded around the television in my study, sitting on the red and green leather chairs, to watch a tall, dignified man with slightly grey hair walk through the gates of Victor Verster Prison, near Paarl. Nelson Mandela held his wife Winnie's hand and raised his other hand in greeting. After 27 years, Nelson Mandela smiled at the world and his beloved South Africa, a free man at last.

I was watching history in the making. It was one of those moments that left me almost speechless, with a feeling of goodwill too intense to describe.

'What's wrong? What's going on?'

I arrived at the Huntersvlei nursery school one morning a couple of months later – 19 April, to be exact. The two nursery school teachers and women from the stad stood huddled between the swings and jungle gym. They were wailing and sobbing into handkerchiefs. Children whimpered, not understanding what was happening.

I put my arm around a terrified child and turned from woman to woman. 'Has someone been hurt?'

'It's the police in Rammulotsi. They're shooting the children. Five of them they are dead.' A woman with an angry tear-stained face looked up. 'It's too much, Mrs Evans. We thought when Mr Mandela came out things would get better. All they want is schools and places to live in, and the police are killing them.'

Things didn't get better. Over the next few years, the police and defence force killed thousands of people who were trying to present them with petitions. Violent clashes between political parties left even more people dead, as did attacks on civilians by APLA, the Azanian People's Liberation Army. But on that particular day in 1990, youngsters in Rammulotsi had marched to the municipal offices with a list of 'demands'. As had happened a few years before when Moses's nephew had been killed, the police had opened fire – with devastating results.

Not long after this tragedy, people moved in their hundreds from the crowded corrugated-iron shacks in which they'd been living to open land next to Rammulotsi.

'Some of the Comrades came to see me today,' Anthony said to me one evening at about that time.

'Why?'

'I think they just wanted to talk. They told me that if they weren't provided with enough land to build their own shacks and houses on by the municipality, they'd just take it, and that Mr Nel, the township manager, must *thula*, be quiet.'

And so it is that the area became known as 'Thula Nel'.

33

LETSITELE

In a town where the road signs warn you to watch out for hippos, the old South Africa was still stuck in its ways.

A STOCKY MAN OF about forty, wearing khaki shorts, brown boots and a short-sleeved khaki shirt, advanced on us as we stood outside the nursery school. Letsitele – that small subtropical town in the north of the country with its abundance of orange, mango and litchi trees and vibrant purple-and-white bougainvillea, the scent of frangipani and camellias, and signs warning pedestrians to watch out for the hippos that lumbered out of the Letaba and Letsitele Rivers, which flowed at the edge of the orchards – was, with Ntataise's help, establishing farm nursery schools, its 28 teachers all trained by Maria. The teacher at this particular nursery school was unenthusiastically throwing a ball at a group of children. There was nothing about her to suggest she was enjoying herself. I commented on this to the advancing farmer.

'Mevrou Evans, don't you tell me what to do with my workers.' He'd all but told me to *thula*.

Maria and I had parked our car on this, my very first visit to Letsitele, in front of a rambling, and rather dilapidated, building with flowers and trees painted on the mud-splattered walls. Swings and a jungle gym were set in the hard ground. Behind the nursery school were rows of oblong brick houses, taps and pit toilets in their yards. Washing was laid out to dry over bushes. Many of the people working on the Letsitele citrus and fruit farms had their homes in the 'homelands' not too far away. The farm was, for them, a weekly stop-off point, temporary accommodation.

Refugees from Mozambique also poured across the border to these farms, men and women desperate for work, children who needed healthcare and food. I caught a tennis ball, braced to balance myself against the scantily clad children playing catch around my legs. There was no response to my greeting, but the teacher greeted Maria and Thandi Ngobeni, the woman Ntataise had employed to run this project, with a volley of words.

'She doesn't want to be a nursery-school teacher. She wants to go back to her job in the pack house,' Thandi explained. 'I told the farmer.'

'What did he say?'

'He said he'd think about it.'

'There's a great divide between the way you and the Ntataise trainers see the nursery schools and what the parents and farmers want out of them,' Anthony said when I got home. The parents wanted care and food for their children; the farmers wanted more women to work in the avocado and citrus pack houses; Ntataise wanted to provide children with early learning skills.

In the Letsitele Valley, some thirty kilometres up the road, Rebecca prepared to run a training course on another group of farms. Her accommodation, she found on arrival, was a garage with neither light nor air, her bed a wooden door propped up on bricks with a foam rubber mattress. 'I don't have anywhere else to put her,' said the Rural Foundation developer.

The problem, apart from that woman's embedded racism, was money. Ntataise paid for the trainers' time and travel and the materials for the training programme, while the host organisation provided accommodation and meals. Usually this was not a problem. The training staff were far more forgiving than I was. Their concern was for the trainees. Rebecca said she would sleep in the garage. In the event she stayed with the Rural Foundation developer, in her house, leaving her makeshift bed tipped up against the garage wall.

On our way home from this field visit, we visited Margaret Solomon and Winnie Mashaba in Nelspruit. There were now 40 farm nursery schools in the Ntataise Lowveld project, little beacons of hope and laughter set in farm villages surrounded by lush sugar cane fields and orchards of citrus trees, their leaves green and shiny, their fruit orange and heavy. We had employed a second full-time trainer. Her name was Daphne Nkosi. In many of the nursery schools the dog-eared books and frayed carpets of our previous visit were gone. Shaded by high wooden roofs, the hot tropical air flowing through the open buildings, children sat at plastic tables of different colours. Some painted squiggles on sheets of computer paper, some pounded lumps of playdough, others paged through children's books.

The next day we arrived at yet another nursery school and Daphne led us proudly to the entrance of the building.

'Hellooo?' She came back out, looking puzzled. Apart from a caretaker who ambled out, roused by her shouting, there was no one there. A long conversation took place in siSwati. It was orange-picking time and it turned out that the children had slept at the school the previous night while their parents were on night shift, and they had now gone home. A sunburnt man, wearing a traditional khaki shirt and shorts, came up to the wire fence to find out what the noise was about.

'We are very disappointed,' said Margaret in Afrikaans, drawing herself up to her full five feet, red hair blazing. 'It's nine o'clock in the morning and the children have gone home? They should just be getting here.'

'Disappointed?' the farmer yelled, leaping over the fence. Who were we to be disappointed? He would send the children home when he wanted them to go home. Margaret advanced, I retreated. It was another *thula* moment.

When I arrived home, furious, Anthony was philosophical. 'You win some and you lose some,' he said. 'These are the everyday realities of South Africa. Keep challenging them.'

34

SHARP SHARP

As funding starts to pour in, a last-minute
altercation over an axe-wielding trainer.

THE HONEY LOCUST TREES, as old as Ntataise, gave welcome shade to the training centre the day we celebrated the organisation's tenth birthday in 1990. We had trained more than a thousand women and reached some twenty-two thousand children. We employed ten trainers in three provinces. Paul Houmoller, managing director of the Van Leer Foundation in South Africa, was our guest speaker. He handed Maria and me a framed copy of a centuries-old print of children throwing balls and pushing hoops, their long skirts dragging on the ground. I looked around me at the faces of the women, some of whom had been working in the lands when I arrived on the farm but were now competent teacher aides. I looked at Rebecca and Bonny, Maria and Alice. Their training and travels had done so much to develop their confidence and self-esteem.

But on that day of celebration, there was also sadness. Lydia Khoabane, one of our founding trio, was leaving us. It was, she said, time for her to retire. She was over sixty years old and she said she was tired. A line of women – trainers, teachers, parents and trustees –

sang a praise song and draped a traditional Sotho blanket over Lydia's shoulders, honouring her for the work she'd done, calling her a 'mother'. We hugged her and put presents at her feet. She kept two large boxes to open last. On the table for us all to see, she put the sewing machine she had so badly wanted and the dinner service she had chosen.

There were only two of the original founders left. At last, Maria Mohlahleli agreed to be deputy director of Ntataise.

That night, I woke in a sweat. Ntataise was ten years old. I was over forty. We were about to open two new projects. One was in an area called Levubu, on farms with prolific crops of citrus, bananas, avocados and macadamia nuts. They lay to the north, not far from the Mozambique border, but to me they could have been in another country. The other was to be on sugar farms on the KwaZulu-Natal north coast. I didn't know how I was going to run projects that far away, even with advisers, or how I would raise enough funds to keep it going.

The next morning, I made my way to the Huntersvlei nursery school. 'Mme Janey, Mme Janey!' I knelt down and hugged the children. 'Sharp sharp,' they said. Little thumbs pressed against mine. I was surprised to see visitors and I stood up as Ishmael Mabitle introduced me to John Hirsch, the new American consul general in Johannesburg, and his wife, Rita, a teacher from New York. They had been visiting Ishmael's school in Rammulotsi and he'd brought them to visit the Huntersvlei nursery school.

'What's your biggest challenge?' John asked me.

'Funding,' I replied. 'That's our biggest challenge.' Summer rain fell on the corrugated-iron roof. We battled to hear each other. I would become good friends with John and Rita over the years and through them Ntataise was introduced to USAID (the United States Agency for International Development), an invaluable introduction.

Tony Reeve, soon to become Sir Tony, the new British high

commissioner to South Africa, was another invaluable friend. On the day he came to visit at the Huntersvlei nursery school, the playroom was beautifully laid out. He smiled at children painting strokes of red and yellow on sheets of computer paper. A little boy sat on his heels and balanced blocks precariously on top of one another, a circle, a square and a rectangle. Four-year-old Mpho lay on her tummy, her fingers tracing the words of a story book open on the carpet.

The ambassador said he was enchanted. After lunch, he climbed into his chauffeur-driven car for the three-hour drive back to Pretoria. As the car started to move, he put his head out of the window to tell us that the British consulate would fund another dormitory building for the Ntataise training centre. I felt deep relief. As Maria took over responsibility for the Ntataise training programme, I was becoming responsible for raising what seemed like larger and larger sums of money.

'This is nerve-wracking,' I said.

Anthony asked, 'What is?'

'Asking people for money.'

'You're not asking for it for yourself, and you're not asking individuals,' said Anthony 'You shouldn't have to ask for it at all, but if you don't the neglect will only get worse.'

Sometimes the sheer weight of raising funds scared me. Apart from anything else it was people's salaries I had to raise and yet, in the main, I thoroughly enjoyed it. I couldn't conceive of anyone saying no to Ntataise's requests. I enjoyed the people I met and I loved telling them about Ntataise, welcoming them to the nursery schools and introducing them to the Ntataise team.

'What's the sigh about?' Anthony asked when he wandered in one day, hoping for lunch.

I pointed to the papers. 'Funding request forms, report forms, invoices, order books. One funder wants an analytical report, another needs a narrative, and this one,' I waved a sheaf of papers, 'wants to know our strategies. I don't know what they are talking about.'

I ferried everything to the office and pinned a list of funders to a blue felt pinboard behind my desk. It was dogged work but I loved it.

One morning, the voice of the executive director of the Southern Life Foundation boomed down the phone. She said she would like to visit us. Virginia Ogilvie Thompson, impeccably dressed in a smart suit and sensible shoes, duly arrived at Huntersvlei. Southern Life, she told me after we'd shown her around, was turning 100.

'Could Ntataise spend R100 000 on a special project to mark the occasion?'

'Of course, how wonderful. But what should we spend it on?'

There were no restrictions, and the donation turned into 100 toy trunks for 100 farm nursery schools. USAID and the British embassy funded an extra 35, which meant we could give one to each of the nursery schools with which we were working. Months later, 135 blue metal toy trunks, with 'Ntataise' sprayed in white paint on their lids, were loaded onto lorries and delivered to farms in KwaZulu-Natal, the Free State, Mpumalanga and Limpopo. Maria and I were to hand over the trunks to each preschool. The first handover was to be attended by Virginia Ogilvie Thompson and local dignitaries.

Maria, her little girl Neo and I arrived in KwaZulu-Natal the day before the first of the toy trunk presentations. Driving us to look at the venue for the following day's presentation, Bronwyn Eb, the KwaZulu-Natal Ntataise adviser, was clearly distressed. 'Our trainer's been arrested,' she said.

'What on earth for?'

'For sinking an axe into her boyfriend's back.'

'Where's she now?'

'In police custody.'

'Get her out,' I said. Virginia Ogilvie Thompson was not the sort of person to take this type of irregularity lightly. I didn't care what it took to get the trainer there. The next day dawned bright and clear. The waves broke noisily not far from the Umhlali Hall, where 35 trunks waited, as did the trainer. I don't know who had done what, and I never asked. The presentation went off without a hitch. The chairman of the South African Sugar Association, Tony Ardington, looking resplendent in a well-cut suit and tie, made a speech. The farmers and their wives, farmworkers and their wives, farm nursery-school teachers and farm children mingled over the toys and tea and cakes. It was a joyous occasion, with no further mention of the axe in the boyfriend's back.

The glow of the toy trolley presentation had faded, and a forlorn-looking Maria sat in my office, a letter in her hand. 'I don't want to go,' she said.

The letter from the Canada Southern Africa Education Trust Fund was an invitation to Maria to spend three months studying early childhood development at the University of British Columbia in Vancouver. 'How do I tell Mac that I am going away again? And what about little Neo? How can I leave my little girl?' she said as we found British Columbia in an atlas covered in mothballs. To me, it seemed an opportunity she should not miss, and it was at my urging that Maria accepted the invitation and joined a small group of South African women for the long flight to British Columbia.

'Jane,' said Maria when she returned after what had seemed to her an interminable three months away from home, 'it was a good opportunity but it was very stressful. Mac didn't support me, he just complained. It wasn't a normal university course, but something developed for NGOs, and it was quite patronising. I could have learnt it all at home. Also, we had to share rooms and fridges to put our food in. Someone accused me of taking her food and it was very unpleasant.'

This was not Maria's first trip overseas. She had been invited some months before to take part in a Van Leer conference in The Hague and in Germany, and to spend a week in England, but that had been a different story. Everyone, according to her reports, had been treated like equals and were there to share and to be listened to. Canada wasn't one of my better moves. I should have listened to Maria.

35

THE SHOPLIFTER

The crime she confessed to was troubling enough, but her views on child-rearing came as even more of a jolt.

'SHOPLIFTING? YOU'RE NOT SERIOUS!' I shouted down the line to the ELRU director in Cape Town. A new trainer from the Ntataise Eastern Free State project, attending a course at ELRU, had been caught leaving a Cape Town department store with unpaid-for clothes hidden under her skirt. Maria asked me what I was going to do. I said that if the trainer told the truth I would give her another chance. In those days, we didn't have formal disciplinary policies.

A few days later, the perpetrator walked hesitantly into my office and sat down. I asked how her trip to Cape Town had gone and if there was anything she wanted to tell us. She looked at her lap, fingers twisting a piece of tissue, then broke the silence. 'There was a problem. I took some clothes from a shop that I hadn't bought. The others dared me. I'm sorry.' She looked at me, then shifted her gaze to Maria, who sat beside me. We talked about right and wrong and she promised she'd never do anything like that again. As an afterthought, she told us she had learnt lots of new things.

'Like what?'

'How to control children.'

'And how would you control children?' I asked.

'I would put them all in a sack and tie it up.'

Her career with Ntataise didn't last long.

There were times, too, when I wished mine would end. One morning I came into work and found a typed sheet of paper on my desk. It was headed 'List of Demands'.

All the trainers' names, apart from Maria's, were typed at the end of the page. I felt nauseous. Why the confrontation? Couldn't everyone just have talked to me?

I called the signatories into my office. The four women shrugged and looked at one another. No one answered when I asked why they had chosen to write the letter. After much shuffling, someone said the problem was overnight pay. 'We're away a lot and we need more money.'

'But Ntataise pays for your accommodation and food,' I said. 'There's a special away allowance.'

'We want money for private kilometres when we are away.'

'What are private kilometres?'

'We want use of the Ntataise cars over weekends while we're away on training. We want to see friends and do things for ourselves.'

'Like what?'

'Shopping, relaxing.'

The trainers had run 13 courses in places other than Viljoenskroon that year. They travelled in Ntataise cars and were away from home for two weeks at a time, some more often than others. We didn't have an official written car policy. It was verbal and had worked fine on trust, until one trainer had clocked up several hundred kilometres in a weekend.

In the end, we compromised. Permission would have to be given for any distance over 100 km in a weekend, and the petrol paid for by the trainer. It was time we formalised our policies. I didn't mind being challenged, but I couldn't understand why the trainers hadn't talked to me about it. They shrugged when I asked.

I stopped agonising and went to fetch Claire from school. 'I'm going to be in the Miss Salomon Senekal competition tonight,' my nine-year-old daughter told me as she got into the car, flinging her school case into the back seat. This meant she should make her hair 'look nice', wear a pretty dress and be back at school by six that evening. 'I need a party dress,' Claire insisted. 'A nice party dress.' We settled on a smocked dress. 'My hair must look pretty too.'

I looked at the lank, straight hair framing her pretty face. Her fringe needed a cut. I phoned Viljoenskroon's hairdresser, but the salon was closed. I would just have to cut it myself. Claire knelt on a towel. David sat cross-legged on the floor; six-year-old Sally offered advice. I stood back to look at my handiwork. It didn't look straight. I cut off a few more centimetres. Claire looked in the mirror. Tears poured down her face. Her fringe had disappeared from one side of her forehead and sloped towards her eyebrow on the other.

Sally and I sat near the front of the school hall that evening. Crickets chirped outside. Spiky flowers stood on either side of the stage. Little girls with cascading blonde curls or puffed-up black hair came onstage, looking like miniature brides in white or pink dresses with billowing skirts. I thought I saw a hint of lipstick on their mouths and a dash of rouge on their cheeks. I hadn't thought of that.

Claire stood at the end of the line, sullen in a sensible, smocked, blue-green dress, her fringe crooked. Her skinny legs disappeared into white socks and black patent shoes.

'Ag, shame, she looks sweet,' said the woman sitting next to us.
'She looks funny,' Sally giggled.
Claire stared ahead. Her lips were closed, her arms stiff, her body

rigid. The judges took their time. They eventually gestured to a mini-bride with blonde curly hair: 'Mejuffrou Salomon Senekal.'

'I'm never going to enter a beauty contest again,' said Claire, safely back in the car.

'And I will never cut anyone's hair again,' I said.

But there wouldn't be another Mejuffrou Salomon Senekal competition for Claire to enter. In early 1992, Anthony and Moses heaved a large trunk into the station wagon. This one was filled with Clifton school clothes, labelled with Claire's name. Only David and Sally were left to hug Claire, stand with Sybil and wave goodbye. We had decided on Clifton Preparatory School in the rolling hills of KwaZulu-Natal's Nottingham Road. It seemed perfect for our tomboy, horse-riding Claire. The four-hour drive to KwaZulu-Natal was agonising. Claire slept on the back seat, and Anthony and I talked about nothing in particular in bright voices. I could hardly hold back my tears.

Lunch for parents, staff, and new boys and girls was set out the next day in the shade of a giant oak tree. Claire, in her brand-new grey school skirt and blazer, clung to us, not saying a word. We drove back down the twisty drive. This time I cried, and Anthony's eyes, despite that strong exterior, were misty.

We had barely arrived home that evening when the dormitory mistress phoned. Claire was in her pyjamas, she said, happily throwing pillows at the other new girls.

36

ELECTION DAY

High hopes and deflated tyres, on the day change came to the farmlands.

'MR ANTHONY, MR ANTHONY!' Sophy Ntsoeleng – Bonny's mother-in-law, who had worked in the house for Sybil for many years – pounded on our back door. She stood outside wringing her white apron in her hands. 'Come quickly. The old Missus won't wake up.'

Anthony and I ran along the gravel path and sandy farm road that joined our two houses. Sybil was curled up in her bed. Anthony put his ear to her chest. We felt for breath under her nose. The doctor arrived, his car squealing as it braked in the garden. He held her limp wrist, put his stethoscope to her chest, listened and was quiet. 'I'm sorry,' he said after a few moments, 'she's gone.'

The face-brick Methodist Church in Viljoenskroon was full on the day of her funeral. Those who couldn't get a seat inside the church stood outside in the warm afternoon sun. A procession of cars with their lights on wound its way through town to the cemetery. There, under the gloomy gum trees, her coffin was lowered into the ground next to her husband Rhys's white marble grave. As the Sesotho hymn 'Modimo re boka wena' (God we praise you) was sung by men and women, some of whom had known her since she had arrived there 60 years earlier, I wondered whether Rhys was waiting to meet her.

Sybil's death was the end of an era in all our lives. For Anthony it meant the loss of his beloved mother, and our children their grandmother; for me, well, it meant that Anthony and I were now the 'grown-ups' on the farm, head of the next generation of our branch of the Evans family. Anthony kept his feelings to himself and presented that strong, self-possessed exterior, but inside he was hurting and it was only at the Christmas after Sybil died that tears had poured down his cheeks. It wasn't the same without her.

September of 1993 had seen sadness, an ending in our family. But it was in November of the same year that South Africa, by adopting an Interim Constitution and a Bill of Rights, took steps on the path to its new beginning. Early in 1994, the Independent Electoral Commission turned the Huntersvlei nursery-school playroom into a mock polling station and walked people who lived on the farm through the election process, complete with polling booths and ballot boxes. It was the first time the vast majority of South Africans would vote in a general election. It was the first time any of us would vote in a democratic election.

Not everyone entered into this historic occasion with the awe and excitement that had filled the Huntersvlei nursery school on that mock polling day, however. The right-wingers were making one last stand in a desperate attempt to cling to fast-receding Afrikaner nationalism. Viljoenskroon's streets were lined with defiant white men and women as a parade of tractors drove through town, bearing right-wing farmers, waving the old South African flag, defiantly mourning the passing of apartheid. These terrified men and women erected less-than-sturdy watchtowers and barricades at all the entrances to the town. Were they trying, I wondered, to get back into a laager?

During this incredibly fraught time, I received a call from a BBC Africa reporter. 'Tell me,' she said, 'about the farmers' last-ditch stand.' Deadly serious, she continued, 'Are you good farmers or bad farmers?'

Anthony and I were, I informed her, South Africans and of course we supported the change. We, like so many others, had longed for it.

Polling day, 27 April 1994. The autumn air was cool. Men and women huddled in warm blankets on the back of the farm wagons that were taking them to the polling stations in Rammulotsi. The tractors pulling the wagons turned off the Huntersvlei farm road and onto the main tarred road. The front wagon swerved. The driver stopped and jumped off his tractor seat. The tyre was punctured. The second wagon veered to the side of the road. Another puncture. On the driveway from the house to the main road my car wobbled and pulled to the left. Two flat tyres. I was working as an observer at one of the Rammulotsi polling stations.

Anthony drove up next to me. 'Look at this!' He picked a fist-sized metal ball off the drive. Sharp spikes stuck out of it at every angle. 'They've been scattered on the stad road too,' he said, picking up two more. They were a message for the *pienkes* (the pinks), which is what the right-wingers called those of us who supported change. Desperate to halt the changes taking place, they were stopping at nothing to prevent the transport we had provided to take ourselves and the farm employees to the polling stations in Rammulotsi from getting there.

But a few punctures were not going to get in anyone's way. Lines of voters snaked for kilometres around the township. Old men and women who could barely move shuffled to the front of the queue. People stood in the sun for hours. Entrepreneurs sold cold drinks and food. No one minded how long they waited.

'*Dumela*, Jane,' someone shouted.

'*Dumela*,' I shouted back, feeling a surge, like an electric shock. Not only was I part of this miraculous event – I was also part, in a tiny way, of this community.

37

LETTING GO

The organisation had outgrown the farm, just as it had outgrown my own wildest ambitions.

THE ANC CAME TO power, winning 62.7 per cent of the national vote in South Africa's first democratic elections. It was later that year, with the country still wrapped in the euphoria of these elections, that, under the shade of the tall honey locust trees, their long brown pods and shiny dark thorny leaves rattling in the wind, a hundred or so guests stamped and cheered as Britain's urbane high commissioner, Sir Anthony Reeve, cut the cream silk ribbon we'd carefully tied across the newly painted blue door and declared the Ntataise training centre's new dormitory wing open.

The new rooms, funded by the British consulate with the high commissioner's support, had added ten more beds to our accommodation. We could sleep 25 people. As the cheering faded, the Free State's Member of the Executive Council for Education, Mr Sakkie Belot, said government and NGOs like Ntataise should work closely together. We agreed. It was a *mokete* of note. The formalities over, everyone tucked into a lunch prepared by Huntersvlei wives and mothers.

Bonny had transformed the playroom into an elegant dining area. She'd draped trestle tables in white tablecloths, and swathed plastic chairs in white covers with wide blue bows. 'This is lovely,' said Sir Anthony Reeve as we showed him to his seat.

Along with the British consulate, USAID had been funding Ntataise for a number of years. They were very hands-on funders. Their annual visit to Ntataise took place that year, not too long after the opening of the new dormitories The project officer Jennifer Bisgard was, on this occasion, accompanied by a new project officer. His name was Jonathan Jansen, a man who went on to become the first black vice-chancellor of the conservative University of the Free State. A leading and highly respected South African educationist, he was to become a very close friend. Visits from funders were nerve-wracking – from USAID with its demanding reporting requirements in particular – but despite the penetrating questions this larger-than-life man asked Maria, Bonny and me as we showed him the nursery schools, I really liked him. His interest in our work was as deep as his concern for the children who crowded around him.

Over dinner at Huntersvlei that night, Jonathan told Anthony and me that, as a young boy, he and his family had been removed from their farm in the Western Cape. The land had been declared as being for whites only. He was sharing his history. It was painful to hear and I could see how deep his anger went.

The next morning, I sat behind my desk waiting for Jennifer and Jonathan and their reaction to our work. I was nervous; their ongoing funding was vital to Ntataise. All our shortcomings kept running through my head. I thought of everything I should have said the day before. I sat on my hands to keep them from shaking.

'We can't afford to lose USAID funding,' I blurted as they entered the room.

'Who said anything about losing it?' Jennifer replied. 'We'd like to extend it. Is there anything else you need funding for?'

I could hardly believe it. I pointed to the map pinned to the wall behind my desk. My finger moved from Venda near the Zimbabwe border, down through the Limpopo province in the far north of the country, through Mpumalanga on the east, with farms virtually on the Mozambique border, to KwaZulu-Natal, to the cold, mountainous regions of the eastern Free State, and finally to Viljoenskroon in the heart of the maize belt.

By this time Ntataise employed 22 trainers in those far-flung areas of South Africa. They were training and providing on-site support – mentoring, we'd call it these days – for 583 women from 445 farm- and community-based preschools. There were some 13 600 children in these schools. Some of the preschools experienced high staff turnover, and others were housed in unsuitable, unhealthy premises – there were playrooms with far too many children in them to be functional. But as the farm preschool teachers gained in confidence and experience with the support of the Ntataise trainers, these problems became the exception. There was an unprecedented demand for training from women on farms and in the rural towns. I told Jennifer and Jonathan that the more we trained, the more we rolled up our sleeves and helped the teachers in their playrooms, the better the schools became. On-site support was crucial to our training model. A growing number of children were being fed and their health was improving. Getting their parents involved hadn't been as easy as we'd hoped, but we were persevering.

The crux of the matter for me was that, even with the help of our voluntary managers, running these organisations from Viljoens-kroon, sometimes hundreds of kilometres away, was becoming a nightmare. They needed more immediate leadership. The final straw had been a phone call to me from a sombre Alice Neluheni, the trainer-manager in Levubu in the far north. She had lent her Ntataise car to a friend, who had written the car off and died in the accident.

In those early-morning hours of worrying, when the sun

appeared over the flat Free State horizon, I knew it was time to let some of my Ntataise babies go. It was time to decentralise. Eight of the Ntataise field projects wanted more independence. They wanted to run and manage themselves. This seemed to fit in with the strong regional moves being made by the government. But someone had to raise the funds, pay the salaries and basically run the proposed independent organisations.

'Send us a proposal,' Jennifer said.

Waiting for USAID's reply in 1994 was as agonising as waiting for the original Van Leer reply in 1980. That funding started the organisation; this funding, if approved, would take it to a whole new level. It was approved. About a month later I received a letter from Jennifer and numerous onerous-looking forms to complete. On one hand it felt as though a great weight had been lifted from my shoulders; on the other I felt quite melancholic. The Ntataise organisations were growing up. This funding would allow them to operate as separate entities while retaining the support of the Ntataise head office in Viljoenskroon and the Ntataise training courses. They would 'own' their futures.

Moses – and sometimes Maria – and I drove to all the projects to introduce the new decentralised concept. We talked for hours about roles and responsibilities, and how our relationship with them would continue. In Levubu and Louis Trichardt, in the far north, farmers filled our hands with boxes of mangoes, litchis and bananas. In Nelspruit and Schagen, in the tropical Mpumalanga Lowveld, we were laden with oranges. Boxes of asparagus were pressed into our hands in the Free State's Ficksburg. As Moses and I finally left our last stop, a trainer clasped my hand through the open car window. 'We want our independence, but don't forget us, Jane. We need you and Ntataise.' And we needed them.

This mutual need turned into 36 of us – trainers, managers and admin staff from all the Ntataise organisations – gathering the following year for what became the first Ntataise Conference. We held it at a country hotel set in the middle of pine forests not too far from the Solomons' farm in Nelspruit.

Anthony was cynical. 'I hope it's not going to be just another talk shop.'

I hoped so too.

What the conference did, in fact, do was turn our group of newly independent ECD organisations into a team, the core of what has become the Ntataise Network, and one of the leading ECD networks in South Africa. In modern jargon, the conference was an exercise in capacity-building and networking. As Ntataise grew, so did the size of the conference. It became an annual institution, one which Anthony agreed was important and which he attended, with the other trustees, until he couldn't any more.

38

SCIENTIFICALLY PROVEN

The joy of an official validation that
Ntataise wasn't a nannying service after all.

THE NTATAISE PROJECTS WERE not the only babies I was letting
go of.

'I want to come home,' eight-year-old Sally sobbed down the
phone. She was inconsolable. Beside her, Claire cried almost as
copiously.

Anthony and I had decided that it would be easier for Sally to
settle in if she spent the last term of the school year at boarding
school with Claire in the Natal midlands. The next year, Claire
would be going to high school at St Anne's in Hilton. As it turned
out, it was a bad idea.

Claire's tears were because she wanted to play with her friends,
and Sally's because she was a little girl and if she couldn't have her
mother she wanted her older sister.

Our three daughters were now all at boarding school. Robyn was
already in high school at St Andrew's in Bedfordview. Thank
goodness David was still at home – for a while, at any rate. For
Anthony, going to boarding school seemed the natural order of

things; for me it is something I still agonise over, even though two of my daughters are now mothers themselves.

Apart from the empty feeling I had in my tummy, those many years ago, we now had four children at schools in three different provinces, each with a slightly different school term. Anthony missed the girls as much as I did. The solution seemed to be to spend more weekends in KwaZulu-Natal.

The moment I saw the whitewashed house perched on a hill, I loved it. Clumps of arum lilies grew at the curves of the long, winding concrete drive. Before us, the land swept away to rise into rolling hills. I stocked the little pantry of our new cottage with homemade jams from a Saturday market, bought fresh vegetables, fetched the girls from school and packed endless picnics. Arum Hill, as we named the house, became a weekend haven for our family and for countless other children, their parents and friends. Our six-hour trek from Viljoenskroon via Johannesburg to fetch our weekly boarder, Robyn, to the Natal midlands spilled over into 1995 and would continue in one way or another for the next 12 years.

During this time Maria and I took another trek, this one to Johannesburg.

'President Mandela has hurt his shoulder. He won't be with us tonight.' The master of ceremonies' words were drowned in a loud groan of disappointment from the crowd seated at the tables and tucking into fresh bread rolls. Ntataise was a finalist for the first Presidential Awards for Exceptional Contributions to Education in South Africa. By then, Ntataise's field projects, with the promised help from USAID, had formed their own trusts and assumed full responsibility for their own management and fundraising. 'This change has placed the ownership of each organisation where it should be, in the communities it serves,' a beaming new trustee had said. It was these changes that had helped earn us our nomination.

Maria and I attended the glamorous awards function at the Sandton Sun Hotel in Johannesburg. We stood around in our eveningwear feeling uncomfortable and out of place. We hardly knew a soul in that vast function room, nor at our table. The chatter hardly stopped when, above the noise, we heard the MC announce: 'The award for Exceptional Contribution to Education in South Africa in the field of Early Childhood Development,' the drum roll quietened everyone down, 'goes to,' we gripped each other's hands, 'Ntataise!'

The two of us threaded our way through tables crammed with other hopefuls and guests, onto the stage, the bright lights shining in our eyes, to receive our award from Deputy President Thabo Mbeki.

Away from the lights and the chatter, the real celebration took place when we got home, clutching the trophy with its thin golden leaves. There were flowers on the table in the trainers' room. There were little sausages and meatballs on sticks, sausage rolls and a bottle of champagne. We all clinked glasses and toasted our win. I didn't know how I'd do it, but we were somehow going to get a photo with Mr Mandela and this award. It was, after all, his award. I asked Terror Lekota, who was by now the premier of the Free State province, if he would help arrange it. He told me the President would be in Bloemfontein the following week, and that we should bring our trophy and wait outside the venue. I thought of the crowds jostling to touch or simply catch a glimpse of Madiba, and I knew we would never get near him. So we gave it a miss, placed the trophy on a special stand in the Ntataise office, and waited – for six years.

'Hey, Sis.' My brother Mark phoned me one evening in 2001. 'You said you wanted a photo with Madiba? Zelda says you can come with me when I interview him next week.'

We passed the scrutiny of the guards at his Houghton home and were shown into the office of his secretary and long-time assistant, Zelda le Grange. A deep, familiar voice from the adjacent room said,

'Come in, come in.' Mr Mandela sat on a white wingback chair, in a trademark blue-grey shirt covered in oblong patterns and buttoned to the neck. A red HIV/Aids ribbon was pinned beneath his collar. Leaded windows looked out on to a leafy garden. Looking across at me, the great man said, 'You look so cross. You frighten me.' Far from cross, I was completely overawed. I didn't know what to say to him. I felt like a complete idiot. But, melting in the warmth of his smile and his sheer magnetism, I clutched the trophy, my copy of *Long Walk to Freedom* and a photo of the Ntataise staff.

He gestured to me. 'Come, sit next to me.' I sat on the arm of his chair and he took my hand in his. It was warm, and firm. He signed the book and the photograph of the Ntataise staff holding our trophy. Mark took a picture of us. Madiba had written me a note: 'To Jane. Best wishes to an impressive young lady.' A photo of Madiba holding my hand and his message above it now hangs on my study wall, a happy reminder of a high moment in my life.

Early in 1996, the Joint Education Trust, set up four years earlier by South African business, political parties and trade unions with a R500 million grant to work towards restructuring the South African education system that remained bogged down in the inequalities of apartheid, asked if Ntataise would have the effectiveness of its training independently evaluated. Winning awards was one thing; proving that we really deserved them was another.

This would be one of the first evaluations of its kind in the informal ECD field. The evaluation comprised a formal comparison of children's performance in their first year of primary school: those who had attended preschools, as they were now officially called, with Ntataise-trained teachers and those who had not. Dr Ingrid Herbst and a team of researchers from the University of the Free State did the testing. I hovered outside the classroom, trying to get an idea of how the preschool children were doing. Dr Herbst was polite but firm and totally non-committal. She suggested I didn't hover quite so much. I had to wait for her report, which arrived in a stiff brown cardboard envelope tucked into the green canvas post bag.

'The only conclusion one can come to—' I'd turned straight to Dr Herbst's summary at the back of the report '—is that the Ntataise early intervention programmes developed for the communities they serve, have been scientifically proven to be extremely effective and valuable.'

There was more. I flipped through the white pages. 'The research shows that the Ntataise programme is equally effective for rural, farm and township children. All groups of children we tested who have attended preschools with Ntataise-trained teachers show a comparable and higher level of language development than children who have not.'

'Why are you so surprised?' said Anthony. 'This is a huge milestone for Ntataise. Didn't you think your programmes were good enough?'

I thought they were, but we hadn't tried to prove it before. I sent Rhys Rolfe a copy of the evaluation and he made a special trip to my office. 'Did I really suggest Ntataise was a nannying service?' he said. 'You've pioneered preschool education on farms all over the country. I really didn't think you'd do it, but you have.'

I thought back to the day in 1979 in Rhys's office with the peacocks crying in that unnerving manner outside, when he'd hit his hand on his desk in total disbelief at the idea of farm women becoming nursery-school teachers.

39

TOY TROLLEYS

'Do you know who I am?' Madiba asked, bending over the playing children.

AND SO IT WAS that 1996 turned into 1997 and in January three blue tin trunks stood on the grass outside our house. David, our youngest child, was following in his siblings' footsteps, leaving home for boarding school in KwaZulu-Natal. There was no children's washing in the bathroom, no clothes littered on their beds. No more school lifts, extra lessons, spelling to listen to. No children to chatter to in the car, to hug goodnight. The house felt empty, and I as empty as the house. The only way I could keep that horrible hollow feeling at bay was by incessantly popping into Anthony's office for a cup of coffee and throwing myself into Ntataise. So much so that Anthony said early one morning, 'What on earth are you going to Johannesburg for this time? You're never home.'

'You know that's not true,' I laughed. 'But this could be exciting. I've been invited by the Nelson Mandela Children's Fund to a meeting in their Johannesburg offices.'

The challenge put to me when I'd settled into a chair in the spacious old Saxonwold house, now with the sign for the Children's

231

Fund reading 'NMCF' at its gate, was for me to suggest how the Fund could help with early childhood development in rural communities and informal settlements. Many of the nursery schools I visited, especially in the far-flung rural areas, had no educational equipment, no toys, no storage space and often no permanent structures. They operated from a basic mud hut or in a temporary space in a church or clinic. There was often no water, toilets, or electricity. Driving along isolated rural roads I'd often seen grey plastic supermarket trolleys lying on the side of the road with their wheels in the air. I'd seen others brimming over with someone's earthly possessions tied to them with string, a kettle spout poking through clothes and blankets, or the stock from a small roadside stall unpacked every morning and packed away every night. Those trolleys had given me an idea – an idea I had long been wanting to put into practice and, in its way, not that different from our nursery school van in Viljoenskroon.

'Let's turn shopping trolleys into toy trolleys. We'll have them made in bright colours, fill them with toys and teach preschool teachers and playgroup mothers how to use them.'

'Whoa, not so fast. Why trolleys?' Jeremy Ratcliffe, the fund's director, asked.

'What toys?' added Marianne MacRobert, his second-in-command.

'Lots of preschools are held in churches or clinics or huts. The teachers have to pack away the equipment each night and there aren't locks, they can't secure it, and they don't have much play equipment in any case. The trolleys would be preschools on wheels. The nursery-school teachers would wheel them home every night, and wheel them back each morning. It would be a fantastic project for the NMCF to support,' I said.

There was much discussion between Jeremy and Marianne while I looked out at the green garden, listening to a mixture of bird calls and telephones. Before I left for the Free State later that day, Jeremy had agreed – to a pilot project. One hundred trolleys. The Children's Fund would pay for the toys, which I would have to choose, order and pack. I would also need to identify which preschools would receive them, and have them delivered – and find someone else to sponsor the trolleys.

'Who is going to do that?' Anthony asked me that evening. 'Is it part of Ntataise's work?'

I was so relieved, when I got home in the setting sun, that Anthony wasn't waiting with the message 'Cancel the order,' a repeat of my toilet-lid cover plans so many years before, that I was ready for his questions.

'This pilot project has got everything to do with Ntataise. The NMCF is happy for us to pilot it with our preschool projects. If it works, that will be a different story.'

For the next few months, I dreamt, thought and worked on the toy trolleys. We ordered the same toys we used in the blue toy trunks. I trundled around trolley factories with a hard hat on my head, mixing pieces from different trolleys until I had as close to a rainbow trolley as we could get. Then, early one morning, the sun not even up, Puleng, Alice and I helped 15 children from the Huntersvlei preschool, each clutching a breakfast pack, into a bus. Tightly wrapped in rugs, their parents kissed them goodbye and told them to be good. We were on our way to Pretoria to launch the toy trolleys – at the president's official residence, Mahlamba Ndlopfu.

From what I'd seen of her work, Puleng Motsoeneng was one of the most passionate and committed farm nursery-school teachers in our district.

She'd run an excellent nursery-school on Niekerksrus, the farm of Trix and Jan van Biljon, and done well in the Ntataise courses she'd attended. One day, a couple of years before our early-morning excursion to Pretoria, she'd knocked firmly on my office door. Sixteen years younger than me, with thick black eyelashes and a direct gaze, she'd come to tell me that, for various reasons, she and her family had to leave their work on the farm where they lived and that not only did she not have a job, but didn't have anywhere to live either. She said Alice Ntisa had suggested she come and meet me. She needed to borrow money to build a shack for her and her family to live in, and said that Alice had mentioned we were short of a trainer.

She sat in the chair opposite me. I asked her to tell me something about herself.

'The week I was born,' she told me 'it rained and rained. That's why I was called Puleng, it means rain. There were 11 of us in my family,' she said, 'and when I was growing up we lived in a mud hut with four rooms, which my father built for us on the farm where he then worked. He was the foreman. My mother worked for the farmer's wife in the kitchen.'

There wasn't a school on the farm. Every day, Puleng would walk two kilometres to school and two kilometres home, leaving home as the sun peeped over the horizon. 'I walked with a friend who didn't have any shoes, so we shared mine. We each wore a shoe and a sock. The ground was hard and covered with little stones and thorns which stuck to our feet.' She paused to draw breath. 'It hurt and my mother was horrified when she found out. She took my black shoes that I wore to church out of the cupboard and said my friend must wear those to walk to school in. My friend took them off when we got to school because the teacher said they were too smart to keep on.'

I thought of my sturdy black leather shoes with a strap over my ankle that I used to wear to school over sensible white socks. Puleng took a sip of the hot tea that was in front of her, and ate a biscuit. 'My father said he couldn't bear to see me walking to school and he sold a cow to buy me a bicycle.' Puleng wiped the crumbs off her chin. 'I was 20 when I married and my parents-in-law agreed to look after our new baby Mpho when I went away to study. I wanted to be a nurse.'

But fate stepped in. Puleng's application was approved and her letter of appointment as a trainee nurse mailed to the farm post box. 'The post had to be collected from the town post office but the farmer and his wife had gone on holiday. By the time I got the letter the acceptance date had passed. I begged and pleaded with the hospital to still take me, but they said my place had been given to someone else. Mme Jane, how I cried.'

Sitting there with the sun streaming in through the net curtain, my own cup of tea and biscuits in front of me, I nearly cried myself. 'Oh, Puleng. You must have been so disappointed.'

'Yes, Mme Jane, I was. But then I heard about Ntataise and asked the farmer's wife if we could open a nursery school on the farm.'

Our growth as an organisation depended on people. We needed competent young women like Puleng who were as passionate and loyal as Maria, Rebecca, Alice and Bonny. They were at the very heart of what Ntataise did. It was indeed only a few days earlier that Alice had said to me that I should meet Puleng, and that neither Alice, nor any of the other trainers, for that matter, could take on any more training. Their schedules were overflowing.

I agreed to help Puleng with her shack. It felt to me that this strong young woman who had shared her shoes had guts and a presence that made me, at any rate, listen to her. I asked her whether she'd like to work for Ntataise as a learner trainer. It was another moment of pure serendipity: I worked with her closely over the next few years while she developed her knowledge and leadership.

The toy trolley launch was being held to coincide with the NMCF's annual general meeting. After our icy start, Pretoria, three hours to the north of us, was warm. Jacaranda trees layered its streets with a carpet of purple flowers. We unpacked the bright red, blue and green trolleys in a large hall adjoining the residence. Colin

Hall, CEO of Wooltru, was there to meet us. Wooltru had not only sponsored the trolleys and introduced me to the factory that had made them in the colours we wanted, but also stored them and delivered them to their destinations.

An uncertain hush turned into a roar when Nelson Mandela walked into the room. Hot bodies squashed against mine. We all wanted to see him. Oblivious to the excitement, the Huntersvlei preschool children played with the contents of a toy trolley laid out on a thick plastic play mat on the floor, totally absorbed.

'Do you know who I am?' Madiba asked, bending over the playing children. Majolefa sat back on his knees and stared up at the tall man bending over him. He replied in a sing-song voice, 'You are Mr Mandela.' We laughed and the tension broke. How could one not love a man who so loved little children?

Later, I was invited to lunch with the NMCF trustees and other guests in the official residence. Madiba joined us for a while on the terrace. I couldn't stop smiling; I was overawed at being part of this event. But the euphoria I'd felt that day, with hopes of even more toy trolleys, was eclipsed for me by events at home.

40

MARIA AND ISHMAEL

Changes, challenges and a tragedy.

MARIA SAT IN HER usual place on the chair in front of my desk. 'Jane, it's time for me to retire from Ntataise. Mac is sick and he needs my help in his building business.'

The hammering, shouting and general noise from the farm workshop sounded louder than ever. 'Maria, you can't leave us. What will Ntataise do without you?' I put my hands behind my neck and bent my head downwards. Maria had worked with me and Ntataise for 17 years. Ntataise would lose an experienced and competent leader, and I would lose a confidante and friend. I didn't know what I'd do without her.

We held Maria's farewell party in the Huntersvlei primary school hall. Its wooden school benches were packed with trustees, Ntataise staff, directors of our independent projects, preschool teachers, funders and even government officials. The primary-school's choir, all Huntersvlei preschool graduates, stood in front of the audience in their school uniforms, singing with extra verve.

Maria had made her mark in rural South Africa. Her contribution to early learning in vast swathes of this country was immense.

Women from the Zimbabwean to the Lesotho border revered her and the difference she had made to their lives. I dreaded 1998 without her. There were 48 trainers in the Ntataise network by then, and the number of courses we had written and offered was growing. In addition to the core programmes, nursery-school teachers wanted training in baby care, financial management and running parents' committees.

'I don't know how we will do this without Maria,' I told Anthony. I sat in the cracked red leather chair in our study, curled my legs under me and dropped my head into my hands.

'Of course she'll be a huge loss but you'll find someone else,' he replied.

'The someone else will have to be someone very special. ECD under the new government is like being on a roller coaster,' I said, looking up.

In the bleak days of apartheid, the government didn't seem to care what we did. They didn't help us, but they didn't put any hurdles in our way. Despite this, I'd kept in contact with the Department of Education and Training in nearby Kroonstad. It had seemed to me that NGOs like Ntataise should use all means possible to influence the government's skewed outlook on early education. In those dark years, a solid ECD movement had been born and nourished in poor areas of South Africa by the NGO sector and the women in the communities with which it worked. 'It's like handing the new government an education system on a plate,' I said to Anthony.

'And are they nibbling?'

They were more than nibbling. It was civil society that had developed the ECD movement for children from communities crushed by apartheid. As much as the apartheid government had spurned ECD for black, coloured and Indian children, so the new government embraced it. But with this willing acceptance of early learning for all South African children, particularly those from disadvantaged communities, came bureaucracy and policy after policy. Policies by the various government departments, as my good friend André Viviers from UNICEF recently said, 'elbowed each other out of the way, they juggled for space and everything stayed the same'. ECD had been shifted from one government department to the next and back again. NGOs had scrambled to not only keep up, but to continue to offer training to women in disadvantaged communities.

'It's infuriating but at least you now have your training programmes accredited by the government and the people you train get government-approved certificates. That's quite an achievement,' said Anthony.

He was right. The establishment of quality-control bodies and recognised qualifications in the informal vocational skills development sector was a major step forward, despite teething problems and the plethora of acronyms these new bodies brought with them: SAQA (the South African Qualifications Authority), SETAs (Sector Education and Training Authorities), the NQF (National Qualifications Framework) and, among many others, OBE (outcomes-based education), the catchword for the country's new education system introduced by the Department of Education under the new government's first Minister of Education, Sibusiso Bengu.

'There seems to be massive confusion as to what outcomes-based education actually means, apart from ridding the system of racial discrimination. Do you understand it, or how it will be implemented?' Anthony, my sometime inquisitor, swatted an article on OBE in the newspaper with his hand. 'There are questions from experts in the field about whether it is the right model for the country to follow. I wonder if it will increase standards of education for all children?' He'd carried on before I could get a word in.

'I have to understand it,' I replied. 'It affects ECD and we are going to need to rewrite all our programmes to fit in with it. It seems to be skills-based and not so theoretical.'

When the new curriculum came out 1998, history, geography, reading, writing and maths were all called something else. It was the outcome of learning that was important, reaching a goal – but how to reach it wasn't entirely clear. Ironically, it was the NGO sector at ECD level, I felt, that rose to the challenge. Ann Short wasn't concerned by OBE and its demands. She understood it and set about overhauling the advanced Ntataise training programme – known at that stage as the Further Training programme, later to be called the Further Education and Training Certificate programme – along with a well-developed assessment system to fit in with OBE. It was a substantial body of work, all based on the material we'd already developed and contained in guidebooks for the trainers and the manuals for the trainees.

While Ann wrote, Puleng – who was fulfilling her earlier promise and was now a coordinator and senior member of the Ntataise team – and her team of trainers read Ann's work, tried it out with trainees and made suggestions for any adaptations. It was a long way from the late 1970s when Ann had first come to Huntersvlei. But what hadn't changed in those 28 years was our model, which focused on intensive training of trainers and the most important on-site support to practitioners, as non-qualified but trained nursery-school teachers were about to be called.

OBE proved to be a disaster. Wealthier, better-equipped schools handled it, but poorer schools with teachers still reeling from apartheid education struggled. Comments were made that the administration of the new curriculum was overwhelming and cut down on teaching time; the teachers complained that they had not been properly trained and that, while OBE might work in smaller classes with more intensive individual input, it was not going to work in classes with 40 and 50 children.

In 2010, the Minister of Education Angie Motshekga closed OBE down. It had lasted for just over ten years and caused further upheaval in an education system that was already struggling to find itself.

It was Ishmael Mabitle who had introduced me to the vast inequality between schools in Viljoenskroon and Rammulotsi. As an educationist, he had played a vital role as a Ntataise trustee through the early debates about OBE. One evening, Anthony and I were getting ready for an end-of-year school function at Michaelhouse in KwaZulu-Natal when Anthony's cellphone rang.

His abrupt telephone voice sounded gruffer than usual. The cold Midlands air lay, frosty, on the windows. Inside the house, a log fire burned in the grate. He walked to the window for better reception, listened for a while, then turned to me. 'There have been huge storms at home,' he said. 'The farm's flooded and – he hardly paused '– Ishmael has died in a car accident.'

Ishmael Mabitle's car had skidded on the wet road near the salt pan and overturned in a pool of water. He hadn't been able to undo his seatbelt. He had drowned in a puddle.

I wrapped my arms around myself and cried unabated tears. Apart from the loss to his family, Ishmael would be an incredible loss to Ntataise – and to me, as a friend. What would 1999 bring?

41

NEW YORK

'When we were children playing in the dust, we looked at the aeroplanes flying overhead. One day, I used to say, one day I'll be on that plane.'

IT WAS AN HOUR'S trip by car from New York City to Babyland Family Services in New Jersey. Mary Smith, founder of this private not-for-profit organisation, wrapped me in a warm, welcoming hug when I stepped curiously out of the taxi. She and Babyland's glamorous Gloria Freeman had visited Ntataise earlier in the year. I was in New York, visiting my brother Adam and returning her visit.

The Babyland playrooms rang with laughter. The basic preschool daily programme was much the same as ours. The children came from homes with many of the same problems – poverty and unemployment – but Babyland differed from Ntataise in major ways. There were qualified teachers and social workers working with teacher aides, who were the equivalent of our teachers. The playroom classes were much smaller and better resourced. The food was good, and there was lots of it. The premises were solid buildings, spacious without being grand. There was plenty of play equipment – mostly bought and not, like most of ours, improvised.

What really gripped me was the warmth I felt in the playrooms, the patience and understanding shown by the teachers to the children and their parents. It was an atmosphere that pulled me in. Above all, there were children of all race groups. They were all equal. Babyland was a well-established organisation and reminded me so much of home. The welcome I'd received at Babyland, and an invitation to return 'soon' with some of our trainers, stayed with me all the way home, across the Atlantic Ocean and down the length of Africa, brown and dry beneath the droning plane.

Puleng's words, 'people of the world', had stayed at the back of my mind ever since her return from a study tour in neighbouring African countries three years earlier. American funders had at that time pushed me to send three senior Ntataise trainers to the USA. 'They are doing so well, Jane. What about broader exposure?'

Maria's miserable three months on a programme in Canada not long before rang warning bells. 'Can't we use the funds to send more people to neighbouring countries?' I'd asked.

'Shouldn't you be asking the trainers if they'd like to go to the States, instead of you deciding what experiences they should have?' Anthony, my sounding board, asked.

'Probably, but it would be good to give more people a chance to travel closer to home.'

The funders disagreed with me but eventually made the funds available and ten Ntataise trainers from our projects in Mpumalanga, Limpopo and the Free State spent ten days on a study tour to early childhood programmes in neighbouring Botswana, Zimbabwe and Namibia.

'We ate spaghetti, spaghetti and more spaghetti,' said Alice, who'd lost her passport and her money.

'It was tough being the group leader,' Maria said. 'You think you are part of the group but you aren't.'

Bonny chimed in. 'I needed to go to the loo. We were on a cruise on the Zambezi River. I told them to stop for me. They did, but I had to squat over a hole in the ground. There were elephants all around us. I thought they were going to kill me.'

'It was a great experience,' said Puleng. 'We all learnt a lot. We are now people of the world.'

'You turned our offer down last time, Jane. How have things changed?' The funders, the American Jewish World Service and Nancy Muirhead from the Rockefeller Brothers Fund, had questions. The change was in our trainers' growing confidence in themselves, boosted by their trip to the other African countries, and my trip to Babyland, a place where our trainers would feel at home, learn things relevant to our own situation with mentors who'd guide them, and be able to share their own experiences. It was a tough negotiation – neither funder was a pushover – but in the end they both agreed to fund this trip for our three senior trainers.

This time I asked them if they'd like to go to the USA. Bonny, Puleng and Alice prepared for their month-long internship and training programme at Babyland with excitement and trepidation. It was a long way from home – further than any of them had ever been – and a country they knew little about. 'When we were children playing in the dust, we looked at the aeroplanes flying overhead. One day, I used to say, one day I'll be on that plane,' said Puleng. 'But I never thought it would be to the United States.'

'I can't believe I'm really going to America.' Bonny emptied a packet of beaded necklaces and crocheted doilies made in Rammulotsi, which the trio was taking with them as gifts, onto my desk. I felt all choked up as I stood outside our office on the farm with the rest of the Ntataise staff and hugged the three women goodbye. Rebecca asked us to close our eyes and pray that God would bring them back safely to us. Tears, laughter, wet hand-kerchiefs and last touches, and the three were on their way. The cavalcade of cars containing husbands, children and some of the remaining Ntataise staff set off for Johannesburg International Airport. We huddled around the phone the next day to hear our travellers say, 'We're here, in New York. The buildings, the people, there are so many of them.' Puleng's voice sounded as clear as if she was in the room next door.

'Why were you so determined that the trainers should go to New York?' Anthony asked me when I told him they had arrived safely. For me, travel to new places was the pinnacle of excitement. Maybe I was projecting this on to my colleagues. 'They've never had a chance to see other parts of the world. The programmes we follow are based on programmes in the USA. It'll be great to see that we are not that different, but that there is lots for us to learn and equally for us to share from our experiences here.'

'Like what?'

'Like how to make and play with improvised equipment, like what it's like to live in South Africa, like the work they are doing. I just think it is a great experience,' I said defensively.

There would be another trip to New York a few years later, our first fundraising event outside South Africa – our only fundraising event outside South Africa. The Schomburg Center for Research in Black Culture in New York City was the venue for this event, organised by the Friends of South African Rural Preschool Development, an American charity set up by Ntataise and American colleagues. For some reason, I thought it would be easy to raise funds from individuals in the USA. It wasn't. Our guest of honour, the South African ambassador to Washington, Barbara Masekela, arrived to the beat of an African drum, the stomp of African feet – a group of young Zulu men in Zulu regalia, studying in New York and making some extra money. Having this stalwart of the ANC with us added gravitas to the occasion. Outside, we saw the sights and sounds of Harlem. Inside, South Africans of all ages and colours mingled with Americans of all ages and colours, old friends, new friends, existing funders of Ntataise. 'Our countries may be far apart but what we have in common is our passion for young children,' one guest enthused, spooning bobotie onto her plate. As a party, it was a smash hit. But as a fundraiser, it was a damp squib. We just covered our costs, even with a donation from a supporter.

Scraps of paper blew against my legs and I struggled against a relentless current of people. I was lost in New York City, it was raining, and I was late for my appointment. I frantically tried to wave down a cab, but none stopped for me. 'Nobody gets lost in New York,' my brother said. 'It's the easiest city in the world to get around.' I got lost. I didn't know how the buses or the subway worked, so I walked and walked in the pouring rain, my umbrella getting tangled up with hundreds of others.

'Not to worry,' the charming ex-South African – now a successful New Yorker – said when, bedraggled and wet, I eventually walked across the soft carpets into his office some forty floors up in an intimidating glass building. Dr Agnes Setai, the Ntataise chairperson, and Bonny and Puleng, were already there. Looking down from this dizzying height the cars on Fifth Avenue looked like toys, the people like ants. We talked about children playing in 'dusty' African playgrounds. Ntataise was a couple of thousand dollars richer when we finally left him.

I had one more contact – an investment banker, also an ex-South African. He waited until I'd sat down in the sort of chair it was difficult to get out of, a leather marshmallow, and said, 'So, tell me, Jane, how many children from the Ntataise preschools have become head boys or girls of their schools?'

He had no idea of the conditions in which black South African children went to school; they were a far cry from the private boys' school he'd attended. He gave us $14 000 anyway, about R84 000 at that time. But raising money in the USA was not, as someone said, 'for sissies'. We didn't try it again – not through individuals, at any rate.

'Did you ask those men for a donation outright?' Anthony asked curiously when I got home.'

'Yes.'

'That was brave. Why did you think Americans would give Ntataise donations?'

'They had South African connections, they grew up here. And Americans seem to give, they are philanthropic. They get tax advantages, apart from anything else.'

I'd thought ex-South Africans and people who'd visited the country would support us. They probably would have, but we'd need a full-time fundraiser in the States to make this happen. 'One person who had indicated he might consider serious support gave us two hundred dollars.'

'That must have put you in your place,' Anthony laughed.

'It did rather.' I smiled ruefully. 'I enjoy fundraising, but only through corporates, or foundations and trusts. I can't ask people for personal money. I feel too embarrassed.'

Over the years that I've raised money for Ntataise, I've only twice done it through social events – one being New York, and the other a 'ball' at the Inanda Club in Johannesburg. That yielded regular donations over a number of years, but not enough to warrant a repetition, however great the exposure for Ntataise.

As I climbed into a taxi heading for JFK, and home, Puleng and Bonny took their own taxi to Newark to catch a plane to Orlando, Florida, where they'd been invited to take part in the National Black Child Development Institute's conference, attended by thousands of women from all over the USA. This was a major recognition for these two women and for Ntataise. They were excited and I was so pleased for them. They truly were 'people of the world'.

While our trainers were exploring New Jersey and New York,

those of us at home implemented one of our most ambitious – and, as it turned out, successful – projects. It was with *The Star* newspaper, to help even more people become part of the ECD world. Ntataise joined forces with this major Johannesburg daily newspaper to share educational ideas from Ntataise's new booklets of play and learning activities for three-, four- and five-year-olds with thousands of *The Star*'s readers. Once a week, throughout the year, Ntataise published a full page of these learning activities in the newspaper's special education supplement. This supplement reached the newspaper's 220 000 subscribers.

In addition, *The Star* delivered copies of each supplement to 1 000 preschools, which we identified in the poorer areas of Johannesburg. Along with the print media, twice a month Bonny hosted a radio programme on ECD for Sesotho-speaking mothers on the Free State radio programme Lesedi FM.

The number 1 000 seemed to follow me deep into 1999. After the success of the pilot toy-trolley project two years earlier, I received a call from the Nelson Mandela Children's Fund's Jeremy Ratcliffe. 'We want to do 1 000 more toy trolleys,' he said. 'Will you coordinate it?'

It was to be known as the 1 000 Edu Trolley project. I would decide on the toys, source them, order them, help the Nelson Mandela Children's Fund draw up criteria for which preschools and playgroups would receive the trolleys, and make sure they were packed and delivered. I shivered with delight. I invited NGOs in ECD from all over South Africa to the NMCF's Saxonwold offices to decide on the trolley contents and which preschools would receive them. Woolworths once again agreed to sponsor, store, pack and deliver the trolleys. It took most of that year to complete the project. But before I could accompany struggle stalwart and NMCF trustee Amina Cachalia, to deliver trolleys to remote communities, sadness in my own life intervened.

42

AN EMPTY SPACE

In the valley of the Downs, a memory of
my father's life in the land of silver mist.

'DAD'S VERY SICK. HE is in the Critical Care Unit at Milpark Hospital.' My stepmother Sheila's voice was flat on the other end of my phone. I was surrounded by 1 000 red, blue and green trolleys, which stood in neat rows in the vast Woolworths warehouse south of Johannesburg. Teams of volunteers were sorting and packing thousands of toys. Each trolley had to receive exactly the same selection. It was a highly organised operation. I finished the call and I ran.

I was lightheaded with worry by the time I reached Milpark. A doctor met me at the door to the unit. 'Your father's not going to make it. He's had a massive haemorrhage.'

I tiptoed into the ward. The curtains were drawn around my father's bed. Sheila sat next to him, holding his hand. 'He's in a coma, but talk to him.'

'Oh, Dad.' I rubbed his cold hand. What could I say? Ours had been such a fraught relationship. The acrimony of his and my mother's divorce when I was only three, and Adam only one, had never been laid to rest. We always felt the coldness between them. 'We love you,' I said. I had continued to see my father and his family right through my married life. I talked to him regularly and he took great delight in our children. I felt a greater warmth from him during his later years than I had when I was little. David and Mark had not played a great part in my life growing up, and it was only in the years since Dad and Sheila died that I developed a real closeness to Mark. I was never able to do this with David; he died when he was 55.

The monitor went wild. The cardiologist, who had looked after my father for many years, put his head around the curtain. He leaned over, switched off the machine and said, softly, 'He's gone, Sheila. I am sorry'.

She sat there for a while, just holding his hand. I kissed my father's forehead and waited for her on the other side of the curtains. Anthony and my half-brothers, David and Mark, arrived and said their goodbyes. Dad was wheeled away.

That night, Anthony was awarded a Chancellor's Medal from the University of Pretoria for services to agriculture in South Africa. There was an empty seat next to his at dinner. I should have been with him, but I felt I needed to be with Sheila, my half-brothers and their families. My father had instructed us many times that he didn't want a funeral. So, a few days later, fresh autumn air ruffling the dry leaves on the ground, we joined friends and family in my father and Sheila's garden to the sound of bird calls and the lawnmower from next door. My brother David read from the Old Testament and we closed our eyes while he prayed. My mind wandered above the bird calls, the lawnmower and David's voice. I thought of my father, a person on the periphery of my life.

Standing beside Anthony and our four children, all wearing their school uniforms, I could feel the rough leather of Dad's old green hatchback Volvo. Every two weeks it had been his turn to 'have us'. It was usually dark when he drove Adam and me home to our mother, the three of us singing World War II songs: 'Pack Up Your Troubles' and 'It's a Long Way to Tipperary.'

Sheila asked if we could scatter his ashes at Huntersvlei, but somehow that didn't seem right. 'What about The Downs?' I asked.

'What are The Downs?' Robyn asked.

I stood on the leather-covered stool in our study and lifted a book off the bookshelf, its green leather edges torn, the pages foxed with age. Its title was *Land of the Silver Mist* and it had been written by my father, Harry Klein. 'Listen,' I said, and read his own words as our own private eulogy: 'I was a gypsy with a horse and donkey. I was free, unfettered by office walls. But I had not yet found what I had come to seek. There was something more, I knew, waiting somewhere on the trail ahead.' That something more was a place called 'The Downs'. 'It was set like a gem in a ring of tumbled mountains … with their deep gorges and open glades.'

In 1938, my father, a wanderer and adventurer, had come upon a hidden paradise in the far north of South Africa settled by a man named Orrie Baragwanath. Harry bought five acres of land from him. 'On my hilltop overlooking the loveliness of mountain and valley, where mists sweep in silvery splendour, I built a little shack of wood and iron, it was rough and simple, I called it Hlamonu (Come Here).' Years later, on his last stretch home from the war, my father returned to Hlamonu. By then a lieutenant colonel, he bore the scars of a horrific air crash at Kabwe, in what is now Zambia.

He replaced the wood and iron with mountain stone and it was to this rough cottage, with no electricity or running water, that he took me, aged two, and my beautiful mother, Peggy, and started a logging business. Divorce was not common in those days, but after his business failed and we moved to the Cape, my parents divorced and a new and strange life for all of us began. Running through it like a thread of silver was The Downs.

A short while later I had finished a series of preschool visits in the

Lowveld and was en route to meeting Anthony, Sheila and the boys for our journey to The Downs, when my cellphone rang. It was my half-brother David. His voice sounded muffled. 'My mother's just died.'

Riddled with cancer, Sheila had been overcome by dehydration. 'She can't have died, we're going to The Downs to scatter Dad's ashes,' I said stupidly.

Sharing our sorrow seemed better than being alone. The memory of Sheila's gentle spirit and soft voice urged us up the winding mountain pass. The thriving avocado orchards were but a distant memory. Houses once filled with voices and laughter were in ruins. Wandering vines strangled broken-down homesteads. Mark read from *Land of the Silver Mist* when we reached what, according to the description in Dad's book, must once have been the Baragwanaths' house. Our feet crunched through the undergrowth and we prodded the mass of weeds with sticks, watching for snakes. There was no roof, no windows, and the walls had crumbled. We stood on the remains of a front stoep, blackjacks gripping our clothes, and looked down the sweep of the valley to the heights of Dad's beloved Mamatsweri. The rondavel Dad described in his book was buried under the tumbling plants and wasn't very inviting. I trod lightly over scattered stones, broken bricks and the cracked floor, imagining him sleeping there as a young man, his trek oxen tethered outside, his men talking in the glow of a campfire, coffee boiling on a Primus stove.

We couldn't find the house my father had built for my mother and me. But halfway up a hill we opened the box containing his ashes. To the right of us stood the ruins of bygone settlers, to the left the towering Drakensberg. Dad was back with his dreams. The Downs, my mother told me when we returned, was the only place she and my father had ever been really happy.

When she turned 80 the following year, I suggested we visit the valley within the vast, rugged peaks. My brother Adam and his wife Lindsay joined us from the USA. Margot McNeal, a Swiss nurse who had met her love in a sprawling stone cottage in the purple mountains, offered to be our guide. We stopped in her four-wheel-drive bakkie at a boom. The Downs was now a national park called Lekgalameetse. The mountains slumbered where we had left them nine months before.

'Stop,' my mother called as we reached the plateau. An almost invisible path led into what I could only call a fairy glade. Trees with long, thick trunks reached up to the sky. High above, their leaves entwined. Swirling strands of silver mist crept through the roof of leaves. Rays of sun struggled to push through the thick canopy. Decomposing leaves carpeted the ground.

This was where the Baragwanaths had celebrated weddings and christenings. 'We came to so many parties here,' my mother said. We walked round the glade, which was like a ghostly ballroom, its walls and ceiling made of leaves and silent mist. The dancers were memories of years long gone. It was hot when we came out of the forest and we pulled on hats.

'Over there,' my mother pointed ahead of us. 'I'm sure it was over there.'

The bakkie juddered over clumps of tough grass bleached in the sunlight and through hidden potholes until we saw the ruins of a house all but hidden by dry reeds. Margot parked her bakkie to one side of the crumbling building. There was no roof. All that remained were the lintels that stretched across long-gone doorways.

The valley swept away before us. My brother Adam helped my mother over a pile of broken bricks. Birds whirled high above us.

'We always carried forked sticks in case of snakes.' She told us she'd once washed my eyes with milk after a snake had spat at me.

I could remember neither the snake nor the house. All I could remember was myself as a little girl with long, dark curls, staying overnight with the Baragwanaths. (These are the same Baragwanaths after whom the hospital and an earlier aerodrome had been named.)

The next time I went to The Downs, some eight years later, was after my mother died. I climbed through the long grass. Standing in the ruined kitchen, I cried as I'd never cried before. My father had built that house. My mother and father had stood on that same concrete floor so many years before, tucked me into bed in the small room that led off the kitchen, their lives still before them, full of promise and hope.

43

A NEW MILLENNIUM

*More than two decades had flown by
since we first stood on that patch of
sandy ground.*

DR ADELAIDE TAMBO, OUR guest of honour, told me when she arrived that the timing was not good, as she was dealing with painters in Johannesburg. I quailed before this national icon, one of the bravest members of the struggle, and stuttered our appreciation.

As my mother turned 80, Ntataise turned 20. It was the first year of the new millennium. We celebrated this milestone at our seventh Ntataise Conference, held at Dikhololo, a rambling country hotel on the edge of the Waterberg mountain range in the North West province, with all members of the Ntataise Network.

The first lady of the North West province, Tumi Plaatje-Molefe, welcomed Ntataise. When she arrived she was accompanied by her husband, Popo Molefe, the premier, and his entourage. We had not expected him but, no doubt drawn by Dr Tambo, he was there. 'Where is he going to sit?' I whispered desperately. Anthony leaped up and offered him his seat. Dr Tambo's warmth and strength touched every beating heart. We ululated and danced in the aisles after she opened the Conference, telling us that the struggle for equality for our children was not yet over.

We gave her a container from a Viljoenskroon pottery, with 'Ntataise' printed in blue on its white glazed side. It was filled with sugared peanuts grown and roasted on the farm. She wore an Ntataise cap on her head. A long, snaking line formed behind her when she was ready to leave, and escorted her to her car. We waved until she disappeared down the dirt road. She phoned me later to thank me for the peanuts. I promised I'd send her more.

We celebrated our 20 years in the Free State in a large white marquee set up on the dirt road between the Huntersvlei farm primary school and the Ntataise training centre. Mrs Anna Buthelezi-Phori, the Free State MEC for Social Welfare, welcomed the hundred or so guests, all women and men who had been involved with Ntataise since its inception: nursery-school teachers, government officials, farmers and, of course, the Free State Ntataise trainers and the Huntersvlei nursery-school children.

Later in 2000, one of these trainers, Alice Ntisa, left Ntataise to become the new director of the Ntsoanatsatsi Educare project, one of the Ntataise network members based in the rugged hills of QwaQwa in the eastern Free State. I was thrilled and sad at the same time to see her go, but as Anthony said, 'That's a compliment to you. You trained her, you helped get her to this position.'

Alice was one of our 'people of the world'. She was tough and determined. She would do well. Alice had hardly left when Rebecca retired. It was 23 years since Rebecca and I had stood on the sandy patch outside the farm clinic and asked the workers' wives if they'd like a nursery school for their children; 23 years since the mothers told a clueless girl from Johannesburg that they'd choose the teachers and that I had better find out what to do in such a 'crèche', the farm nursery school that led to the formation of Ntataise.

Like Maria, Rebecca had made an invaluable contribution to early learning for the children of farmworkers in South Africa. She'd scooped women up in her wide smile and said, 'If I can do it, so can you.' She'd become a woman to be reckoned with. I felt a gaping hole when she left us. Rebecca knew what it was like to work on a farm – long, hard, often back-breaking days picking up fallen mealie cobs, weeding the fields. She'd got up before first light to boil water for her family to wash with and to use to make pap for the children to eat before school, to make her husband's food, then to tidy the house and get dressed herself. What Ntataise had done for her, as she told me many years before, had not only made her want to give her children a better life – but also allowed her to do so.

44

SELENA MOLOKE

As the candles flickered, I spoke of the memory of her smile, and the legacy of learning she had left.

SIXTY MEMBERS OF THE Ntataise Network from seven of South Africa's provinces sat in the green leather chairs of the historic Council Chamber of the Free State's Fourth Raadsaal. The Free State legislature had seen provincial governments come and go, and history being made, since it opened in 1893. This Ntataise annual conference was in 2001, our 21st year, and was held at Thaba 'Nchu, a Free State town east of Bloemfontein, the province's capital. We felt it fitting that the province's premier, Mrs Winkie Direko, be invited to open the conference. Dr Agnes Setai, who had taken over from Anthony as chairperson of the Ntataise Trust that year, successfully issued the invitation to the premier. Not only did she agree to open the conference, but she agreed to do it in the Raadsaal. The pleasure of this event was soon lost when later that year HIV/ Aids claimed its first Ntataise victim.

Selena Moloke, Maria Moloke's eldest daughter and a Huntersvlei nursery-school teacher, sat listlessly on a child's plastic chair in the playground. Her usually smiling face looked bleak. A hacking cough racked her body. She buried her head in her hands and then looked at me, her eyes pleading. I knelt down next to her. She told me she had TB and was too weak to play with the children, too sick to work. She told me how much she loved the nursery school and that she'd be back as soon as she was well. A chill ran through my body.

When I got home I phoned the doctor. 'She might have TB,' I said, 'but what if she has Aids?'

'There's nothing we can do, Jane. We don't have antiretrovirals. We could try to get them through private providers but basically the medication is unavailable.'

The government was in denial. There was no subsidy for anti-retroviral treatment. Young men and women were dying in their thousands.

Selena got thinner and thinner. Her curves and dimpled smile faded. I visited her in her mother's house where she lay under the bedcovers, too weak to sit. Her hand rested on the blanket. I was shocked at how thin she was. I stroked her forehead, which was damp and hot. Maria sat on the bed, trying to pour drops of water into Selena's crusted mouth. Her eyes were wet with tears. Selena's little boy pulled at his grandmother's skirt. He didn't understand what was happening to his mother.

I soon received the message I'd been dreading. Maria Moloke had lost a second child.

The day of Selena's funeral was clear and fresh. From the early morning I watched taxis line the dirt road alongside the Huntersvlei farm primary school. Anthony, Claire and I were shown to chairs at the front of the school hall next to the Moruti, the church minister who would conduct the service. 'Tsamaya hantle Selena' (Go well Selena) was written on the blackboard behind us in white chalk. The hardboard partitions had been pushed to one side of the room. Men and women, boys and girls, were crammed onto wooden benches and white plastic chairs. Maria and her family sat to the side of Selena's polished wooden coffin, huddled together, covered with blankets. Loud keening filled the room. The sun's heat intensified and the corrugated-iron roof expanded with a noise like gunshots. The coffin rested on a metal trolley in front of us. The fragrant scent of fresh flowers mingled with the smell of plastic wreaths. Mourners placed envelopes alongside the flowers, containing gifts of money for the family. Selena's friends, dressed in black, formed a guard of honour around the coffin, the candles they held flickering softly.

I wondered how many South Africans would succumb to this illness, which was sweeping through the country with relentless momentum – gathering men and women, young and old, and leaving little children lost and bewildered. The voices of the congregation – schoolchildren, young men and women, parents and grandparents – soared in song. Through the open windows I saw nursery-school children chasing one another across the school grounds. The MC called my name and asked if I would say a few words to the family. What could I say to Maria, the woman who had carried my children on her back, fed them when they were babies, helped nurse them when they were ill?

I talked about Selena and her work at the nursery school, her willing smile and the legacy she left through those young children who'd learnt from her. I talked about HIV/Aids. No one wanted to talk about it, no one wanted to hear about it. It meant death and fear. But it was too catastrophic an illness to ignore. This needn't have been. For me the greatest tragedy was the number of households in which both parents died, and children were looking after each other, helping each other get dressed for school, getting food from I don't know where. Aids was tearing families and social structures apart.

When I had finished speaking, people, including my daughter Claire, were sobbing so hard that they ran out of tissues. Wads of toilet paper were passed to them down the rows of mourners, to dry their wet cheeks and streaming noses. Later, we stood silently at the primary-school gate as the coffin carried by Selena's friends and family passed us. The graveyard was a patch of veld in the stad, not far from the main road. It felt cold and grey, the way we all felt. Gum trees towered above us, blocking the sun from warming the graves, from warming the mourners. We stepped carefully over mounds of earth. Some of the graves were covered with granite slabs, most with grass and soil. Here and there a headstone told us the name of the person buried there. But mostly people's births and deaths were commemorated on strips of wood embedded in the soil.

Soon after Selena's death, as the number of child-headed households grew, I came across a quote in a magazine from a few years earlier. It helped me articulate the feelings deep inside me that just couldn't find the words to come out, feelings which made the work we were doing at that particular time even more relevant. It read: 'My dear young people: I see the light in your eyes, the energy of your bodies and the hope that is in your spirit. I know that it is you, not I, who will make the future. It is you, not I, who will fix our wrongs and carry forward all that is right with the world.' They were the words of Nelson Mandela. I had always been driven by the light in children's eyes. Watching it being extinguished broke my heart.

Keeping that light shining wasn't always easy. I seldom felt the tug of children's hands on mine, little thumbs against my thumb. I didn't have time to drive along bumpy dirt roads to outlying pre-schools, through dongas and puddles to township schools. The more the government embraced ECD, the more forms there were to read and complete, the more standards there were to meet. The more Ntataise's services were in demand, the more money was needed, the more funding proposals there were to write, the more reports to send. I bound newly documented policies and disciplinary codes into books. Job descriptions and employment contracts stood in neat files on the office shelves. Ntataise was accountable, we practised good governance. I felt overwhelmed with administrative matters.

At the same time, funders were asking what I was doing about succession. Wasn't it time for Ntataise to have a black leader? We were a new South Africa, after all.

45

THE QUEEN MOTHER

'You strike a woman, you strike a rock'.

THE HOT SUN BEAT down on us as we joined a throng of people making their way into the Royal Bafokeng Stadium in Phokeng near Rustenburg, some three hours from Johannesburg. The Bafokeng nation was getting a new king, and Anthony and I and Ntataise senior staff had been invited to his inauguration.

By 2003, our network had swelled to seventeen members working in more than a thousand preschools. Ntataise training had reached more than 10 000 women and 300 000 children. Our trustees supported and encouraged us and now we had a chance to support one of them – Dr Semane Molotlegi, Queen Mother of the Bafokeng, a great woman and a tireless community worker. Young members of the Bafokeng nation handed us bottles of iced water, a box of juice and fruit as we walked into the stadium. South Africa's first lady, Zanele Mbeki, was welcomed, as were Nelson Mandela and his wife, Graça Machel. Archbishop Desmond Tutu nodded graciously as his name was called. Modjaji, the Rain Queen, took her place on the stands. The smells, the sounds and the traditions of Africa bound the crowd for that day into one. Business leaders, members of NGOs, government officials and the people of Phokeng watched in hushed silence as the young man, who had not been born to be king, made his way around the stadium. Kgosi Leruo Molotlegi was to replace his brother, who had died. His subjects welcomed him with full-throated ululating. It was all about succession.

Shortly before this royal occasion, I had attended another, very formal in style. Queen Elizabeth II was visiting South Africa and I'd been invited to a cocktail party at the British High Commission in Pretoria, along with hundreds of others. The Queen of England looked like my mother-in-law, warm yet aloof, curly grey hair neatly in place. We all stood behind a white line marked on the grass, like a tennis court. We inched forward, wanting her to notice us, to shake our hands. But she walked right past, stopping only to chat to a beaming bishop and his wife. She too had children in the wings. Succession must often have tried her mind.

'The answer as to whether it is time for someone to succeed me in leading Ntataise must be yes,' I said to Anthony.

'I agree, you've been there a long time and it is probably time for new energy. But can you let go? It's so much your baby.'

The sun was setting. We were sitting on the stoep talking about succession, the new King of the Bafokeng, who had never anticipated such a life for himself, watching the early stars appear in the sky as it got darker. It was about new energy – but in the South Africa of 2004, it was about so much more. The matter of succession hung heavily over me. I wanted to make changes, I just didn't quite know which way to go. Mmemogolo, the Queen Mother, and trustee Maggie Nkwe – along with our chairperson, Agnes Setai – provided invaluable guidance.

For me it was vital for the future of Ntataise that we appoint a leader who would understand the communities in which we worked, the nuances and the undercurrents that seemed, increasingly, to be passing me by. It was difficult to pinpoint those nuances and the often political undercurrents, in the educational sense. In the end much of it did boil down to language. I had tried to learn Sesotho, but I had not tried hard enough. I could greet people and ask their names, but not very much more. Many of the meetings I attended in the Free State were in Sesotho. If a word of English was thrown in I often got the gist of what was being said, but getting the gist was not enough – nor were translations. I lay awake night after night in an agony of indecision. Deep down, I really didn't want to be replaced. I was frightened of losing my relevance in the field; apart from anything else, Ntataise was one of the reasons I got up each day. But it was time to make the change.

'I don't know if I can, but I will have to let go,' I replied to Anthony.

Maria Mohlahleli had been my obvious successor, but she was submerged in the building business with Mac. They had successfully been awarded contracts to build a number of houses and Maria could not even think of returning to us, although she would do so in the future to run a parent programme. 'Look for someone in your organisation,' said an influential black businesswoman I turned to for advice.

'Maybe Puleng is that person,' I said to Anthony.

'Why do you think she'd fill that role? What does she have that the others don't?'

'She's clever, she's got the courage to stand by her principles and from all my interaction with her she has the ability to make decisions and implement them. She's not frightened of expressing an opinion and, in my mind, she's a leader. People respect her and listen to her.'

When I'd broached the subject of leadership with Puleng a few months earlier, she'd said, 'I'm not ready for that, Mme Jane. In any case, I'm too busy with the accreditation to think of it.' She was one of Ntataise's senior members of staff and had worked with Ann

Short on our programme development. Puleng was as vital to the Ntataise training programme as Maria had been before her.

'It is a significant achievement,' Dr Setai, our chairperson, said when the Ntataise advanced Further Training programme was granted full accreditation by the Education, Training and Development Practices SETA, the new government quality assurance body that had given us such a compliance headache and whose name was such a mouthful to say. Ntataise was one of the first ECD training providers in South Africa to be so accredited. The accreditation meant that our courses complied with the required government standards of learning and assessment – but above all, it meant that those who completed them would at last receive a longed-for nationally recognised qualification.

Like it or not, succession was a matter for discussion at our AGM in May 2005. There were almost sparks of anticipation in the Ntataise farm offices where the AGM would be held. The entire staff joined the trustees for lunch in the Cottage on the farm before we sat formally around the wooden table in what had been Anthony's wood-panelled boardroom, and his father's before him. Anthony's mother's house, our first home, had been turned into offices for Anthony and his management and secretarial team. There was considerably more space, which they needed. This freed up his offices for Ntataise to use.

On the table, the minutes of the previous year's meeting and the financial statements waited to be approved. The business of the day completed, the last item on the agenda was succession. Despite her reluctance a few months earlier, Puleng faced the seven trustees to be interviewed for the post of director of the Ntataise Free State operations. The air was tinged with anticipation and the smell of manure from the feedlot outside. The pictures of tractors and prize-winning bulls long gone, pictures of nursery schools filled the walls. Everyone was relaxed and the questions flowed easily.

'Are you ready for a leadership role, Puleng?' asked Agnes.

'Like a baby, I have been through all the stages of development with Ntataise. At first I crawled, then as I gained confidence I sat, then stood, and finally I'm running. I'm ready for the challenges of managing, delegating and monitoring.'

'In isiZulu it is said: *"Wathint' abafazi, wathint' imbokodo"* – you strike a woman, you strike a rock. I think Puleng is our rock,' Agnes said when Puleng left the room.

I had no doubt. The decision to appoint Puleng Motsoeneng as the first black leader of Ntataise, one of the first black leaders of an ECD training and resource organisation in South Africa, was unanimous. It would be for her to develop the voice and the vision to strengthen the organisation, to make its work move ahead, make an even greater difference.

She sat quietly the next morning, listening attentively as I offered her the role of Director of Ntataise Free State, on behalf of the trust.

'I'm ready, I'd love the job,' she said. 'But what are you going to do?' There was a definite tone to her voice.

I promised that, whatever I did, I would do my very best not to interfere with her work in the Free State. And I haven't.

'Aiii aiiii ai!' someone shouted when I announced the board's decision to the trainers and fieldworkers gathered in the Ntataise training room. Puleng disappeared into a flurry of excited arms. The mechanic popped his head round the door to ask if anything was wrong. For once, the jubilation from our office outdid the noise from the workshop.

'This,' I said, 'calls for a celebration.'

46

POSITIVE

The diagnosis was grim, but the prognosis
was a new way of looking at life.

IT HAD ALL THE promise of a breathtaking summer's day. I had an interview with the *The Star* newspaper in Johannesburg later in the day, and I wanted to look good. I wore a new flared beige skirt, cream silk cami and high-heeled shoes. But my first stop was a long overdue mammogram.

'Don't get dressed yet.' The nurse popped her head round the curtained cubicle. 'The doctor wants to do another ultrasound.'

The silk cami slipped through my fingers. 'I am all right,' I asked, 'aren't I?' My legs felt shaky.

'I'm going to do a biopsy just to make sure,' said the radiologist.

'Make sure about what?'

She didn't answer me. She rubbed a local anaesthetic cream over my right breast and I felt a sharp pain. 'All done,' she said. 'I'll have the results tomorrow. Get dressed and come through to my office.'

I was shaking so much I could hardly stand. There was a cup of tea and a biscuit for me on the doctor's desk. I took a sip. It was hot and sweet. The doctor's voice was calm and matter-of-fact. 'I might be wrong, but I don't think so. When we have the results I'll tell you what to do.'

I stood in the antiseptic corridor outside her rooms trying frantically to phone Anthony. I couldn't get a signal. Porters pushed hospital beds past me on their way to the theatre. Nurses and doctors with white masks walked past, their shoes squeaking on the polished tiles. It smelled of disinfectant. Outside in the sunlight, car doors slammed. Babies wailed.

'Yes, my girl.' Finally I heard Anthony's gruff 'don't interrupt me' telephone voice.

'I had my mammogram. The doctor thinks I might have a problem.'

There was a pause. 'Okay. If there's a problem, we'll sort it out together. Just come home.'

Before I could do that I had my interview at *The Star*. The summer day now seemed empty; the sunlight had lost its warmth. The lift took me to a worn-looking newsroom. The feature writer, a colleague from my journalism days, thrust out a welcoming hand. We sat and chatted about Ntataise and its 25 years, but I couldn't concentrate. I couldn't stop thinking that I might have breast cancer.

Positive. That's all I heard when the radiologist phoned me the next day. I was back home, at a Ntataise meeting.

'It's not bad. Please don't worry,' she said, but to deaf ears.

I was shaking with shock. As it welled up, my legs felt like jelly, my voice became husky. She suggested the names of two surgeons I should see. I returned to the trainers' room where Puleng waited for me with Sophie Masilela from the Middelburg-based Sithuthukile Trust and Karin Boyum from Thusanang in Magoebaskloof. We were approving new training programmes.

'I've got breast cancer,' I blurted out, in total disbelief.

Someone pulled out a chair and pushed me into it.

Anthony stood next to my bed, his anxious face hovering above me. A tube protruded from my right side. The white hospital gown felt thick and rough. I retched uncontrollably into the stainless steel kidney dish the nurse held in front of me. Anthony told me the operation had gone well.

'Don't touch,' said the nurse. It was too late. I felt the ridge of white plaster that covered the concave indentation where my right breast had been.

'You have to eat something,' said Anthony. Green jelly and yellow custard wobbled under my spoon. I pushed it around the plate.

'Come on mum, just one spoon.' Sally's eyes tried to smile.

I managed a laugh. 'It seems just the other day I was saying the same thing to you.'

For their sake I swallowed the slithery dessert.

Vases of roses and mixed summer flowers stood on every conceivable trolley and counter. Anthony showed me a long list of people who had phoned to find out how I was. It was all these people who finally dragged me back into the world, past the depression and shock.

Visiting time turned into a party. 'There are too many of you. Can't you see she's exhausted?' A nurse shooed friends out into the corridor. 'Some of you must stand outside. Take turns.'

Through it all, my mother sat quietly near my bed, her walking stick in her hand.

A stick figure stared at me from the mirror in my bedroom. A livid scar ran from my right shoulder to under my rib cage. It was hidden under a strip of plaster. A haematoma had turned the right side of my body purple. It had bled profusely, soaking my sheets until they were bright red. 'You need a blood transfusion,' our GP had said.

'What you do need,' said Anthony, 'is to relax and stop worrying.'

I dressed and propped myself on pillows with a fluffy pink mohair rug covering my feet.

'You came to see me when I had my hysterectomy, now I've come to see you,' said Bonny, sweeping clothes off the chair in my bedroom and sitting on it. She was one of my first visitors. Her five-year-old grandson Kamu stood shyly in the doorway, holding a bunch of flowers.

'Hello Mme,' he whispered.

'Come in, Kamu. Come and sit.' I patted my bed.

He gave me the bunch of pink-and-yellow flowers wrapped in cellophane and tied up with a thick pink ribbon. It was 20 years since Bonny had thrust flowers into my hands after passing her driver's licence test. It was even longer since she, a 17-year-old, and I, a 29-year-old, had first met each other next to the fledgling honey locust trees which, like the nursery school, were spreading tentative young branches.

Bonny wanted to work and make a life for herself. 'I didn't realise that was work, it was like I was playing because I loved it so much. I wanted to work too, to find purpose in my life. I've come such a long way since then.' Bonny balanced her cup of tea on her lap.

'Lesenyeho, my husband, and I got married very young,' she went on. 'We both dropped out of school and watched our friends go to high school and teachers' training college in QwaQwa. We couldn't do that but we worked very hard, Lesenyeho in the lands at Huntersvlei and me with Ntataise so we could learn and grow and do just as well as our friends.'

'How do you feel now, Bonny?'

'Hai, Mme Jane, Lesenyeho worked so hard, he became a farm manager and we got a lovely house to live in. And me? Ntataise gave me another world. You expected things of me which I didn't think I could ever do, but I did them. I still can't believe it is me, Bonny, teaching other women, travelling overseas and to other parts of this country. Talking at a conference in Miami, going to Los Angeles, meeting people of high calibre which I would never have thought possible. When I was a little girl I had a nickname, 'Mainangwana'. It meant that I was shy, too shy to look up at people. It doesn't seem possible now, does it? I always want to come home after my travels. Ntataise and Mr Evans gave us chances Lesenyeho and I didn't even dream of. It's my turn now to help younger woman achieve what I've achieved. And you know, Mme Jane, it wasn't only me. Think of all the women we've worked with who never imagined that they would have a qualification, enough money to help their children at school and to make nice homes.'

She looked at her grandson. 'Kamu, finish your Coke, Mme Jane looks tired. We've talked enough.' Bonny got up to leave.

As I finish writing this memoir, the honey locust trees where we met have grown even older. Bonny is 60. I'm in my 70s. We've been friends since we were girls.

A few days later, the Ntataise staff sat solemnly in our study. Earlier, Puleng had handed me a bowl of red roses. Now she handed me a cup of tea and a solid-looking oatmeal biscuit. 'Mme Jane, you are too thin. You must eat.'

I took the cup of tea she held out. The cup rattled against the saucer. 'My family says I must relax. I'll try to. It's now up to you, Puleng, but I'll always be here to help you. I'll be back at work next year.'

Puleng wiped tears from her eyes.

'People really care about me,' I said to Anthony later, wiping my own eyes.

'There's nothing to cry about,' he said, putting his arm around me. 'Of course they care about you. We all do.'

I don't know what I would have done without my family and my friends – especially Anthony. From the moment I phoned him, shaking, and said, 'I might have breast cancer.' And the moment he told me to come home and we'd face it together, I stopped shaking.

It is hard to explain the sheer terror I felt (and still feel) every time I had an X-ray, another test. Every ache or imagined pain sent my blood pressure rocketing. What was that small bump on my wrist? Why was my neck sore? What was the pain in my stomach? I realised how vulnerable we all are. It put many things into perspective for me. The stresses of work seemed secondary. Having the people I loved around me was all that mattered then, and still does now. But I couldn't lie under a fluffy pink mohair blanket forever.

Anthony lured me out of bed with walks and drives on the farm, a stop in the maize fields to watch the sunset. He brought me books to read, pointed out interesting articles. He did whatever he could to take my mind off my healing wound and the shock of my operation. My children all helped me in different ways, like coming with me to bone scans where I was sandwiched between two parts of the X-ray machine, feeling claustrophobic and not allowed to talk for the duration of the procedure, and making smoothies loaded with nuts and bananas to tempt me to eat.

One of the most frightening things for me was not being able to eat, managing only ice cream and milkshakes and smoothies. There was no reason for me not to eat, my oncologist said. It was pure anxiety. The children brought me glasses of every sort of juice one could think of, including vegetable juice and orange juice. They talked to me, brought me flowers, and generally made me feel loved. The need to lessen their worry spurred me on to recover.

Gradually, life seemed to carry on much as before, but in other ways it would never be the same again. How little we knew that the ravages of cancer would inflict a devastating wound on our family in years to come.

It was 2006. The new year had barely dawned.

'It's time Ntataise moved off the farm,' I said to Anthony.

'Sounds like a good idea. Where are you going to go?'

'To Rammulotsi. That's where most of our work is. We'll build a training centre.'

'Where will you get funds to pay for it?'

'I'll raise the funds.'

Raising funds was one thing, but finding a suitable plot of land in Rammulotsi was quite another. 'Don't stress, we'll find one,' said Puleng, after we'd looked at yet another plot, deep in the township, accessible only along potholed dirt roads.

At the municipal offices, once the scene of angry protests and brutal police retaliation, paint peeled off the walls and windows flapped on their hinges. A rapid conversation took place between Puleng and the clerk. He thrust a large map in front of us, its ends frayed and brown, and stabbed it with his finger. 'Here.'

'Where's here?' I asked.

'There.' Our eyes followed his finger. We peered out of the window. 'You see that plot, the one with long grass? Next to it. I'll show you.' He set off at a cracking pace. We followed him out of the building, out of the high wire gate, along a short dirt road. 'Here, this one's available.'

The plot was just off the main road into Rammulotsi, opposite the municipal offices. It was where I had met with Mr Nel, the township administrator, many years before. The Boitumelo preschool that he had asked me to raise funds for was diagonally across the road, behind its high concrete wall. Puleng and I paced it out. Her legs were longer than mine and we came up with wildly differing measurements. But whatever it came to, it seemed very small.

'What about buying the next-door plot too?' the official suggested.

The plot held a corrugated-iron shack. We looked at the tangle of weeds, the waist-high grass, the corrugated-iron shack stacked with sheets of scrap metal, and the rats, snuffling like hungry pigs in the dirt. Puleng said she'd find out who owned it.

'The good news', said the lawyer to Puleng a few weeks later, 'is that the plot is zoned for business and training.'

'And the bad news?'

'The bad news,' he said, 'is that the person who owns the land owes the municipality money. You can't buy it until he's settled his debt.'

The trouble was that the owner couldn't settle his debt until we bought the land. It was a conundrum. While we waited, we had plans drawn up and submitted them to the municipality.

47

THE VIGIL

Worlds apart, tears fall for my namesake and my mother.

'JANE.'

The voice over the phone from Johannesburg was desperate. 'Bonny's not here. There's a room full of women waiting to be trained.'

I'd hardly put my phone down when it rang again. This time, it was Bonny. Her voice was strained. 'Mme, I'm in Johannesburg but my daughter Jane's in hospital in Klerksdorp. I have to go to her, please send a trainer in my place.'

By lunchtime our trainer Tibi was on her way to Johannesburg. Bonny's usually cheerful face looked blotchy when she came to our house to see me on her way home. Jane, she said, was HIV-positive. She'd known that, but hadn't wanted to tell me. Now Jane was in hospital, seriously ill. Bonny's pain and despair was beyond anything I had ever seen.

Anthony and I sat in our study. We watched TV in a desultory way, but mostly we talked about Aids. We were discussing what we should be doing to help when the phone rang.

Anthony put down the receiver. He looked at me. 'Jane has died,' he said quietly.

My cellphone rang. It was Bonny, sobbing. Jane had died before she'd got back to the hospital and she hadn't managed to say goodbye. It took us ten minutes to drive to the manager's house at the top of the farm. Bonny's husband, Lesenyeho, waited for us at the front door. I held Bonny tight. Her chest heaved and her cheek was wet against mine. Kamu sat on his grandfather's knee, his face buried in his neck.

I waited with Bonny and her family a few days later until Jane's open coffin arrived for an all-night vigil. Cars and truckloads of people from all the farms around us arrived for Jane's funeral the next morning. A tent had been erected on the lawn. To the side of the house, women cooked meat and mealie meal in large pots. Bonny and Lesenyeho were well-known. Lesenyeho was a Huntersvlei farm manager and, in addition to her Ntataise work, Bonny was active in the church. Men and women, many of whom I'd grown to know well over the past 30 years, filled the tent. Young women took turns to hold candles around Jane's coffin, to look after their friend, to guard her and guide her into the world beyond.

Bonny and Lesenyeho were very composed. Kamu, dressed in a miniature suit and tie, stood awkwardly with his cousins. When I was asked to speak, I could think only to start by saying to Jane's family and the congregation: 'One of my proudest memories since coming to live at Huntersvlei was the day Bonny told me her new baby girl had been named after me. I watched her grow into a beautiful young woman.'

A grieving Bonny returned to work. 'At least we've got Kamu,' she said to me.

I felt dread, and begged her to have him tested. She did; he tested negative.

While Jane Ntsoeleng had been losing the battle for her young life, my darling mother had been fighting for hers. We'd cancelled a family holiday overseas to be with her. Instead, Robyn came home from London, where she was living.

'You look terrible. I suggest you go away for a few days while she's in hospital,' the doctor told me. 'She'll be well looked after.'

Tucked under a white sheet in the Milpark Hospital's high care unit, my mother gripped my hands, pushing them hard against the bed. I don't think she knew, at that moment, who I was.

'I can't leave,' I said to Anthony, my heart breaking.

'You need a break. We'll be back soon.'

Anthony, Robyn, Claire and I packed a picnic lunch to eat on the road for our few days away but my heart was heavy.

The dining room of the Coach House in Agatha, not far from The Downs, was candlelit. We sat at a table with friends and scrutinised the leather-bound menu. I answered my cellphone on the first ring and took it outside into the balmy night air.

'My mother's just died,' I told Anthony, the children and the other guests, walking straight past them out of the dining room. My family followed me. Tears poured down the girls' faces. Anthony's eyes were wet. I was too stunned to cry.

The entire Ntataise staff and our trustee Maggie Nkwe were among the many friends who packed the Temple Emanuel synagogue for my mother's memorial service. It was a perfect Johannesburg day. The slight chill of early summer was offset by blue skies. I heard the cars on Oxford Road. I smelled roses.

The rabbi's words washed over us. My brother Adam contained himself as he talked about the mother who had loved and cherished us. I closed my eyes tightly to prevent the tears as my cousin David Sonnenberg gave the eulogy. Sally and Robyn read the beautiful words of Christina Rossetti's poignant poem: 'Remember me when I am gone away, / Gone far away into the silent land ...'

Adam and Lindsay went back to New York, to their daughter Georgia. Only Anthony and I attended my mother's cremation. It was only as her plain pine coffin moved over the belt to the ovens beyond that I was able to cry.

48

TOYI-TOYI

*A ceremony of celebration puts the cap
on a dream made real.*

THE WOMAN'S BLACK ACADEMIC gown flapped behind her as she ran to catch up with me. Smiling, she held her side and panted: 'I had to talk to you. I never thought this would happen. Me with a qualification. For all of us, it is a dream come true. Before the preschools, we sat at home. Now we have knowledge, we have confidence, we have skills, we have jobs and we have certificates.'

It was our dream too, and it had come true in 2006 when Puleng had burst into my office brimming with news. All 54 of the preschool practitioners she and her training team had been training over the past 18 months had received their National Certificate in Early Childhood Development – our first government-recognised certificates.

Newly washed jeans, T-shirts and shorts pegged to rickety washing lines lent colour to the dreary township roads the day we made our way to the Mphatlalatsane school hall in Rammulotsi for the graduation ceremony. The faces of the young women who filled the front rows were solemn, unsmiling. Their families and young children fidgeted on chairs in the rows behind them. Marie-Louise

Samuels, head of Early Childhood Development at the National Department of Education, presented the certificates. Simon Moka-lodise, a Ntataise trustee and soon to become high-school principal, placed sashes around the women's necks.

Husbands, sons, daughters, mothers, fathers, wearing their church clothes, blasted vuvuzelas and toyi-toyied in the aisles. A church women's group ladled generous portions of steaming fluffy white rice, stiff mounds of maize meal, chicken and beef stew in rich, thick gravy from stainless steel pots on tables at the back of the hall when the ceremony was over. There was enough for all 300 of us, and even for extra guests who had wandered in. I'd never seen a group of women so proud.

In April that year I, too, had worn an academic gown. The University of Pretoria awarded me the Chancellor's Medal for Services to Education. As the audience stood, I followed the vice-chancellor, the dean of Education, Professor Jonathan Jansen, and other academic staff onto the stage. Young men and women about to graduate sat in rows on the stage behind me. The assembly of parents and friends stretched before me in the dark auditorium. I smelled a jumble of perfume, sweat and anticipation.

Anthony and Claire sat in the front row and waved. The vice-chancellor read the citation and called me to stand next to him at the rostrum. I blushed with embarrassment but I accepted the award and the applause with a somewhat tremulous but happy smile.

After the ceremony we joined the dean and his guests, and Maggie Nkwe and her husband, Bishop David, for a cocktail party. Jonathan Jansen made his way over. Asking everyone to be quiet, he turned to me. 'No one will ever know,' he said, 'how I felt on being welcomed into your and Anthony's home the first time I visited Huntersvlei with USAID.'

The warmth of his words, the obvious depth of his emotion, brought tears to my eyes.

49

TOMORROW

As the rain showers its blessing on the white tent, the baton is handed over.'

THE BROWN EARTH WAS dry and hard. Puleng and I tried to turn the first sod, but we made little progress. We wouldn't give our spade to the builders. We wanted to do it ourselves. Slowly the ground gave way. We had finally received permission and raised the million rand we needed to build the centre.

Erf number 1617, Rammulotsi, was Ntataise's.

Relentless winds blew. It was November, and quite unseasonal. The tent pulled at its metal struts; I had visions of white canvas taking off and flying over Rammulotsi. At last the rain came, settling the thick brown dust. It was a sign of good luck.

The new Ntataise Training Centre was about to be opened. Every dignitary in the district was there. Drum majorettes from the primary schools marched along the wet roads to usher in our guests. The Centre, which housed Puleng's spacious new office, desk space and a locker for each trainer, a training room and a toy library, looked new and serene compared to the chaos in its grounds. Our guest of honour was Professor Jonathan Jansen, whose address summed it all up so much better than I ever could: 'It is a typical South African township. The few tarred roads are filled with potholes, young men with cloudy eyes drift aimlessly down the streets and young women who should be in school carry babies. Little has changed in this township, which has carried its share of apartheid oppression, such as the terrible time in 1990 when police opened fire on primary-school children, killing five and dispersing their desperate teachers.

'In a small corner of the community all gloom fades. The sound of music beckons me. Women from the community are swaying in song under a white tent. Toddlers move in dance and song to cheers of encouragement from the seated crowd. A trainee teacher in early childhood development gives an animated talk about how she has been transformed by her training. One speaker after another praises Mme Jane for how she tirelessly trained teachers, raised donor funding and motivated young black women to take leadership positions. As the rain showers its blessing on the white tent, the baton is handed over. The centre of training will no longer be on the farm but in the township inside a modest but sparkling new building. As I unveil the inaugural plaque I notice an unusual crowd. Black and white, young and old, middle-class blacks and poor farmworkers, small children and aspirant teachers, government officials, university trainers from Tukkies, parents, local politicians, donors from Johannesburg and activists from Rammulotsi …'

The wind dropped. Lunch was over. Our guests dispersed. Puleng stood next to my open car door. 'Mme Jane, you and Mr Evans have hosted Ntataise for so many years. It is our turn now. You'll never really know what it's all meant to us and all the other women and the communities they reach. We're not very far away. Come and see us.'

'Good luck, Puleng,' I said. 'I'm coming back for a cup of tea soon.'

I drove through Rammulotsi, through puddles of water, past young girls still wearing their drum majorette uniforms. I drove up the farm's long tree-lined front drive, small stones tumbling behind my wheels. The cattle in the camps ignored me.

At the big house under the arch, Anthony waited. 'Tomorrow's another day,' he said, and he hugged me.

EPILOGUE

AUGUST 2016. ANTHONY HAD died.

Grief and pain strangled my heart. I reached out my arms to my four children. We steadied one another as our world shattered around us.

Forty years had passed since I had arrived at Huntersvlei. On my left ring finger, the blue of my sapphire engagement ring took me back to our earliest days together. On my right, a ruby glinted; we had just made 40 years. We had both hoped for so many more.

Neither of us had reckoned on the ravages of cancer and the indescribable pain and discomfort that Anthony would suffer. It had never occurred to me that Anthony and I wouldn't grow old together. The strong man who had been the rock on which our family was built had gone. There was a great, gaping hole. I gasped for breath. Anthony had not wanted to die. There was still so much for him to do, grandchildren he had longed for but would never meet.

'He'll always be with you through your memories,' people would say. But a memory was not a pair of warm arms holding me tight. It was not someone to talk to, to argue with, to share problems with, someone to love.

Adrenaline and sheer disbelief got us through those early days. In a daze, I greeted the hundreds of people who joined us under the shade of the oak and white stinkwood trees, and the white marquee on the Huntersvlei front lawn, to say goodbye to Anthony. Even as I finish this book three and a half years later, I try to hear his voice, to listen to his advice.

'Stop listening and finish the book,' says Sally. 'Dad said I must make sure you do.'

It was only a few years earlier that I had sat through the earthquake in Rebecca Sothoane's living room. Members of her family and Ntataise had sat in sympathy, then terror, as the earthquake had torn through Rammulotsi. On this day, Puleng, Bonny and Maria sat on the red and green leather chairs in my study, offering me comfort after the earthquake that had torn through my life. The leather on the chairs' arms had cracked with age and use, the colours had faded. Anthony's Labrador Amber lay restlessly at my feet. She couldn't understand why Anthony wasn't there, sitting in his chair scratching her neck.

'I can't believe they are so grown up.' Puleng pointed at the photographs of our four children that hung on the wood-panelled study wall. There were four babies, then four young adults in graduation gowns: Robyn with an M.Phil. from Oxford; Claire with her MA from the London School of Economics and who now runs our farming business; Sally, a first-rate investigative journalist with her Honours degree from the University of the Witwatersrand; and David, with his MBA from the Gordon Institute of Business Science, who now lives in England.

And then three brides. The photos told the story of the passage of time.

On another wall hung the photo of me and Mr Mandela taken with the trophy Ntataise had won in 1995.

For all my fears about country life, the Free State was now part of me – it was as much my home as it had been Anthony's.

It seemed to me ironic that, with Sybil, Rhys and Anthony no longer with us, I – once a stranger – was now custodian of Huntersvlei.

'Can you remember how everyone used to complain about food in the training centre and Monica had to cook it here in your kitchen?' Maria said. We all laughed.

'And the time all our materials landed in the mud on our way to Vaalwater?' Bonny hooted with mirth.

'And the first Ntataise graduations?' said Puleng.

I'd been as good as my word, and stood far enough back to give Puleng the space she needed. We still work together. The network of ECD organisations started with USAID funding so many years ago stands at 22 member organisations spread over eight of South Africa's nine provinces. In 2016, its 38th year, the Ntataise Network reached 4 000 practitioners (as ECD teachers with a vocational qualification are now called), 2 500 preschools and 132 000 children. I am now an advisor and a Ntataise trustee.

ECD is firmly entrenched in the South African government's vision of essential education. There have been successes and there have been failures, good times and bad, but ECD NGOs that worked with courage and determination with disadvantaged communities during those dreadful years of apartheid had laid a good foundation for the new government to build on. The communities served, the NGOs and the Departments of Social Development and Basic Education need one another, both nationally and provincially. Immense progress has been made, but there is still a long way to go. Less than 50 per cent of children in the preschool age group in South Africa are reached by an ECD programme – and even then, the quality of the education offered in some of those preschools needs to be improved. There will soon be professional qualifications in ECD for universities to offer. But the role of the NGOs and solid vocational training and support for women in isolated, disadvantaged communities will remain vital to the continuing spread of good-quality ECD in this vast land of ours.

'Ntataise,' Anthony had once said, 'set out to provide early learning for young children. It did this, but in so doing it became a major force for the empowerment of women. It gave them confidence, knowledge, standing in their communities and jobs. It gave disadvantaged communities and thousands of children feet on the first rung up that long education ladder. Good-quality ECD helps children, especially those from disadvantaged communities, to understand not only early concepts, pre-reading and writing skills, but early socialisation, getting on with each other, and development of their emotional needs.'

For me, as the young bride who left the big city to settle with her husband on a farm on the edge of a small, conservative town in the Free State, with its vast blue skies, kilometres of maize fields, grazing cattle and signs pointing to separate doors for '*nie-blankes*' and '*blankes*', Ntataise was a pathway to purpose, a portal to a journey of self-discovery that has shaped the way I see the world.

I shared my journey not just with Anthony and my children, but also with the many remarkable women who have overcome great personal challenges, all with one overriding, unifying aim in mind.

To lead a young child by the hand.

ADDENDUM

DECEMBER 2019. THE FIRST murmurings of a new, fast-spreading and often fatal disease, COVID-19, were heard. By March 2020 South Africa, along with many other countries, was in full lockdown. Businesses and schools closed; people were called upon to stay in their homes. Millions of people, including ECD practitioners, lost their salaries, and many their jobs. Social distancing, handwashing and sanitising, mask-wearing, a ban on alcohol and cigarettes, working online and holding Zoom meetings became the norm. Hospitals prepared themselves for thousands of sick people. People were frightened and confused. South Africa was protecting its citizens from this pandemic which had thrown the world into an unimagined space.

August 2020. Ntataise was to have celebrated its 40th birthday at its annual conference. It did, but not in the way anticipated. The more stringent levels of lockdown were eased in South Africa, and the country began to return to a 'new normal'. Social distancing, sanitising and mask-wearing were here to stay for an indeterminate time. The struggle to re-ignite the economy began. Schools, including preschools, needed to comply with government directives before they could open.

Ntataise celebrated the milestone of its 40th birthday online. Participants, who had not seen one another for months, waved and blew kisses as their pictures came up on the screen.

Along with the uncertainty and fear it brought, COVID-19 highlighted ongoing challenges faced by people living in the poorer areas of South Africa: the state of schools; the lack of water, toilets, electricity and functional buildings; and the inability of out-of-work parents to pay school fees.

After 40 years, Ntataise showed the resilience and strength of its network. When the government struggled to reach the most desperate citizens in far-flung rural areas, Ntataise, through its established network, was able to step up and help. The worth and value of a network of this nature goes far beyond training; it is part of the lives of the communities in which it works. From her base in Johannesburg, Sarah McGuigan, who leads the Ntataise Network, and her team offered ongoing support and leadership to the 22 organisations that form the Ntataise Network, and introduced many directors, managers and trainers to working online, developing the necessary digital skills to do so.

I had hectares of maize fields to move around in, family living with me – including my grandson, who arrived at three weeks old and left with his parents after five months. And I was part of Ntataise. Lockdown or no lockdown, work carried on, online. In the Free State and North West provinces, Puleng and her team trained practitioners through Zoom and Google Meet get-togethers. With the Ntataise Network, they identified and acted as conduits for the delivery of government, business and private donations of food to the families of thousands of preschool and playgroup children.

It was the mothers and even grandmothers of current ECD practitioners who started with Ntataise in the 1980s, against all odds, to bring early learning to disadvantaged communities. The practitioners, trainers and ECD leaders of today have their own challenges. But they are also resilient and determined. I have no doubt that they will overcome the hardships they currently face.

ACKNOWLEDGEMENTS

THIS MEMOIR HAS BEEN a work in progress for well over ten years. Many people have helped me along the way to turn my thoughts, words and inhibitions into a book. To each and every one of you, I say a most sincere thank you.

It was Jo-Anne Richards and Richard Beynon who spent many hours prompting me to 'show, not tell', including my feelings. Pat Tucker asked pertinent questions to fill gaps in my writing. Throughout the process Jonathan Jansen encouraged me, and gave me confidence when mine waned.

Over the past few years it has been Gus Silber and my daughter Sally Evans-Amoretti who have critically read my manuscript. Gus helped me tighten up my writing and put events in context. Sally has been forthright in suggesting different ways of looking at things and in helping me to make the book come alive.

It has been a great pleasure for me to sit with my Ntataise colleagues, going over 'old times'.

Maria Mohlahleli, Bonny Ntsoeleng, Rebecca Sothoane, who is sadly no longer with us, and Puleng Motsoeneng, I thank you for your help in drawing things out of our combined memories and sharing your own memories and feelings with me. I treasure your friendship. I would also like to thank Emily Rammile and Peter Khoarai, who shared their memories of the horrific shooting of schoolboys and young men in Rammulotsi with me.

My thanks, too, go to Eric Atmore, who made his master's and doctoral theses, which delved into the history of ECD in South Africa, available to me.

Rhys Rolfe, an integral part of my years on the farm and my sometime antagonist, I thank for sharing his wealth of knowledge of the early days of Huntersvlei with me.

It was my beloved children who, when I was procrastinating, asked, 'How's your book coming on, Mum?' Robyn, Claire, Sally and David, I thank you for keeping me writing, for making Ntataise part of your lives, too, and for being there at any time of day or night, especially over the past few years.

I do not have enough words to thank Anthony. He didn't read my manuscript until a few months before he died, and it was not in its finished form. His deep interest in education, his cajoling and his never-ending support helped me make a remarkably fulfilled and happy life on the farm, and Ntataise, a reality.

To my publisher Nkanyezi Tshabalala and editor Angela Voges I also add words of sincere thanks.